EXPERIENCES
NEVER
STOP

PART 3

D1457835

REBECCA WALTERS HOPKINS

BALBOA.PRESS
A DIVISION OF HAY HOUSE

Balboa Press books may be ordered through booksellers or by contacting:

Balboa Press
A Division of Hay House
1663 Liberty Drive
Bloomington, IN 47403
www.balboapress.com
844-682-1282

Because of the dynamic nature of the Internet, any web addresses or links contained in this book may have changed since publication and may no longer be valid. The views expressed in this work solely those of the author and do not necessarily reflect the views of the publisher, and the publisher hereby disclaims any responsibility for them.

The author of this book does not dispense medical advice or prescribe the use of any technique as a form of treatment for physical, emotional, or medical problems without the advice of a physician, either directly or indirectly. The intent of the author is only to offer information of a general nature to help you in your quest for emotional and spiritual well-being. In the event you use any of the information in this book for yourself, which is your constitutional right, the author and the publisher assume no responsibility for your actions.

Any people depicted in stock imagery provided by Getty Images are models, and such images are being used for illustrative purposes only. Certain stock imagery © Getty Images.

Scripture quotations are from the ESV Bible® (The Holy Bible, English Standard Version®), copyright © 2001 by Crossway Bibles, a publishing ministry of Good News Publishers. Used by permission. All rights reserved.

Print information available on the last page.

ISBN: 978-1-9822-7773-4 (sc)
ISBN: 978-1-9822-7775-8 (hc)
ISBN: 978-1-9822-7774-1 (e)

Library of Congress Control Number: 2021924069

Balboa Press rev. date: 11/24/2021

CONTENTS

ACKNOWLEDGEMENTS

I thank *God, my guides, my father* protecting, and guiding me daily from heaven.

I thank my beloved husband, *Michael*, for his understanding and unwavering love throughout this journey.

I thank all *my friends* who have shown support and love, especially *Jessica, Dottie, Dana, Gloria, Katie,* and *Susan,* for their encouragement, support, and interest in my work.

This book was intense to write. Your love and kindness from each of you, aided me in my writing.

I have done it all for God.

Love,
Rebeccca Walters Hopkins

MESSAGE FOR THE READER

- Experiences Never Stop Part 3 are my accurate accounts of my life between March 19, 2020, through May 6, 2021.

- These experiences happened through my gifts of empathy and mediumship.

- God's words italicized so you will have no problem finding what our heavenly father spoke to me frequently.

- I want you to realize God's tremendous power and understand what God looks like, speaks, and thinks.

- I document time throughout the book because these encounters happen randomly.

- I share thirty-seven dream visits from spirits communicating with me through my gifts from God.

- The power of prayer is mighty. I share how God changes my life through prayer and God's lessons.

- I hope you learn how prayer will benefit and change your life after reading this book.

- God is always listening and there is much more to come…

EXPERIENCES NEVER STOP PART 3

March 19, 2020

I felt overwhelmed as an empath and medium, sensing the world forced to deal with COVID-19. I sensed the tension of uncertainty growing, particularly on my birthday. It felt pleasant in the eighties, perfect weather in West End, North Carolina. Our governor issued an executive order for everyone to remain home. You could merely enter society for essential goods and if your job deemed necessary. How could I celebrate? I could do nothing but pray.

I hear music through my gift of clairaudience from my three spirit guides and my deceased father. Then they speak. My master guide is an angel. This year I learned my master guide's name is Gabriel. He sounds masculine, firm, and direct when he speaks. Gabriel always plays the "Shout," song by Tears for Fears before I hear from him.

Gabriel instructed three days ago. "Pray for what you need. Pray for the ones you love. Pray for strength and guidance."

I broke down several times on my birthday, feeling the vast stress encroaching. I could not work and must remain home on my birthday. I sensed doom and wickedness hovering over us all. My spouse strived to make my birthday special. He is Italian, handsome, compassionate, loving, kind, and has a wonderful sense of humor. He has short, dark brown wavy hair and brown eyes. He owns a local bakery in town and is my best friend.

My husband presented me with gorgeous yellow daffodil flowers and baked a chocolate layered cake covered with shaved chocolate. He grinned with pride at the supplies he found. He bought two filet mignons for dinner.

I struggled to smile and pretended I felt overjoyed. I could not concentrate on anything but this virus. I sensed misery and panic coming. These were the changes my guides had advised me to prepare for. *How long would this virus last?*

We cooked the filets medium rare. The steaks tasted succulent and savory. The chocolate layered cake looked delicious. We gazed into each other's eyes and relished each bite.

I held back tears and whispered in my husband's ear, "Thank you for making my birthday special. I love you."

Later, Noodle and I wandered into "the room" to relax. Noodle is our beloved schnoodle and weighs twenty pounds. She has light gray curly hair, lovely small brown eyes, floppy ears, and a pom-pom tail like a poodle. We named our extra bedroom "the room." It became a joke between us. The room is a modest twelve by twelve area with a full-size bed with luxurious blankets and velvet pillows. My husband installed a massive TV. God speaks to me in this room when I meditate. We all love this space. This room feels safe and cozy, like a nest.

At 8:30 p.m. I watched on Amazon Prime, "The Bible, In The Beginning," Episode 1, directed by Christopher Spencer, Crispin Reece, and Tony Mitchell. In the series, God told Abraham he would father children. He needed to lead his people. Abraham would change future events and God blessed individuals as the story unfolded.

Dad exclaimed, "Beck, put this in the book. God is glad you are watching it."

My father died on March 13, 2012. He plays gospel music frequently and a couple of other songs before he speaks. He calls me Beck, not Rebecca. He is not a guide, but God allows me to hear him. Dad was a lovely, caring, hardworking man and loved to joke. He had dark brown, wavy hair and blue eyes. He was short of 5 feet 6 inches tall. God appointed my father to help me write for you.

Gabriel announced, "God is with you, Rebecca. That is right. Like Abraham, you will help people. These are God's words. God wants you to write these things. You are his messenger. God will tell you what to write."

I watched how Abraham's knowledge was given to him by God. His family did not believe in him. Abraham continued on his journey and listened to what God advised him to do. I noticed how my life mirrored what I witnessed in the show. God tested me like Abraham, and I passed the tests. Many of my prayers had been answered by God.

I heard "Don't Speak," by No Doubt from Dad. He coached me. "Beck, God is glad you are watching the program. Many of your questions will be answered."

My eyes are greenish blue. I am in my fifties, petite, strong-minded, and have long blonde-brown hair. I am clairaudient, an empath, a medium, an author, wife, and salon owner. I was Octavian Augustus in a past life.

Ilene added, "God is smiling for all these things have happened. Moses was strong as Abraham's faith was."

Ilene Fitzgerald lived in Ireland in 1589 and has been my spirit guide since birth. I saw her during a meditation. Ilene loved to ride horses when she could. She was a stunning, beautiful woman. She had creamy white-skin, extensive reddish dark-brown hair, dainty hands, and happy living at the Ross Castle.

At one part in the movie, Moses demanded his people to be released from the Pharaoh. The Pharaoh chuckled. Moses informed the Pharaoh he was not a god and to release his people. Moses warned the ruler that God would send ten plagues if his people were not released.

Dad stated, "God said this is true."

Later in the movie, after the plagues, the Pharaoh told Moses to take his people and leave his land. Moses did.

Dad cheered. "God enjoyed this part. Saving his people."

Moses cast his staff in the water and split the red sea and crossed safely.

I thought, *"I have learned anything is possible when you have God in your corner. God is extremely powerful."*

He laughed. "God liked what you added, Beck." God watched what I logged into my journal and knew what my thoughts were.

Moses crossed safely, and the pharaoh's people drowned.

Dad beamed. "God loves this part."

I heard "Santa Claus Is Coming to Town," by John Frederick Coots and Haven Gillespie. Ilene added, "God is loving and kind and always protects those that believe in him."

Noodle needed to pee, so I paused the movie. When we came back into "the room" it was almost 10:00 p.m., and I heard music from Dad.

I asked, "What does all the information in this movie mean? What am I to do? Write it? Is this about this coronavirus growing? Should I suggest how to pray on social media?"

Dad replied, "Yes, Beck, God wants you to do these things. It will help people."

I asked, "What should the prayer be?"

Gabriel spoke, "Do unto others as you would have them do unto you. Pray for the things you need, and God will provide for you. Pray for strength and guidance. If you do not choose to do these things, do not. God is showing you the way."

I posted on Facebook, Twitter, and my personal page about what to pray for during the coronavirus. I continued to watch the movie. God gave Moses the Ten Commandments. The movie talked about the Arc of the Covenant.

Dad beamed. "God is pleased, Beck. You have listened to Gabriel. Many will benefit from your courage and diligence."

Gabriel announced, "God is pleased with your decision. It will help hundreds of people in the next few days."

Ilene played "Lean On Me," by Bill Withery. She added, "Pray for strength and guidance, Rebecca. God is by your side. Remember to do these things."

Gabriel announced, "God is always listening. He is a kind, loving God. He is merciful to those who ask for it."

I gasped. "Wow, this was a lot of information at once and all on my birthday."

March 21, 2020

Dream One: At 6:00 a.m. I woke startled and realized I had a visit from my ex. We were still together. We looked in our twenties and my current spouse was in the dream. We were all friends. I was attracted to my present husband in the dream. I noticed my ex's brown hair, medium length, with blonde highlights. I sensed his immaturity. He was not an intelligent man. He liked to play music and perform different band gigs. He craved to be a Rockstar, which we understood he would never be. He was skilled, but not *that* talented. My ex showed me the person I truly loved didn't want me. I couldn't have him. I stared at my ex and my red and white cocker spaniel, Freck. My dog, which died many years ago, seemed okay. We all walked outside to hang out. My current husband's sister was there as well. She appeared younger than she is today. Everybody looked in their twenties and we all knew one another. The sister bored listening to my ex. He craved to play childish games outside. I spotted him in the yard, struggling to play the game by himself. I observed the green grass and the scorching sun shining above. The sister wandered inside. Me and my current partner worked out on gym equipment. I desired to be with him and wanted nothing to do with my ex.

I looked down. My cocker spaniel sat beside me. I sensed she protected me. I knew she was in heaven because I saw her before in heaven in dreams. She died over thirty years ago, and I miss her.

We lost Noodle in the dream. I could not find her. She had lost most of her hearing. I wasn't able to call for her and searched desperately. I frantically sprinted to a dog I thought was Noodle. It wasn't her. My heart dropped. I screamed at everyone to help search for Noodle. I felt panic rising in my chest. I learned she was last seen in the park, close to where we were. She loved to mark areas. I scrutinized over forty distinctive types of dogs in this playground. Enormous dogs and small ones too. No Noodle.

I spotted her and rushed towards her, my heart pounding. I grabbed the dog and realized it did not smell like Noodle. *It wasn't her.* Devastated, we continued the search. Hours passed. We could not find her anywhere. My heart felt shattered and broken.

I sensed my current husband did not want to be with me. He flirted with other women in the dream. We were not together and anxiously looked for Noodle. I *never* found her.

I woke and heard Noodle cough beside me. Relieved, I sobbed. I walked downstairs and took her outside. When we came back inside, my husband slept in "the room." When he did not sleep well, he ended up in "the room" not to wake us during the night.

I bawled. Tears flowed down my face. My ex *attempted to harm me from darkness*. He needed to torment me and wished me to feel *his pain*. He did these things through my gift of mediumship. My husband and my dog are my weaknesses. My ex knew and sought to use it to harm me. Still overcome what I had endured. I woke my husband and laid with him. I never went back to sleep after this horrible dream. The pain in my heart was still there. My ex wanted me to feel. He was a bastard, even in darkness. Ilene had told me before my ex was in darkness because he did not believe in God. This was what evil did to him for eternity, made him feel the pain repeatedly. He showed me his anguish. He hated I felt happy with my current husband, and I never wanted him. He attempted to trick me again.

I felt comforted in my husband's arms and smelling Noodle lying close to me. I bawled. We loved each other more than anything. This was the difficult part of my gift. I prayed for protection from these vile spirits. They still could sneak in and sought to harm me. This happened because God wanted me to write this for you.

I recalled my ex's anger, hurt, pain he projected onto me. He wanted to hurt me deeply, and he made me feel it.

I finished logging into my journal. I stated, "What a freaking nightmare and now I must get ready for work at the salon." I remembered coronavirus was another ongoing nightmare.

Dad whispered, "He tries to hurt you, Beck. But he cannot."

Ilene added, "We protect you."

Gabriel stated, "God is with you. This man can never do you any harm. Only tries to. God protects you."

I replied, "So wonderful to hear."

I knew these things were true. It felt outstanding when they reminded me. I still felt the hurt I sensed from the dream.

March 23, 2020

Dad beamed. "God is pleased with what you have done today."

I asked, "What do you mean?"

The last couple of days I struggled whether to close the salon this week or next week because of the coronavirus. I had prayed for guidance. I remembered last night when I kissed my husband good night. I heard, "There is your answer."

My ex's dream visit showed me who was the most significant, my husband and Noodle. I realized how much they meant to me if they weren't there anymore.

Sunday, me, and my husband discussed at great length about the virus. I would close the salon temporarily to protect our family.

We worked on the pool, prepared it for the three-inch concrete base. It amazed me when we placed the boards in the hole's bottom for the concrete frame. We checked to see if the platform appeared level. It was perfect. It seemed odd because nothing was that easy. It surprised my husband, too.

He asked, "Check it again."

I knew at that moment God had something to do with it. I prayed for help to dig the pool using a backhoe and a shovel. It wasn't likely the hole was level, but it was. I smiled, realizing what God did. He answered my prayer.

At 10:00 p.m. Noodle and I laid in "the room."

Ilene instructed. "God will speak to you in a few days. You need to prepare."

I felt glad and surprised I would hear from God, but terrified of the changes coming. God would protect me. The unknown made me feel unsettled. I could not shake the dread which hung over my head and sensed there was more to come. I struggled to focus on the future, like Gabriel instructed the other day.

How was I to focus? I must close the salon and not work. Later that day, I worked on a video of Psalm 23 and published it on YouTube. God wanted me to do these things. The video needed improvement, but I did my best. I worked on more videos while the salon was closed. I needed to work on writing and tasks around the house and stay busy for my sanity.

Dad beamed. "Remember to pray. God loves you, Beck. He's excited about speaking with you. He has much to share with you. You must remember to pray for the things that you need. God will show you the way."

I heard a new song from Ilene. "Wonderwall," by Oasis. I heard it on TV yesterday. It was Ilene, playing it for me. She did this often.

I remembered I saw 1111 and 111 earlier in the day. This meant you were on the right path and to keep positive thoughts. I saw signs, numbers, from my guides often. Later that afternoon, the governor announced all salons were closed. We were in quarantine until further notice because of the coronavirus.

I sighed and worked on dinner. I made baked salmon, olives, and broccoli for myself. My husband left for the bakery. He needed to finish a few orders since I wasn't working.

Ilene added, "God loves you. He is showing you the way. You must be strong during these times."

Gabriel announced, "Prepare the house, for your Lord will speak to you. I will tell you when God is ready."

I prepared the house by burning sage and frankincense through the entire house. I asked God to fill the house with God's love. I ate my dinner and wondered what God would say. I felt excitement growing inside me.

March 24, 2020

For the last several days, I prayed for encouragement and signs. Last night, I dreamed of Dad and Mildred.

<u>Dream Two:</u> Mildred wanted to speak to me. I saw through the window her husband, a child, and a cousin in her car.

I sighed. "The games are beginning. She brought other people with her. I could not confront her about the actual issues, how she betrayed me. I didn't want to speak to them, but they were in my driveway. I felt the dread rising in my heart."

I opened the front door and there stood Dad. He looked tan, youthful, and in his thirties. His brown hair appeared thick, wavy, and slicked back. He wore a loose yellow-orange shirt. The material looked of silk but not smooth in texture. It reminded me how if you washed silk, it crinkled after the wash. The yellow-orange shirt wasn't tucked in. It hung loose, blowing in the wind around his hips. I noticed the short sleeves rolled up over his biceps.

Dad smiled. "Surprise, it is me."

I heard Mildred's husband behind him. He looked worn down, tired, and skinny. He didn't want to be there. I hugged Dad, ignoring these toxic people behind him. We embraced a while. It felt amazing to feel my father hold me in his arms. It made me feel protected. Dad entered my home and walked away from these people, stopping by unannounced. I continued to talk to Dad. He leaned over the counter and joked as he pulled his shirt over his head. I observed his back hunched over to make a shape of an arch. His skin looked smooth and young. There was nothing wrong with his back. He was joking around.

Dad laughed. "Stick a needle in it. It's hurtin."

He teased. I dug frantically in the kitchen drawer, searching for a needle. I pulled out the turkey injector and laughed.

I kidded, "I can't find it."

He laughed and waited. I forgot about all the bodies outside my door, wanting to speak to me. We were having a marvelous time.

I woke and realized immediately I had a visit from my father. He reminded me to keep these people out of my life because they do me harm. I felt the dread again. I remembered how they made me feel before from their lies, deceit, and betrayal. I must stay on this path without them. It was difficult for me. I cared too much sometimes.

Dad looked fabulous, healthy, young, jolly, and thrilled to see me. He protected and reminded me to do these works for God.

Last night my guides reminded; God would speak in a few days. I needed to prepare the house. I hoped God would tell me what to expect in the upcoming days dealing with the coronavirus. A client booked a reading that morning. God told me to write more than give readings with my gift, but it was an opportunity to make money. I needed to. I did not know how long the salon would be closed.

Noodle wanted to walk after lunch. I felt wonderful on the trail, no stress like two days earlier. I enjoyed the cool breeze and the morning air. I heard, "Don't Speak," song from Dad.

I asked, "You looked so good in the dream. I wondered if you were on a Caribbean island somewhere. You had an awesome tan. Your laid-back clothes wrinkled like linen. Where were you?"

Dad laughed. "In heaven, Beck, you can do whatever you want. I can't wait for you to see it."

I whispered, "Me too. I can't wait. I know it will be awhile."

He stated, "Many, many years, Beck, many years. God has a lot for you to do."

I strolled down our dirt road and pondered these things. I wondered what heaven would be like and what I would do for God.

He whispered, "You'll be speaking to people."

I gulped, "Wow, I guess it will happen when I am ready."

Noodle and I stepped into the back yard. I heard music from Gabriel. I thought of the reading I did for my friend Jess. (She is a lovely lady in her late sixties. She has short, blonde hair and mesmerizing brown eyes. She is extremely optimistic. I learned over the years Jess was my stepfather in a past life. I shared this information in my first book, *Living Life as an Empath and Medium, by Rebecca Walters Hopkins.* Jess is a dear friend I could trust.)

Jess told me during the reading, she prayed and asked things from Gabriel to help her children. She was raising two teenagers. They were her deceased husband's grandchildren they adopted as toddlers. It was difficult for Jess, being a single parent at her age. When she shared this information, it made me smile. I knew I wasn't allowed to tell Jess; Gabriel was my master guide. I had meditated before the reading. I asked my guides to answer questions Jess had I could know. Gabriel answered all the questions, and Jess did not know where the information came from. I told her the information came from my master guide.

I asked Gabriel, "Why can I not tell Jess who you are?"

Gabriel replied firmly, "God has told you to do these things. You must obey your Lord."

I whispered, "I understand. I will obey. There's no reason I wouldn't. I just thought it was funny this morning. She prayed and asked for help from you, Gabriel. You're my master guide."

Noodle had enjoyed her walk and seemed worn out. She marked constantly during the walk. She loved to mark and needed these social interactions with other animals.

I thought again about work. I wondered if it would be near the end of April. The stock market dropped and made me uneasy too.

Ilene instructed. "Pray for what you need. God will provide for you."

I prayed. I thanked God for all the things he had already done. He had blessed me with many things.

March 26, 2020

I woke and heard the "Shout" song.

Gabriel instructed. "Prepare the house. God will speak to you today."

I inquired, "When?"

Gabriel stated, "God is busy. I will tell you when God is ready."

I gasped. "Wow, today I will hear from God."

Noodle and I climbed out of bed. I called my husband. I explained how excited I was to hear what God had to say about the COVID-19 situation and our lives.

At 8:50 a.m. I drank half of my coffee. Gabriel announced, "God will speak to you when you are ready."

I gasped. "Wow." I chugged my coffee and burned sage and frankincense throughout the house.

At 9:16 a.m. I prayed and meditated. I heard from my guides, "God is waiting."

Gabriel announced, "God is coming. You must remember to pray for the things you need."

God spoke in a firm, gentle voice, *"Hello, Rebecca, it is God the Almighty. I come to you. You must listen when I speak. Many things have happened in the last several days. You must remain calm, centered. I will protect you. You mustn't be weak. These things I say to you. Time is of the essence. You must do these things for your Lord and Savior, Christ the Almighty, himself.*

You must prepare for the many changes coming; they will disrupt your life. These changes will pass. You must remember to pray. I will guide thee. Do unto others as you would have them do unto you, thus saith the Lord.

Remember, I am always here, ask, and I am there. You have been dutiful with your studies. I have been watching, listening, guiding. Remain centered and calm through these times. They will be difficult. These things my messenger must do. You must protect yourself. I will protect thee. The many changes that are coming will affect your future. These are the things you have prayed for. You mustn't worry. These things will bring you joy. You must remember to pray daily during these times. It will be important, and it will help you stay calm and centered. Remember, this will pass. It will be many weeks. Your husband will provide. I have made these things available to you. He will be protected. I protect those who believe in me.

The changes will affect your future, mustn't worry. I will be by your side, thus saith the Lord, God the Almighty, himself.

Be strong and pray for diligence, strength, guidance, mercy for those who need it. I am here with thee. Do you have any questions? You may ask them now."

I asked, "Lord, do you want me to do readings to make money during these times?"

God answered, *"No, Rebecca, it isn't necessary. I want you to write. Work on the writings. These things I say to you."*

I inquired, "How long will this last before it passes?"

God replied, *"Many weeks, months, before it is gone completely. You must remain calm during these times. I will provide for thee."*

I asked, "Can you tell me what changes I must prepare for.? What did I pray for? I have prayed for so much I can't remember."

God answered, *"These things you must wait for them to unfold, the blessings, I have given to you. These things will make you very happy, thus saith the Lord. You are weak. You must remember to pray for diligence. These things will help thee. Time is of the essence. What other questions do you have for me?"*

I asked, "Lord, we won't get sick, will we? I don't want this virus near my husband. Will he be, okay?"

God replied, *"Yes, Rebecca, you will be safe. Pray and do these things I say to you, daily. I will protect thee. What other questions do you have?"*

I inquired, "Am I doing everything you want me to do? I don't know how I am gonna be able to publish the book if I can't work."

God answered, *"You must remain calm. These things will pass. I will provide for thee. Your husband will help you. I have shown him the way."*

I asked, "Lord, will our businesses be afloat during these times?"

God answered, *"Yes, Rebecca, these things will pass. You must remain calm and believe in me. Pray daily. It will strengthen thee. Work on your studies. They need to be finished."*

I inquired, "Lord, how am I going to have people find the books? They are not finding them. I don't know what to do. I have sold ten books."

God answered, *"You must be patient for things to unfold. These things I say to you. People must seek these things on their own. Remain calm and continue to write. There is much more to come."*

I questioned, "Lord, are my gifts growing? You said they would mature the last time we spoke."

God answered, *"Yes, Rebecca, they are changing, maturing. You know these things are true."*

I replied, "I can't think, Lord."

God replied, *"Do not worry. I am here with thee."*

I asked, "Will my landlord help me during these times?"

God answered, *"Yes, Rebecca, he will be understanding and kind to you. Pray for the things that you need. It will help thee. What more do you ask from your Lord? What questions?"*

I cried feeling God's presence. I sobbed. "What can I do to help my husband during these times?"

God answered, *"You must stay grounded. Encourage him to be safe and I will protect him. He will provide for you during these times."*

I asked, "Lord, will you protect those I love from this virus?"

God answered, *"Yes, Rebecca, I have heard your many prayers. I will protect them all, thus saith the Lord."*

Tears rolled down my cheeks. I asked, "Should I stay home and not go to any doctor's appointments?"

God answered, *"Rebecca, you should be aware who you are, my messenger. You must protect thyself from these things."*

I asked, "Lord, when will we know it will be okay to resume life as normal?"

God answered, *"I will show you the way. I will be with thee, guiding thee, thus saith the Lord. Do not worry. I will come to thee, again. You must remember to pray for the things you need, and I will give these things to you, thus saith the Lord, God the Almighty, himself.*

Do unto others as you have them do unto you. These things shall come to pass. I am your Lord, by your side. You're dutiful and kind, loving to those that you care for. I must go now, for time is of the essence. My messenger must be strong, diligent. Pray for these things, I say to you, God the Almighty, himself. Pray for what you need, and I will provide for thee. I must go now, for you are weary."

I begged. "Please don't leave, God. I'm sure there's something else I need to ask. I can't think."

God replied, *"I will speak to thee again. I love you, Rebecca. Do not worry. I am by your side. I will show you the way. Goodbye."*

Gabriel announced, "Your Lord is leaving. You must remember to do these things that your God has told you to do."

Dad whispered, "Beck, God loves you."

Tears flowed down my face. I could hardly hold my head up. I could not swallow. My chest felt elated. I could not stop bawling. God knew everything in my heart. I have told no one. I needed to end the meditation. I asked my guides, God, angels in heaven, to continue to protect me. I prayed for diligence, strength, tranquility, guidance, and calmness during these times. I asked for protection of the ones I love from this virus.

At 9:46 a.m. It was thirty minutes again. It felt like ten minutes went by.

Gabriel stated, "God is your Savior."

I sobbed. "God, thank you for speaking to me. I am humbled. Thank you."

March 27, 2020

I settled into bed, and my heart felt heavy. My brother asked us to come over to celebrate his wife's birthday tomorrow. We were in quarantine. This was not a grand idea, especially after what God told me. I whispered my prayers and heard, "Livin' on a Prayer," by Bon Jovi. It was from Dan. Dan, my spirit guide, was my boyfriend who died on October 23, 1989, in a car accident. He was tall, funny, and adventurous. He had sandy blonde hair to his shoulders and blue eyes. He always smiled and had an outstanding personality.

I asked, "Where have you been? I haven't heard from you in days."

Dan beamed. "I've been busy. God keeps us busy."

He continued, "I have a gift for you. Tell your brother I love him and miss him. He was my best friend for some time. I cherish the memories we shared, and I hope to see him again."

I laid in bed, tears streaming down my cheeks. Dan listened to my husband and I talking about why we could not go. I thought it would hurt my brother. It wasn't wise hanging around one another, not knowing about the virus any more than we did. They invited more people too. We just could not risk it. I asked Dan to remind me in the morning exactly what he told me so I would not forget.

March 28, 2020

I woke and heard music from Dan. I smiled. He reminded me of what he told me last night.

Dan added, "Tell his wife that I love her too."

I recalled I had another dream visit from my ex.

Dream Three: We were still together. He made me think this each time. He looked handsome and dressed up. My ex had become a talented musician. I stood by his side. I saw a party held in a fancy hotel room. I glanced at a fabulous spread of whatever you wanted to eat and drink. My ex prepared for the performance. His manager wanted him to travel and perform in many places.

I felt excited about these events. He pulled me aside and scoffed, "I am really not attracted to you anymore. I don't want to be with you." He sauntered away. I felt devastated.

I cried. "What? I am fifty-two years old, dating again? How would I find someone at this age? What does he mean he is not attracted to me anymore? I am attractive. I have much to give."

I sobbed and felt awful inside. I woke and realized he attempted to hurt me from *darkness* again. He *wanted me* to feel how *he felt* when I left him. He was a drunk and his life was going nowhere. I walked away and said I didn't want him anymore. I knew this was his payback. It was pathetic. He could never hurt me from *darkness*, but he persisted.

I gave my brother a call at 5:00 p.m. to wish his wife happy birthday. I wanted to give Dan's message to the both of them. I explained to his wife what Dan told me. They were busy with their guests and too busy to talk. I had the nag. I sent a text message to my brother from Dan. I hoped he read it.

At 7:40 p.m. I walked into the bathroom and heard from Gabriel, "God is pleased with your work today. You have followed your heart today."

I smiled and recalled what Dad told me earlier at 7:00 p.m. I asked him to tell me when he read the text. Dad reported at 7:00 p.m. "He is reading it now." A few minutes later, "He is reading it again." I hoped he believed me.

I made spaghetti for dinner, funny my brother's favorite meal.

At 7:48 p.m. Gabriel announced, "You have warmed your brother's heart today."

Gabriel continued, "Your brother doesn't understand, but he is wondering about what you said to him."

I replied, "Gabriel, I hope his guide will help him understand. I know it is not my place. Only if he asks."

Gabriel added, "He loves you, Rebecca, trusts you."

At 9:43 p.m. Dad whispered, "He is looking at it again."

Gabriel added, "Your brother is thinking about what you sent him."

I asked, "That's good, isn't it?"

Gabriel responded, "He must decide."

Later in bed, I woke at 4:20 a.m. I saw the number on the clock today, my iPad and now in the middle of the night. I learned before when I saw 420 it was from Gabriel.

I thought, "Wow, today was outstanding."

March 30, 2020

I turned on my phone and it was 5:55 p.m. I gasped. "Wow, I wonder what changes are coming. I keep seeing 555 from my guides."

March 31, 2020

I drove to the salon to pick up mail and water the rosemary plants outside. I dropped off a package at the UPS store and needed to make a deposit at Wells Fargo. I finished all my errands and rubbed my hands with sanitizer. I recalled Turk and Chicken needed food and drove to the feed store. (Turk was our turkey and Chicken was our one black sexlet chicken.)

I traveled through downtown Southern Pines and noticed the stores were closed. The town looked empty.

I cried. "God, I am glad I have you in my corner. I know you will take care of me and my business. Many people don't believe in you. I feel they won't make it."

Ilene whispered, "It will pass soon."

I drove down Midland Road towards home. I cried. "God, I feel after this is over. People will forget what is happening."

God spoke softly, *"The ones who have lost their loved ones will never forget."*

I replied, "That is true."

I felt grim, driving home. I turned onto our road and heard, "Jesus Loves Me," by Joey + Rory. I smiled.

Dad whispered, "Don't be sad, Beck. It will be over soon."

Halfway down our dirt road, I noticed two neighbors drove toward me. One neighbor wasn't trustworthy. Our road narrowed in parts. I pulled over to let them pass. I remembered what God told me. Do unto others as you would have them do unto you. I waved as they passed. It felt right. I locked the gate at our entrance and felt safe again. I did not feel safe out doing errands. I washed my hands and logged into my journal about what happened.

Gabriel stated, "God is glad you're writing these things down. They are important for people to remember and to be kind to one another. Especially during hard times. Remember to pray for those you love and for what you need. God will provide these things for you."

I heard Psalm 23. "The LORD *is* my; shepherd; I shall not want. He maketh me to lie down in the green pastures: he leadeth me beside the still waters. He restoreth my soul: he leadeth me in the paths of righteousness for his name's sake. Yea, though I walk through the valley of death, I will fear no evil; for thou art with me; thy rod and thy staff they comfort me. Thou preparest a table before me in the presence of mine enemies: thou anointest my head with oil; my cup runneth over. Surely goodness and mercy shall follow me all the days of my life: and I will dwell in the house of the LORD for ever, Amen."

Later, after lunch, I edited my book. 2:30 p.m. and felt sleepy. Noodle and I took a nap. I woke at 3:33 p.m. I smiled and thanked God, the angels, and my guides for being with me. That was what 333 meant.

Later, I walked downstairs, turned on my phone and listened to Governor Cooper. I glanced at the clock, 4:44 p.m. I smiled; this meant the angels were with you. I needed them.

At 7:42 p.m. I baked salmon and kale for dinner.

Gabriel announced, "Prepare the house. God will speak to you in a few days."

I wondered, "What would God say? We haven't gotten to the peak of the coronavirus. I am feeling people's panic. This was the hardest part, staying home in quarantine."

I received calls from people who wanted me to do their hair at their home. They attempted to bully me into feeling guilty from their panic. I could lose my license and arrested if caught. I did not cave in their attempts. It felt rude and selfish of them to even ask.

April 1, 2020

I woke and heard music from Ilene. While I made my coffee, Ilene stated, "God is waiting for you to prepare the house."

I finished my coffee and took a quick shower. I prepared the house and needed to find projects during the quarantine to keep busy. I cleaned out closets and checked messages.

I asked, "Dad, anything you can tell me?"

He whispered, "God loves you, Beck. He has been watching you this morning and is looking forward to speaking to you soon."

I sighed. "I hope he has delightful news."

Dad reassured, "He will, Beck."

Ilene stated, "God is by your side and with you today. He knows this is difficult for you. You must pray for what you need."

I prayed, "I need people to be patient with me. I cannot open the salon during mandatory lock down. It hurts. People are only thinking of themselves and not the welfare of others and me."

Gabriel exclaimed, "God is listening. This will pass. Must be diligent in your work, the writings."

I replied, "I will, Gabriel."

April 2, 2020

Gabriel announced, "Prepare the house. God will speak to you soon. You must be ready."

I took a shower and prepared the house. I walked upstairs to grab socks. Dad whispered, "God is watching you, Beck."

I replied, "He is?"

Dad answered, "God is glad you prepared the house for him. He will speak to you tomorrow."

I beamed. "I cannot wait."

Noodle and I went for a pleasant walk. It was breezy and fifty-six degrees outside. The cool, fresh wind felt fantastic on my skin. I felt calm inside. I prayed for calmness for days. We enjoyed our walk together. Noodle seemed blissful and content. I wondered, "What will God say tomorrow?"

Gabriel reminded, "Work on the writings."

I replied, "I will."

At 3:21 p.m. I logged into my journal what I heard earlier. I planned to lie out in the sun. It was a gorgeous afternoon. I needed to rest for a while and would continue editing *Experiences Never Stop Part 2*.

Stress returned while I was outside. Evil sought to put thoughts in my mind to make me worry. I had not worried all day. I prayed, "God, remove the thoughts evil is trying to harm me with. I ask in the name of the Father, the Son, and the Holy Spirit, in Jesus Christ, I pray, Amen."

Gabriel announced, "God has removed them."

I prayed for the things I needed. Gabriel instructed. "God wants you to pray for what you need."

I gasped. "Wow. I thought I had prayed for what I needed."

I searched deep in my heart and prayed, "God, I need this coronavirus gone permanently from our lives. I need my husband, me, and our dog healthy and safe. I need you to guide and provide for me. I need hope I can touch someone again and not be afraid. I need hope to enjoy my future of the changes coming I have prayed for. I need to enjoy life with the ones I love. These are the things I need. I ask these things in the name of the Father, the Son, and the Holy Spirit, in Jesus Christ, I pray, Amen."

Gabriel announced, "God has heard your prayers and will answer in due time. God will speak to you in the morning. Do not make him wait."

I smiled. "I will not make God wait."

April 4, 2020

Dream Four: I woke several times between 4:00 a.m. and 7:00 a.m. I dreamed three hours about my ex. His hair looked black to the shoulders. Not blonde like it was when he lived. He wore black shorts, a black T-shirt and looked scrawny. He wanted to make me think we were still together. He struggled to tell me why our relationship wasn't working. It was all my fault. He grabbed a beer out of the refrigerator. I glanced at the clock. It was 8:00 a.m.

I commented, "Drinking in the morning doesn't help either."

He scoffed, "I drink when I want to drink."

He wanted to have sex. I attempted to pretend to go through with it.

When I submitted, he barked, "I don't want to now. I am not attracted to you."

He strutted away and returned, "You never want to do anything. That's another problem. You just wanna stay at home."

I replied, "All you crave is to go to bars and party. You're not interested in doing anything with me. You just want everybody to see you."

I thought, "He is narcissistic and selfish."

I spotted people laughing and joking in another room. They wanted to hang out with him. I did not and left. I stood in my ex's sister's house. She missed him terribly. He did not care. He showed me a paper. The paper read he was sorry for the things he did to me. It made me cry. I never finished reading it. I saw pictures of himself as he drew more on other papers. He had no remorse for what he did. He explained how he treated her. I glanced at the paper on the bed and saw pictures of my dog, Noodle. He described how she would die. He scribbled on the picture with a black marker. I stopped listening to him and looking at the papers. He sought to hurt me. I felt his anger. I grabbed the papers and threw them at his sister. He explained she had to move because her house was torn down.

He blurted, "You have nowhere to work or live." His anger projected towards her. I woke at 7:00 a.m.

I gasped. "Wow, I dreamed this for three hours."

I heard music from Dan. I asked, "Why does he keep doing this?"

Dan replied, "The one thing he couldn't have is you. Evil is tormenting him every day. He cannot hurt you. We protect you. He tries to, but he cannot."

I gasped. "Wow. This dream felt intense and full of his rage. Same behavior when he lived. He drank in the morning before I moved out. I gave him papers on how to split our belongings. He *knew* how much I loved Noodle which meant he can see her and me. He still was furious at his sister. He blamed everyone except himself for his cruel behavior. Nothing changed, *even in darkness.*"

April 5, 2020

I slept horribly and felt evil kept waking me. Noodle and my husband woke me many times as well. Noodle attempted to vomit on the bed. I comforted her, and she stopped.

Gabriel announced, "God will speak to you when you are ready this morning. Do not make him wait."

At 8:10 a.m. I climbed out of bed, made coffee, and called my husband. I guzzled the coffee and prepared the house. I grounded, prayed, and meditated.

At 8:42 a.m. Gabriel announced, "God is coming, Rebecca. You must be ready when your Lord comes."

I replied, "I have been trying, Gabriel, fast as I could."

Dad beamed. "He is almost here."

God spoke firmly, *"Hello, Rebecca. It is God. I come to you. You did not make me wait. You honor your Lord and Savior. You have been diligent, praying daily, like I asked you to do. You must remember to pray more. These things I say to you, your Lord and Savior, God the Almighty, himself.*

There are difficult times ahead. Must prepare. It will soon pass. You are my messenger. You write these things I say to you, your Lord, God the Almighty.

You must listen when I speak, for the coming of the Lord is upon you. You must be ready for these changes."

I stated, "It is difficult to hear you, Lord."

"You must remember to pray for those that you love. They need guidance during these times. Focus on the writings. There is much to do. I am by your side, showing you the way. My messenger needs to be strong, vigilant, and merciful. Do unto others as you have them do unto you. Remember to pray it will help guide thee. You are my servant, and I am your master, thus saith the Lord, God Almighty, himself.

Do unto others as you would have them do unto you, thus saith the Lord.

Be kind to those who need it. Be diligent in your work. You mustn't tarry. The changes are coming. Must prepare. I will help thee, these things I say to you, your Lord and Savior, Jesus Christ the Almighty.

You must believe in me. These will be trying times. It will pass. These things I say to you.

Be strong, persevere, and I will help thee. Must remember to pray often. It will help guide and strengthen thee. I come to you today to help my messenger. What questions do you have for me, thus saith the Lord, God?"

I inquired, "How long will this coronavirus last? Before it is gone?"

God answered, *"Many weeks, months, years. These will be trying times. I will help guide thee. Protect thee, and show you the way, thus saith the Lord."*

I asked, "What do I need to pray for, Lord? That will help me during these times?"

God answered, *"Strength, diligence, guidance, mercy for those who need it, calmness, these things I say to you, my messenger, says Christ the Almighty. Time is of the essence. What other questions do you have?"*

I stated, "Your voice is firm today, Lord. Are you upset with me? Are you angry?"

God replied, *"No, Rebecca. You were sensing the power of God the Almighty. It is powerful. I am a loving, kind, giving God. Ask and I am there, these things I say to you. You must be diligent in your work. It will help your future. In the coming days, you must prepare for the changes, for there will be many. I will provide for thee. Must be careful where you go. Time is of the essence. You must remember to pray for the things that you need, thus saith the Lord, God the Almighty, himself."*

I asked, "Lord, when will I work at the salon?"

God answered, *"Many weeks before life will resume as once was. These changes will disrupt your pattern of life as you know it. These things will pass. I will be with thee, guiding thee, thus saith the Lord."*

I asked, "Lord, will you protect us from this virus? Keep it away from my husband and the ones I love?"

God replied, *"Yes, Rebecca. You asked me to do these things in your prayers. You must pray often, daily. It will protect and ground thee. These things must be done. It will help thee. Remember to pray often. I am always listening. Pray for what you need. I will give these things to thee, thus saith the Lord, God the Almighty, himself.*

Thee must prepare for the many changes that are coming. Some you have prayed for; these changes will happen for some time. You must remember to pray. It will help thee. I am by your side. I will show you the way. What other questions do you have for me?"

I stated, "My mind is blank. When will we get through this, when? Lord, you will protect us. I know you will. How will it change my future? Can you tell me about the changes coming?"

God answered, *"The changes are a disruption to the things that you know. They will pass. It will be many weeks, months, before it is gone. Prepare for these changes. Ground thyself daily. It will help thee. Be careful where you go, my messenger. I will protect thee. You must remember to pray for the things that you need, and I will grant them."*

I asked, "Lord, when do you want me to. How will I be able to publish part 2?"

God answered, *"These things will happen in the future, thus saith the Lord. Do not worry. I will show you the way. Continue to work on the writings. These things are important. It is God's will. These things will help those understand that I am real, thus saith the Lord, God the Almighty.*

Do unto others as you would have them do unto you. Remember to pray. Ask for what you need, and I am there. I must go now, for time is of the essence. Do these things I say to you, my messenger, says God the Almighty, himself. Take care, I love thee, Rebecca."

I blurted, "Oh, wow, are we already done? Don't leave God, please. Thank you for talking to me, helping, protecting, and caring for me."

God answered, *"You are welcome, thus saith the Lord, God the Almighty. I must go now, for time is of the essence. I will speak to you again. Goodbye, Rebecca."*

Gabriel announced, "God is leaving. Your Lord has spoken to you. You must do these things for your Lord. Remember to pray. We will help guide you."

I wondered, "Why so fast? I don't feel overwhelmed this time. My heart feels full and calm. God sounded extremely firm today. God was in a hurry."

I prayed, "Surround me with the white light of the Holy Spirit. Protect me today and the upcoming months until this virus is gone. I pray for strength, diligence, guidance, vigilance, mercy for those who need it. Please guide me and show me the way, Lord. I ask these things in the name of the Father, the Son, and the Holy Spirit, in Jesus Christ, I pray, Amen."

Now, I felt overwhelmed and cried. It was 9:07 a.m. This was the shortest amount of time God spoke. He was in a rush. My guides rushed me this morning. I felt dizzy, lightheaded. My heart felt full of God's love.

I finished proofreading. It stunned me what I read. I must push forward. My heart felt broken from the news from God.

April 6, 2020

At 10:30 p.m. Noodle and I laid in "the room." I finished a movie about Jesus being crucified. I turned it off. My guides were silent. I asked, "Where are you? It is quiet tonight."

Ilene instructed. "You need to pray for the ones you love."

My sorrow overwhelmed me after the show. I inquired, "What do I pray for?"

Ilene instructed. "Encouragement, guidance, strength."

I prayed, "Lord, I pray for those who I love. I ask for encouragement, guidance, and strength. I ask these things in the name of the Father, the Son, and the Holy Spirit, in Jesus Christ, I pray, Amen."

April 7, 2020

I edited and glanced at the word count, and it had 666 in the count. 666 meant wake up your higher spiritual truth and focus on balance. My iPad beeped a notification. I opened it at 2:22 p.m. and laughed. These numbers meant balance, too. My spirit felt out of balance and difficult to focus.

Later that evening, I glanced at the stove clock at 5:55 p.m. I choked. "More changes are coming."

April 9, 2020

At 7:00 p.m. I leaned on the railing of the deck, enjoying the breeze on my skin. It felt fantastic hearing the soft sounds of the new crystal chandelier chimes I ordered months ago. They arrived today. I thanked God for guiding my husband and I during these troubled times.

I heard, "Blessed Assurance," song by Frances J. Crosby. I had not heard from dad in a while. I asked, "Where have you been? It has been days."

Dad chimed, "I've been busy doing this and that. God keeps us busy. There's a lot of people that need our help."

I gasped. "Wow, that's how you help people when you're in heaven."

He beamed. "Yes Beck, God can't be everywhere. So, we do things for him. He tells us what to do to help others."

I gasped. "Wow, that is incredible. I did not know that's how it works in heaven. Are you happy there?"

Dad beamed. "Yes, I have never been happier. I miss you and the others, my family. I hope to see you all again. You know who needs help, Beck."

I whispered, "I am trying, Dad."

Ilene instructed. "Thee must believe in God to enter his kingdom."

I replied, "I know it must be that person's choice. I pray every day to help in any way I can. I know they must do this on their own."

I asked Dan, "Do you have anything to say?"

Dan whispered, "He loves you, Rebecca. He believes in you. I hope he will listen, eventually."

I replied, "I know. I hope he believes in me. I have never lied about anything."

He added, "God is listening, Beck. He is pleased with what he has heard."

I gasped. "Wow, Dad, you're gonna make me cry. I am glad God is pleased."

Gabriel exclaimed, "God has heard what you have been saying and is happy that his messenger is learning his teachings. These things will help anyone. You must prepare for the changes. Many that are coming. God will be with you. Remember to pray daily for the things you need. God has instructed me to tell you these things for his messenger needs reminding."

I listened to music from Dan and Dad as I stared off, watching the wind blowing the leaves of the popular tree. The sun glistened on the leaves.

Dad beamed. "God loves you, Beck. We both can't wait to see you in heaven."

I blurted, "Wow, Dad. I can't wait to see heaven, you and God."

At 7:14 p.m. When I tuned in. I heard a lot. There were people sick from the virus all over the country. I hoped the sick people who died believed in God.

Gabriel announced, "God is pleased with what you've written."

It astounded me, *"God is listening all the time,* which is outstanding."

April 11, 2020

Dream Five: I woke many times during the night. I had a visit from Jim Catcher. I saw two women in their sixties. I watched them performing sexual acts with aqua blue dildos. I laughed and viewed while they played with the aqua dildo. One lady placed it in her mouth. She enjoyed herself so much she forgot I watched. I observed her full mauve lips around the dildo as she slid it in and out of her mouth. The other lady giggled and acted silly, waiting her turn.

I stared at the computer screen and checked messages. I realized one lady left a message. I attempted to read it and could not open the message.

I left in the dark and got gas at a small store similar to a Rite Aid. I entered and noticed Jim Catcher. I sensed he was sexually excited. He teased and inquired, "Ladies, what are you doing?" He knew somehow, they played with the aqua blue dildo. I sensed he enjoyed sexual performances.

Jim wore a black baseball hat, long black trench coat. He held his head down. But I recognized his face. He looked thirty. It surprised me to see him.

I explained, "They have lots of things in here and aspirin too."

He questioned, "They have aspirin?"

He was hung over and needed aspirin.

I signed the receipt, and it fell to the floor. I reached to pick it up. I placed the receipt on the counter. The owner of the store appeared behind the counter. He looked in his sixties with wavy gray-black hair. His blue eyes looked round and *bulging* from the sockets. The owner spotted Jim and my signed receipt.

He warned, "I do not want him in my store. Take him to your book signings if you like. I don't want him in here."

Jim stole drugs from the store. I became curious how the owner knew about my book signings. Why would I take Jim to a book signing? He was dead.

I woke and asked Gabriel, "Was it Jim?"

Gabriel warned, "Yes, it was him. He is not with God. He is trying to communicate with you. Evil is trying to get at you. Do not speak to him. He is in darkness. He can see you because of your gift."

I blurted, "Wow, it felt off."

He was a thief hiding in the store. He needed pills and aspirin because he was doing drugs again. Gabriel meant not to contact him while I wasn't dreaming. I would never do that.

I mentioned in my first book, *Living Life as an Empath and Medium,* page 213. In that dream, I didn't know where Jim was. I sensed he had an abundance to learn and wasn't overjoyed. He seemed lost and glum in the dream visit.

Jim wasn't hopeful in this dream, either. I recognized his voice when he spoke. I saw his face. It was him.

I blurted, *"Wow, I have seen darkness again."*

When he lived, Jim liked to party, do drugs, and had lots of sexual partners. He was hung over a lot when he visited at my home. He repeated this in darkness. He felt isolated, lonely, unhappy, and lost. I always liked Jim. But I would never see him because he was in darkness.

At 9:41 p.m. I finished a movie in "the room" on Amazon Prime and wondered, "Why is it quiet?"

Ilene beamed. "God is excited about tomorrow. God's son rose from the dead."

Dad added, "God is listening."

I asked, "What is God thinking?"

Ilene added, "God is preparing for tomorrow. It is a special day. It is a time for giving and receiving from those you love. Many people will be sad tomorrow because they cannot go to church. God will be with them all. You must remember to pray for those you love. They need guidance and strength."

Gabriel announced, "God is with thee, Rebecca. He has been watching you today. Working at your home. God is pleased with your project. Remember to work on the writings, these things are God's will."

I answered, "I felt God watching me today. I will work on the writings tomorrow."

Gabriel instructed. "You must remember to pray for what you need. God will grant these things to you."

I asked, "What will happen to people tomorrow with churches closed?"

Ilene answered, "They will pray to their God, and he will listen."

Gabriel instructed. "God wants you to work on the writings. God will be waiting. Remember to pray. God will be with you."

I gasped. "Wow, we installed part of the pool today. I was beat. It was a lot of work moving sand and concrete. I must pray for endurance and strength."

April 13, 2020

A terrible storm came through last night. The wind, rain and tornadoes touched down in our area. People experienced power outages. We had power and no problems. God again answered my prayers last night. I asked God to protect my family and our home.

The storm gave me a horrible headache from the barometric pressure changing. My husband and I rested most of the day. I edited for an hour and a half. Then rested on the deck with Noodle while she enjoyed hunting for lizards.

Later, My husband and I drank wine on the deck. We discussed what was happening in the world. We shared and laughed, Noodle by my side. My husband walked to the waterfall at our pond to adjust the flow of the water. It appeared clogged with trash from the storm.

I heard music from Dad and Ilene. I asked, "Is there anything I need to know?"

It was almost dark. I had opened the front door to let fresh air into the house. Ilene warned me before not to leave doors open at night. Spirits could come inside.

I asked Ilene, "Is it okay to be outside with the door open?"

Ilene warned, "Yes, but not for long."

I asked, "How long?"

Ilene warned, "Before the sun goes down. That is when spirits come out."

I inquired, "Where do the spirits come from?"

Ilene explained, "The in-betweens come out when the sun goes down from the in-between. It is not safe for you to be out then. Close the doors."

April 16, 2020

Today was tough. I found it hard to focus on anything, tired, not centered, and out of it. At Easter, I felt fabulous and had an enormous amount of energy and motivation. Today I felt trashed inside. God told me this disruption would be difficult, and it was.

At 10:09 p.m. I laid in "the room" with Noodle watching a movie. *Abe of Uprising: The Legend of Michael Kohlhass,* directed by Arnaud des Pallieres on Amazon Prime. I heard music, "Sorry Seems to Be the Hardest Word," by Elton John. I felt this way about someone close to me. They wanted me to do what they needed during these times of crisis. I did not follow through. It felt wrong what they asked of me. Was this why Ilene played this tune for me? Yes.

April 17, 2020

I showered and dried off.

Gabriel announced, "Prepare the house. God will speak to you in a few days."

I dressed, Gabriel reminded, "Prepare the house. God will speak to you in a few days."

I burned sage and frankincense throughout the house. I strolled outside to work in the garden and looked forward to hearing from God. I wondered, "What will he say? I needed God's guidance."

At 10:00 p.m. Noodle and I laid in "the room." I munched on potato chips.

Dad reminded, "God will speak to you in a few days. Prepare the house tomorrow."

Ilene beamed. "God is excited about what he will speak to you about."

I gasped. "Wow, I can't wait. I hope God is pleased with my studies."

Gabriel instructed. "Your Lord is with you, Rebecca. Remember to pray for those you love. They need guidance."

I blurted, "Wow, this happened out of the blue. It was quiet all afternoon."

Dad beamed. "God is listening, Beck. He is looking forward to speaking to you in a few days."

I replied, "I am too."

Gabriel added, "God will speak to you soon. Prepare the house. Pray for what you need, and God will grant them."

April 18, 2020

I woke, grounded, and prayed. Gabriel reminded, "Prepare the house. God will speak to you soon."

I walked in the bathroom and told Gabriel, "Thank you for reminding me."

I prepared the house after my shower and coffee.

April 19, 2020

Dream Six: My ex visited again. This time, it was a nightmare. He always wanted to become a Rock Star. He had his chance to perform in England, a tremendous opportunity. I viewed the dream because I am the medium.

He showed we were still together. He added new band members who were better musicians than himself. I witnessed the excitement on his face. His hair teased like one would wear in the 80s. I noticed an agent arranged the venue in a hotel room with a huge spread of food, drinks, and drugs. I sat in the bathroom, waiting for him to get me. He made me wait for him often when he lived.

He never came.

I viewed where they performed, and no one attended the event. My ex wondered, "Where is Dad? Why didn't he come?"

His father would have attended the event. So, my ex thought. His Dad was not there. He remained in limbo and had no clue where his son was.

I watched the massive aircraft crash on the runway. The airplane stood upward on the tail end; nose pointed in the air. The plane looked crumpled and blocked other aircraft from attending the show.

It devastated my ex. No one heard them play. He returned to the bathroom, looking for the band members. My ex looked high, possessed with evil. He held three small axes to kill each band member. His eyes crazed with anger. He *hunted* them. The band members slept in their hotel rooms. I watched him enter and speak to the singer. He appeared groggy and not upset the show wasn't a success. My ex walked over and sliced his throat with the ax. The blood oozed from the wide gash on his throat. The singer did not know he had intentions of murdering him.

I spotted the manager talking with the Queen's servant, asking for help.

The manager barked, "No, I will not help you."

The show was a catastrophe. He felt devastated. I woke.

I asked Ilene, "Was this a visit?"

Ilene replied, "He is trying to frighten you. But *he is the one frightened. He is in darkness.*"

I sensed immediately evil taunted him with what was important to him. Then snatched it away. *Evil made him* murder his crew so he could never play again. Evil made *him* do it. He looked mad and possessed. I saw wickedness in his eyes. Evil relished him slaying the singer and making *him* do it.

I blurted, "Wow, I could still see my ex's face, eyes deranged, high, and out of control. The blood gushing from the singer's neck. It terrified me to watch the singer's hand clutching tightly around his deep wound. I saw the blood dripping between his fingers. My ex could not hurt me but continued to try."

Gabriel announced, "Prepare the house. God will speak to you tomorrow."

April 20, 2020

At 8:20 a.m. I quickly made coffee because I would hear from God this morning. I heard music from Dad, "Go Tell It On The Mountain" by Fred Hammond.

Dad warned, "God is waiting."

I replied, "Let me drink my coffee and prepare the house. I'll be ready."

At 8:45 a.m. I prepared the house. Noodle and I laid in "the room." I placed amethyst, labradorite, and selenite around my being. I grounded, prayed, and meditated. I heard music from my guides, "God is waiting."

Gabriel announced, "Your Lord is coming, Rebecca. You must be ready. Your Lord is your Savior. You must remember to pray more."

God spoke firmly, *"Hello, Rebecca, it is God. You did not make me wait. You honor your Lord and Savior. These things I say to you, Jesus Christ, himself, God the Almighty. Thee must be diligent in the writings. It will affect your future. Write things I say to you. You have much more to do, for your Lord has asked you to do these things for God. You must remember to pray. I will show you the way. Ask for the things that you need, and I will grant them."*

I replied, "I'm feeling nervous."

God continued, *"Do not be afraid, for I am a kind, loving God. You have been diligent in your work. I have been watching and waiting for these things to be done. You must remember to pray for those that you love. They need guidance during these times. There is much more to come. The disruption will continue for some time. Pray for diligence, strength, perseverance to overcome these obstacles, mercy for those who need these things, saith the Lord, God the Almighty,*

Finish the writings. These things are God's will. Focus on what is at hand. Prepare for the many changes. These things I have granted thee. Your prayers answered by God, himself.

Thee must remember to pray more during these difficult times. It will help thee overcome the obstacles that you face. I will show you the way. Pray for guidance and I am there. You must do these things for your Lord. You are my servant, and I am your master. Remember, these are God's will. This is why you were born, Octavian, to do these things for your Lord and Savior. I have granted many things to thee. There is more to come, the blessings, these things you've prayed for. I will grant them. My messenger is strong, diligent, honors the Lord daily. I know these things, for I am God.

God knows all things. I am by your side every step of the way. You must be diligent in the writings. There is more to write. Honor your Lord. You will enter my kingdom because you believe in me. Those who do not will never enter my kingdom. No evil resides there, only God's love. I will grant mercy for those who asked for it. Only if they ask, thus saith the Lord, God the Almighty, himself.

Remember to pray for those that you love. They need guidance, strength, and mercy for those that were around them. Be diligent in your studies, these things I say to you.

Your gift is growing. You feel it, sense it, and know these things are true. You must remember to pray more. Be earnest in your studies, these things I say to you, my messenger. You write these things for me, your Lord and Savior, God the Almighty. You are humbled in my presence because you know that I am real."

I whispered, "I am Lord. I am humbled."

God continued, *"Do unto others as you have them do unto you. These things will help thee through these difficult times. Pray daily for those that need it, for I am listening. Ask and I am there, thus saith Jesus Christ, himself, God the Almighty. Do you have any questions for me, my messenger? I am waiting."*

I replied, "I am nervous, Lord. When will I resume work again? When will this virus subside from our lives?"

God answered, *"These things will take time. Pray for what you need. It will be many weeks, days before life resumes to once was. Many changes have occurred. Things will be different for some time. What other questions do you have for me?"*

I asked, "What do I need to pray for now, Lord, which will help me?"

God answered, *"Diligence, forgiveness of others impatientness, vigilance, strength, perseverance to overcome. Do unto others as you have them do unto you, thus saith the Lord, God the Almighty, himself."*

I replied, "I've been trying to write every day, Lord. It is tiring and hard to focus. Are you pleased with what I have done so far? I feel like I have not done enough from what you've said to me today."

God answered, *"You are diligent in your studies. There is much more to come. You must continue daily writing. Time is of the essence. Remember to pray for strength, calmness, and I will grant these things to my messenger during the writings."*

I inquired, "Lord, what do I need to pray for those I love?"

God answered, *"Strength, guidance, mercy for those around them. Protection from this virus, these things I say to you. Time is of the essence. Do you have any more questions for me?"*

"I can't think, Lord. It's hard to think." I asked, "Will you be with me, by my side, every step of the way? I need you to be there with me."

God answered, *"Ask and I am there. I will show you the way, my messenger. These things you were born to do for your Lord and Savior. You have asked for these things. I have given thee a second chance to do these things. These things must be done. Remember, this is the journey you have chosen. Honor me, your Lord. Do these things for your Lord and I will grant thee eternal life. You will be by my side and in my kingdom for eternity, thus saith God the Almighty. I will grant these things to you. You must remember to pray often. It will help thee, strengthen thee during these difficult times. Time is of the essence. What other questions do you have for your Lord?"*

I replied, "My gift is changing. What do I need to do to prepare for the changes I am sensing through dreams?"

God answered, *"I am showing you the way. You have seen darkness. It is the opposite of heaven. This is where evil resides. There is no love there, no kindness, only evil souls and torment for eternity."*

I asked, "Lord, Kellee White said the veil was thin. Is this true? Between the two worlds?"

God answered, *"These things are not for you to worry about. Your gift is strong. You must remember to pray to protect yourself from evil. It is always watching, lurking, waiting, to harm thee, my messenger. It knows who you are, at all times, these things I say to you, God the Almighty. I will protect thee. I will show you the way. Evil never wins. God is powerful. These things you experience are for the writings. So, people will understand* that these things are true. I will show you the way. What other questions do you have for me?"

I asked, "Lord, every night I have been dreaming bizarre things. I feel like it's all mixed up with evil in my dreams. Some are true, and some are not. It is like intertwined. Can you clarify what I am seeing?"

God answered, *"Evil will sometimes try to confuse thee. Trust your instincts and your gift that I have given thee. These entities cannot harm thee. Pray for protection every day, forever. I say these things to my messenger. You must do these things, for the gift I have given thee is powerful. It is to be used for God's grace."*

Gabriel announced, "God is getting ready to leave."

I begged. "Oh, Lord, please don't leave. I have waited to speak to you." Tears flowed down my face. "I can't think. Is there anything I need to pray for Noodle? Or my family, my husband?"

God answered, *"You must remember to pray for each other, for strength and guidance. He is by your side. I will show you the way. The truth has set you free. Your life is changing because of these things. The things you've prayed for. Embrace these changes. Do these things for your Lord. I will speak to thee again. I must go now, for time is of the essence. Pray for strength. Ask and I am there. I love thee. Goodbye, Rebecca."*

I whispered, "I love you, God. Thank you for speaking, helping, protecting, and being with me. I am honored to be in your presence."

Dan played "Walk This Way," by Aerosmith.

Gabriel announced, "God is gone, Rebecca."

I sobbed. I did not want God to leave. I couldn't think in God's powerful presence. My head and face felt numb. I could not feel my feet. Tears rolled down my face. It was hard to speak. I felt overwhelmed. God's authority felt powerful. I just wanted to be where God is. I felt overcome with emotions. My heart swirled with God's love and my face still numb.

I ended the meditation and prayed, "Dear Lord, please protect me. Surround me with the white light of the Holy Spirit. Protect me throughout the day and keep evil away from me. Protect my family, the ones I love.

I pray for strength, mercy, guidance, and perseverance to overcome the obstacles that we need to overcome. I ask these things in the name of the Father, the Son, and the Holy Spirit, in Jesus Christ, I pray, Amen."

I looked at the clock, 9:14 a.m. I panted and felt incredibly overwhelmed with love. I sobbed uncontrollably. What I heard from God felt like ten minutes had passed and now it was over. God sounded firm and direct today. But kind and loving at the same time. I was not writing fast enough and must proofread.

I blurted, "Wow, God said a lot today. I must get busy."

April 22, 2020

I intended to call my friend Phil and see how he was doing. I heard music from Ilene, "American Woman," by The Guess Who. I wondered what this song meant. I read the lyrics online and tried to understand the meaning of the tune.

Gabriel warned, "Focus on the writings. God has plans for him. God does not want you to contact him. He must do these things on his own."

I gasped. "Wow, I won't call."

I worked on the pool and the writings for the next several days.

April 25, 2020

At 10:40 p.m. I turned off my iPad and TV. I laid in "the room" with Noodle and my husband slept upstairs.

Gabriel announced, "God is pleased with the work you have done today. You are almost finished."

I edited for hours today and was almost finished. I mentioned to my husband earlier I was close to the end of the rewriting process. I had edited since the COVID-19 lockdown started. It kept me busy.

Ilene added, "You have much more to do. God will show you the way. Remember to pray. We are with you."

Dad whispered, "God loves you, Beck."

I chuckled. "I am glad, Dad. I love God, too."

April 26, 2020

I slept in and made us a large breakfast. We needed fuel to do the tough work we had planned.

My husband and I continued pouring sand-concrete mix around the fiberglass shell of the pool most of the day. We enjoyed a wonderful day together. The weather seventy-two degrees, breezy and felt perfect outside. I noticed the clouds in the sky, and this helped us from getting overheated.

Later that evening, I called a friend to discuss something I remembered Mildred told me about my father. We chatted on the phone until sunset. I shut the front door before dark and turned on the LED strip lights to a striking light blue on the deck perimeter. I noticed the motion activated solar-powered LED lights in the yard came on and nothing there to trigger them. I sensed a spirit set off the lights. Chicken and Turk roamed in the garden. I ended the call and told my husband I needed to lock the coop. He offered. Relieved, I didn't want to walk out there in the dark.

I entered the bathroom and realized the window was open. I asked, "Ilene, did any spirits come into the house because the door and window were open?"

Ilene warned, "Yes, two spirits came in."

I panicked and prayed, "God, please remove all spirits from my home. Protect my home and land. I ask in the name of the Father, the Son, and the Holy Spirit, In Jesus Christ, I pray, Amen."

Gabriel announced, "God has removed the two spirits. Do not leave doors or windows open. It is not safe for you, his messenger."

I sighed and felt relieved. I must be more careful.

April 27, 2020

I woke and wondered about the weird dream, intertwined with different spirits and entities that tried to communicate with me.

I asked Gabriel, "What was I dreaming?"

Gabriel answered, "Spirits are trying to communicate with you through your gift. They are in darkness."

I asked, "All of them?"

Gabriel replied, "No, some are with God. They're in the light."

Dream Seven: I stared at a man and understood he was reincarnated. He returned as a five-year-old little boy. I observed his chubby pink cheeks, a gigantic smile on his face. The child's eyes looked bright blue and seemed thrilled. He was forty years old when he lived. This was his second chance. He needed people to love him and be there, no matter what. The five-year-old boy was dying of cancer and lived in an enormous mansion. I witnessed people everywhere in the house. I roamed and viewed what took place. The crowds roared, joked, and loved being with the child. He loved to give people five dollars when they arrived. It was a joke; he bought their love. The individuals didn't want to except the five dollars. But reluctantly they did. He laughed and grinned while he showed me these interactions.

The boy declared, "All these people love me for who I am." He handed me a five-dollar bill. I didn't want it either but took the money and smiled at him. I watched the individuals in the massive room enjoying themselves. He showed me his second chance. He became a better man, even though he appeared as a child. People adored him. In his previous life, he was not friendly or a generous man. He was the opposite of what he was as the young boy. His soul emitted warmth and love.

My dream shifted to dark, wicked places. I saw no walls in the many rooms. I arrived to receive a mammogram. An older woman appeared with a huge tray of metal instruments. She planned to use all the gadgets on my body. She offered me something to eat. But I saw no food there. She prepared a small bed in an open, dark area. It looked like a massage table and not a hospital bed.

I stated, "I must pee."

I put on a white robe and roamed around this vile place. It looked in ruins. All the bathrooms did not function. I spotted a filthy young girl. She struggled to find somewhere to go to the bathroom. Every door she opened appeared grimy, mucky, and sticky with piss and feces. The toilets had no seats. I found a dark green glass bowl I struggled to pee in. A middle-aged woman sauntered by and mentioned details of her miserable life. I did not want to talk to her.

I warned, "Go away, I am trying to pee." I closed a broken bathroom stall door to block her off. I could not pee.

A different woman stalked me. Her bright red hair pushed to the side with heavy bangs. Her name was Beverly.

Beverly bitched, "I am waiting for you. We are ready for you."

I replied, "I haven't peed yet. You told me to come in here and change my clothes. This place is disgusting and there is nowhere to pee. I can't go. Go away."

The sinister nurse glared at me. I slammed the door in her face and grabbed the glass bowl and tried to pee again. I still could not go.

I viewed an open gray, misty area and heard a woman. I peered closer and examined her frail body crammed into a small metal locker. Her laugh sounded disturbing, as if she were crazy. She grunted at me like I was the looney one. I saw her arm hanging out of the rectangle door. I slid a dirty, transparent plastic curtain in front of me for privacy. I could not pee and felt I was at the brink of an orgasm attempting to pee. I woke.

I blurted, "What in the hell am I dreaming?"

I touched my bladder and did not have to pee. I laid in bed and sensed I was in *darkness*. All the people struggled to communicate with me. What I discovered was random and appeared in open dark rooms. The murky, dreary place felt of doom, filth, and looked nasty. Relieved, I woke. These people felt trapped there. The little kid before seemed overjoyed, ecstatic, and alive in the dream. I recognized my gift changed and matured. It made my dreams more intense and intertwined. I could sense who was good and bad; who was dead.

I gasped. "Wow, what a dream."

Later, after 10:00 a.m. It looked beautiful outside. I took Noodle for a walk. I enjoyed the wonderful breeze blowing my hair. It was sixty-five degrees, perfect weather. We strolled up our driveway and Noodle started running. I ran to catch up with her and recalled yesterday she acted worn-out, lethargic.

Gabriel announced, "God has blessed her again."

I beamed. "Wow, God blessed her again? This is outstanding. She seems high-spirited, content and full of energy."

I prayed daily for God to continue to help Noodle. God had answered my prayer. I grinned with joy. Ilene played music.

I asked, "What can you tell me?"

Ilene replied, "God has given her more time, Rebecca."

I smiled. "Ilene, I love hearing from you. It's breathtaking to hear from you and the way you speak is loving and caring. I sense the feminine part of you in your voice."

Noodle and I strolled toward the house. I beamed all the way, enjoying the wind. I whispered, "I love being home. If I have what I need, there's no reason to go anywhere."

Six weeks had passed since lockdown. I enjoyed being home with Noodle and my husband. I did not miss the drama and problems of others. When arrived inside. I logged into my journal about what happened.

Gabriel added, "God is pleased with what you have written."

God was awesome. He listened and watched the whole time. I felt it.

April 28, 2020

Dream Eight: I stood in a small town. You walked up to cafes on the street and ordered food. I heard two men talking. One fellow looked obese. He wore a brown leather belt and a tan shirt. His hair looked gray. He stared at me and stated, "This is the best food ever."

The other man dressed better. He wore a gray suit like a business executive. They appeared very different types of men, but both loved the meal. I wanted to try it. I grabbed my phone and called in an order. The person told me to pick it up at lunchtime. I strolled to the small cafe. I stood at the counter and waited. I spotted the owner behind the counter a few feet away. He looked twenty-eight to thirty years old. His black hair disheveled and cut short on top, almost shaved on the sides. I looked into his dark eyes. His face was not round, more sculpted at the jawline. I observed his clean-shaven face and recalled I saw this type of skin before. A man with a heavy beard, clean shaven, gave a greenish- bluish shadow beneath the skin.

He gazed but seemed friendly. The restaurant wasn't what I expected. The dirt floor swept clean to look like concrete but wasn't. I noticed the green plants stacked on the floor for the cook. It looked like plantains, a cactus, or a coconut plant? The shells of the plants laid on the floor. I did not understand why the plants were there, but knew it meant something. I stood in Mexico and the area appeared poor. I saw two small, square wooden tables with two brown wooden chairs at each table. The counter length looked four feet. The gentleman behind the counter owned the establishment. I sensed he was shy, reserved, diligent in his work and satisfied. He looked young and worked hard for his business. He loved to cook.

I waited in line and noticed Peo stood in front of me. It surprised me to hear his voice and see him there. Peo wasn't dead, he was alive. I sensed it was the 80s or 90s in Mexico. He joked with the owner. He giggled and ready for his order. The guy behind the counter glanced at me again and realized he could not give him a deal for the order. I would hear him.

The owner stated, "It's $10.50."

Peo chuckled. I recognized his laugh. I spoke to him before when we ordered concrete from him for the pool's foundation.

I watched Peo write on a piece of paper. It read, "$4.87." He kidded, "How will that be?"

He laughed and loved picking on this man. The owner and Peo were friends. I sensed from his tone and his manner they were best friends and loved one another very much.

I was next and leaned on the counter. I leaned inches away from the owner. His eyes looked dark brown, full shaped, dark eyebrows, clean-shaven face, eyes appeared a little slanted in shape. He wasn't tall but thin, not fat. He looked about 5 feet; 8 inches tall.

I stated, "I am here for my order." The owner looked stressed and worried.

He replied, "I sold out earlier to a large group of people that came to my store. They ordered all I had."

The people bought what I ordered. Peo requested something else. I felt disappointed because this was my lunch. I didn't have time to go anywhere else before I returned to work. I woke.

I asked Ilene, "Was this a visit? It felt like one. What was the guy's name? I was in Mexico."

Ilene replied, "Rodriguez, Terry."

I asked, "Was he with God?"

Ilene replied, "Yes, he is with God. He misses his friend."

I gasped. "Wow, I knew they were friends." I still felt his presence and recalled the details of the owner.

I grounded, prayed, and climbed out of bed. I sat on the couch and logged into my journal the dream.

Gabriel instructed. "God wants you to call Peo and tell him about the dream."

I searched for a while on my phone for the concrete man's number. I dialed it and wasn't sure if it was the right number. I started to sweat. I did not know this man and only spoke to him about the order for concrete. Peo answered. I recognized his voice. I explained who I was, and I am a medium. I added I dreamed of his friend this morning. Peo paused and said nothing.

I asked, "Do you have any relatives named Rodriguez?"

Peo answered, "I know some Rodriguez. But no relatives."

I felt panic. Why would Ilene give me the wrong name? I explained the dream. I described details of the owner's looks, and he lived in Mexico. He owned a restaurant, and he was your friend. I described his character and what he looked like.

Peo whispered, "I knew a man who died of cancer. He died a year ago or so. I wasn't able to see him before he died."

Astounded, I sighed. "It was him. Your friend. He loves you and misses you very much."

I asked, "Did you like to joke around with him? Pick on him?"

He laughed. "Yes, I picked on him all the time."

I asked, "Was your friend shy and reserved? Diligent in his work, a serious man?"

He replied, "Yes, you're describing him exactly."

Peo explained his friend was a baker. He loved to cook. I shocked him and heard sadness in his voice when he confirmed his friend was who I dreamed of.

I reminded, "This happens all the time to me. Your friend is with God and God wanted me to explain to you, he misses you. Believe me, your friend is okay and doing great. He is with God. Your buddy had no problem finding me, the medium, to tell his friend he loves and misses you."

Peo said nothing. I added, "Thank you for listening. I know it is hard to have someone call you at work out of the blue and tell you something of this nature. It was him, your friend. Oh, did your friend have kids or family?"

He answered, "Yes, he had children and family."

I continued, "If you feel comfortable, please call his children and family and let them know he is with God."

Peo laughed. "Wow, I will call today."

I continued, "This may help them heal, as it has helped you."

We said goodbye. I had sweat running down my sides. I felt relieved and thrilled I called.

Noodle demanded a walk. During our stroll, I asked Ilene, "Why did you say his name was Rodriguez?"

Ilene instructed. "You must believe what we tell you."

I understood why. Sometimes it was a piece of the puzzle the person learned later.

April 29, 2020

At 10:09 p.m. I dozed in "the room" and Noodle napped. I sipped the last of my red wine and heard music from Dan. I blurted, "I haven't heard from you in days and hear from Ilene more than you. Why?"

Dan replied, "I am only to help you. Ilene and Gabriel are way above me; they guide you."

I asked, "What else can you tell me?"

Dan added, "I am with you every step of the way. To help you. God allows me. I love and miss you."

I whispered, "I love you too, Dan."

Gabriel announced firmly, "God is listening. Obey your Lord, Rebecca. You must work on the writings."

I gasped. "Wow, I understand and will tomorrow. I hope you understand, God. Today, I felt exhausted working on the pool."

Gabriel replied, "God understands and knows all things, Rebecca. Do these things for your Lord and Savior. He is waiting."

I blurted, "Wow, I am sorry, God. I will work on the writings tomorrow. I am close to being finished with book three. I know you want me to start book four."

The forecast called for rain tomorrow, a perfect day to write. I thought, "Maybe start on book four and edit book three together. Writing is easy. The editing is brutal."

Gabriel announced, "God is pleased."

Ilene added, "God will be with you tomorrow to help you work."

I replied, "That is outstanding."

I walked outside with Noodle and held my glass of wine. Gabriel instructed with urgency, "You're drinking too much. You must remember your God's messenger. You must obey your Lord. You must work on the writings. God is waiting for them to be finished."

I sighed and went inside. I poured the rest of my wine down the sink. I brushed my teeth and told Gabriel, "I will work on the writings tomorrow. It will rain and a perfect day to write."

Gabriel answered, "God will be with you. God is pleased."

May 2, 2020

I edited and heard music, "Go Tell It On The Mountain."

I whispered, "Hello, Dad."

Dad beamed. "God is watching you, Beck."

I wondered, "Wow, he's watching me? What does God think, Dad?"

He answered, "He's glad you're working on the writings. You must finish it, Beck."

I whispered, "I know. It's a lengthy process and takes forever. I want my work to be perfect. This is God's work. The app I am using is slow, but great. I am learning so much."

I thought, "Wow, God is watching me. It is incredible and I feel the pressure to finish."

May 5, 2020

I washed the two-sea foam, blue comforters for "the room." At 7:00 p.m. I remembered the comforters sat in the washer. I panicked. It was already dark outside. Noodle and I wanted to relax in "the room." The bed wasn't made. I marched outside to our laundry area in the garage. The space enclosed and had a regular metal door instead of a garage door. I stuffed the blankets into the dryer and walked inside the house. I set a timer for ten minutes. The timer sounded, and I went into the laundry area again. I took the blankets out of the dryer and shook them. Still damp, I crammed them back into the dryer. I noticed a few large wet spots because they were full size comforters. I sprinted inside the house and set the timer again. Timer buzzed. I raced outside once more. The blankets felt almost dry. I noticed I left the door open to the laundry area. I sensed it wasn't wise to be out at night. I thought about how Ilene warned me. It wasn't safe.

I closed the door and waited for the blankets to dry.

Gabriel bellowed, "Go inside now. There are entities that wish to do you harm."

I asked, "Is there someone in here with me, Gabriel?"

Gabriel warned, "Yes, there are spirits gathering around you. Leave now."

I grabbed the blankets and trotted into the house quickly. I asked when inside, "Are they gone? There not in the house, are they?"

Ilene replied, "No, they are outside."

I sighed and arranged the comforters on the bed. Unnerved, we settled in to watch the TV program.

I asked Ilene, "What just happened outside?"

Ilene explained, "Spirits will try to harm you at night. You attract things. They try to hurt God's messenger the most."

I prayed, "God, remove these spirits from my home and land. I ask in the name of the Father, the Son, and the Holy Spirit, Jesus Christ, I pray, Amen."

Gabriel announced, "God has removed them."

I gasped. "Wow, that was scary. Thank you, God, for protecting me."

Later, in our bed. I woke at 1:45 p.m.

Dream Nine: I saw a Caucasian guy with an oval face and light yellow-orange hair. His hair braided in two cornrow patterns. I glanced at him and decided not to stare. I sensed his spirit was *malevolent.* I observed his light-colored eyes glaring at me and he felt too close. I looked away and saw a minuscule figure, a man two inches tall. The man appeared tiny because he was so far away. I looked closer. The tiny fellow was an African man with a huge round afro. He wore a bright, aqua-colored T-shirt which fell past his thighs. He wore long red shorts to his ankles. The black man jumped up and down, giddy with excitement. I sensed the two of them wanted to harm me.

I woke, startled. Panicked, I freaked out and prayed for God to remove these spirits from my presence. It took a while to drift to sleep. These entities sought to hurt me.

I woke at 8:30 a.m. I asked Ilene, "Who and what happened last night in my dream? It was frightening."

Ilene explained, "Your gift is growing. These two spirits found you last night in the garage. They waited till you slept to try to terrorize you. Spirits that are evil want to hurt God's messenger the most."

I asked, "That is how they felt. Were they in darkness?"

Ilene clarified, "No, these spirits are in the in-between. This is why it is not safe for you to be out at night."

I thought, "I must sage the laundry area. I haven't in a while. I prepare only the inside of the house."

I laid there thinking about what Ilene told me. I felt shaken, still knowing these entities found enjoyment in wanting to terrorize me. My guides protected me. That was why I woke. But they attempted to terrify me in my dreams. It did.

May 8, 2020

Dream Ten: When Dean lived, he spoke calmly, a gentle man. He was charming, depending on his mood. His wife wanted everyone to hear everything she said. I did not enjoy her personality most days. She wanted to make sure you knew they had money. Someone told me Dean died a few years ago. He was an elderly man in his late seventies and his back became hunched over after surgery. The surgery wasn't as successful as he hoped. His back issues affected how he walked towards the end of his life. But in the dream, he looked different.

Dean appeared forty and wore a satin-bluish purple suit. I noticed a bold gold bracelet sparkling on his wrist. He was a big, powerful man at his job. I sensed he made enormous amounts of cash in his business. Dean appeared successful, wealthy, and seemed on top of the world.

He showed me images. His spouse was in her late seventies, too. Her salt and pepper hair kept short. She was not very attractive, and I wondered what he saw in her when they both lived.

I sensed the wife believed she would receive all of her husband's money. I examined the images Dean revealed to me. I spotted his only daughter in the dream and Dean showed me numbers. I looked at what he presented, $541,838.88. Dean then showed me what he left his wife, $38,887.00. I continued to view the dream as the medium. He explained he left the rest of his money to his daughter. I saw someone distributing the funds to them both. The wife, disgruntled and furious at what occurred. She felt she deserved it all. Dean showed how she was selfish and deceived him in their marriage. He assumed she was loving and giving. But her personality was the opposite. This was why he left almost everything to his daughter.

I woke and asked Ilene, "Did I have a visit from Dean?"

Ilene replied, "Yes, he wants to be in the book. He knows your God's messenger."

I smiled and recalled the details. He wanted to be in the book. I laughed. He was still charming from heaven.

I asked, "Is he with God? He felt like he was."

Ilene answered, "Yes, he's with us."

I grounded and prayed. Noodle and I walked downstairs to enjoy our morning. I needed to log into my journal. Dean would be in the book.

May 10, 2020

At 11:00 p.m. Noodle and I climbed into bed. My husband stayed up longer to watch his favorite TV show. I whispered my prayers earlier in the day. Noodle wasn't hearing well anymore. I prayed, "Please improve baby Noodle's hearing. I need her to hear what I say to her. I need her to hear I love you. Please don't take her sight and hearing away as she ages. It would break my heart to see these things happening to her."

God spoke, *"I have granted these things because you believe in me. I have answered your prayer."*

I sobbed. Tears flowed down my cheeks. It was true. God was powerful and always listened.

May 11, 2020

Noodle and I strolled on our walk. She seemed overjoyed. I thought about what happened last night and wondered if I should add this to the book. I heard music from Dad.

I asked, "Is there anything you can tell me?" I watched Noodle while I talked to Dad.

He beamed. "She loves you. She's feeling better already from the blessings. God wants you to put this in the book, Beck."

I smiled and sensed I needed to write it down this morning when I woke. As I logged this wonderful experience in my notes. I cried and knew how wonderful it was to hear things from God. I knew in my heart God had blessed her again.

May 18, 2020

Dream Eleven:

I stood in a lavish house. I noticed my client and his wife. They enjoyed a romantic evening in one of the luxurious bedrooms. My ex stood in the adjacent bedroom. The two bedrooms shared the bathroom in the center of the rooms. I walked through my client's dark, cream-colored bedroom.

The headboard made of tufted beige leather. I saw the couple lying in bed together. It was obvious they had sex. Their clothes scattered on the floor. I observed purple roses on the floor and around the bed. They snuggled in bed together and watched TV. I sensed they loved and deeply cared for each other.

I strolled toward the bathroom. I looked down and saw I wore soft navy leisure pants. A buttoned navy top and a soft white robe. I wore no socks. I entered the bathroom and closed the door. My client's wife tapped on the door.

She stated, "We are done, you can walk back through again."

I already knew this, but I thought she was being kind. I didn't want to bother them and needed to use the toilet. I tiptoed back into the other room and passed their bed. I entered my bedroom and spotted my ex laying on the bed. I climbed into bed and noticed his erect penis. It had pre-cum on the tip. I reached for a pillow and wiped off the pre-cum with it. He wanted oral sex. I did not want to do it.

The dream shifted. I observed him staring at me lying on the bed. I laid on my back with my clothes and robe on. He attempted to kiss my body through the night clothes. I looked at his face sneering at me, chewing gum. He loved to chew gum when he lived.

I listened to the gum smacking. He continued to try to kiss my body through my night-clothes but had no success. He spit on my sides, ankles, and legs. He struggled to spit on me more. I heard the spitting and felt nothing. He wanted me to feel humiliated. It disgusted me.

I woke at 9:00 a.m. I never slept this late. I felt disgusted. He was so close to me and wanted me to touch his privates. I felt violated.

I asked, "Why did this happen?"

Gabriel answered, "He wants you to think that he had sex with you. He did not. He did not touch you. We protect you."

I thought, "He wants to confuse me and make me feel horrible *still from darkness.*"

Ilene replied, "We protect you. He cannot harm you. But he tries to do these things through the gift that you have. He tries to torment you through your gift because he knows you are God's messenger."

I needed to write this in the book.

Ilene replied, "Yes, God wants people to understand how evil will try to harm his messenger."

Relieved, this did not happen. I felt him spitting on me. It felt vile and made me feel violated. Relieved, I wore clothes. I trembled, recalling what I felt.

May 21, 2020

I heard Gabriel's music. I asked when I settled in "the room." "What did you say?" It was difficult to hear in the living room with the TV loud.

Gabriel announced, "God is pleased with the writings. You are almost finished. Must prepare for the many changes coming. They will weaken you. Pray for strength, guidance, and protection. We will be with you, guiding you."

I replied, "Thank you, Gabriel. I am glad you are my master guide."

Gabriel added, "God wants you to pray more. It will help thee."

I prayed, "I ask for strength, guidance and protection from the people and the virus. I need calmness and tranquility to help me stay grounded and centered. I need you, God, and my guides to help me. Protect me from all negative energy and evil. I ask in the name of the Father, the Son, and the Holy Spirit, in Jesus Christ, I pray, Amen." I crossed myself.

Gabriel announced, "God has heard your prayer and is pleased with his messenger. He will show you the way."

I sighed. "Thank you."

I had not prayed enough. I edited for weeks and almost finished with *Experiences Never Stop Part 2*. One more day, done. That was why I had not prayed. My mind overloaded with editing and worrying about working at the salon. I dreaded it and missed Noodle already. I never was with my friend every day for weeks, months. I felt blessed and did not want it to end. But it was over tomorrow. My belly bloated already with the stress upon me. I needed my life to change direction. How? God had a plan. My patience tested once more.

May 23, 2020

Dream Twelve: *Evil* entered my dreams. I started back to work. *Evil* terrified me all night. *It* reminded me I would not be with my dog. Evil showed me my dog, horrified and afraid. Noodle trembled with fear. I sensed my fear as I aged, not able to walk. I watched my legs dismembered from the ball and socket joints lying on the floor. My pelvis rested on top of a small metal ball and rolled. My hip joints fastened to the metal ball. I watched part of my body rolling on the floor with no legs. I saw myself chopped in three different pieces. *Evil showed what it craved to do to me.*

I woke, startled, and terrified. It horrified me. I reached under the covers. I grabbed my hips and legs to make certain they were attached. I shuddered, recalling how my body looked dismembered and rolling on the floor in pieces. Shaken, I climbed out of bed and walked to the bathroom to pee. I returned to bed and drifted to sleep.

The dream continued. *Evil* continued to enter my brain to terrify me. It did. I crashed early because I must work tomorrow. I had not worked in weeks. I needed rest and energy to handle the upcoming day. I dreamed of *evil trying to hurt me* all night long until 6:00 a.m. Parts of the dream blocked from my memory. My guides protected me this way. But I still sensed *evil's presence. It wanted to show me how it would hurt me and my dog.* Which I understood would never happen because my guides, God, protected me. I will go to heaven when I die.

Again, evil knew my weaknesses and used it against me. I woke terrified and exhausted, fighting throughout the night. Now, I must deal with the stress of work and facing COVID-19.

May 24, 2020

Today was perfect. My husband and I enjoyed the pool today. We swam, even Noodle. The weather in the upper 80s. The two drum fans blew to make a fake beach breeze. The wind felt fabulous blowing through my long hair. We swam and enjoyed each other's company. Noodle looked for frogs and loved the breeze, too. I watched her ears blowing in the wind. I realized at that moment I have never been happier. I gazed into my husband's eyes, "You do not know how happy you make me."

I shouted over the noise of the fans, "Thank you for putting the pool in for me. I love it and you."

He smiled. "You're welcome. Thank you for buying it."

I added, "I have to pay for it. Gotta make some money since 'Rona'... but it's good. This is what I expected. I am glad we are enjoying it together today."

Later that afternoon, I heard a new tune from Ilene. "I Just Want to Celebrate," by Rare Earth. I searched for the lyrics online. She cracked me up. I felt this way... inside.

I whispered, "I love you, Ilene."

At 5:00 p.m. I edited. I promised God I would. I noticed a coincidence in my editing of the timeline. My coworker confronted me on October 23rd. Tracy's surgery scheduled on October 23rd. Dan died on October 23rd. These events happened different years, but the same month and date. I did not believe in coincidence.

I thought, "Wow, all these things that happened brought positive changes in my life. At the time, I didn't understand any of them. They were painful. I had to go through the changes. When Dan's death occurred. It took me a long time to heal. The other two changes were quick. Wow, God works in mysterious ways."

At 9:00 p.m. Ilene reminded, "Remember to work on the book tomorrow. God is waiting."

I needed to work on the book in the morning. I was close to wrapping it up and needed a few thousand dollars to print it. I had not worked in months. God pressed me to finish.

I thought, "I will do these things for him, and God will provide for me."

May 25, 2020

Dream Thirteen:

I saw a business that used men to deliver and take care of tasks in people's homes. I entered a home and talked to a few people inside. Things seemed okay. I glanced around the sunroom and saw to my right a man and woman sitting. The man wore dark long pants. He sat with his legs crossed, reading a book.

I explained, "Everything will be fine."

I wandered to the corner of the room. I placed a record on the turntable. It played.

The woman warned, "It's too loud. Can you turn it off?"

I turned off the piece of equipment. I noticed as I got closer to the woman it was Joy. I looked to my left and saw her husband, Ken. I felt surprised to see her. (Joy and Ken mentioned in *Experiences Never Stop Part 2.*)

Joy's face appeared orange red. I listened to her talking while I watched. She seemed to have on extremely heavy makeup. Her face, hair, lips, skin, eyebrows appeared orange red.

I wondered, "Oh my, is she hot?" I sat down across from them in the sunroom.

I stated, "I am surprised you are here. I finished editing my third book. You're in it."

Joy joked, "Wow, how can we be in it? We are still alive." She smiled.

I stared at her, "Wait a minute. No, you're dead. You're in it. Don't make me second-guess myself."

I sensed evil tried to make me second-guess myself and dismissed the idea. Joy and Ken were with God. Joy had a sense of humor when she lived.

The dream shifted to an unfamiliar place. I observed my aunt standing at the front of the business that looked like a house. She stood at her daughter's home. I studied her walking towards the front door. My aunt was aware I followed her. She wore a mint-green leisure jacket and pants with a floral white blouse. Her hair teased and styled like she wore when she lived. Her figure looked perfect. She strolled into her daughter's house. I followed in behind her and sat across from her in a room. I spotted her daughter in the background bent over blow drying her long dark hair. Her daughter looked twenty years old. She did not know we were there.

I learned in these dream visits the spirit showed me a time that made them joyful. Her daughter was in her late fifties now.

I asked my aunt, "Were you excited to see my Dad?"

Dad told me after her funeral he was ecstatic when he saw her in heaven with him.

My aunt shook her head from side to side, which meant no.

I reflected, "What do you mean?"

I inquired, "You can't talk?"

She replied by shaking her head from side to side. No again. She died from a stroke was why she wasn't able to speak.

I woke, startled. What did I dream? The dreams intertwined. But three spirits visited me.

I asked Ilene, "Did Ken and Joy visit me in the dream?"

Ilene answered, "Yes, they are learning that they could have been kinder to you when they were alive."

I figured out, "Wow, that's what I dreamed the other time. I saw them at their funeral. Few individuals came to their funeral. This showed Ken and Joy they should have been more compassionate when they lived."

I asked about my aunt, "Why couldn't she talk to me?"

Ilene instructed. "God allowed her to visit you. But she was not allowed to speak to you. She still is amending for hurting his messenger."

I gasped. "Wow, this felt crazy. She looked fantastic. She was my favorite aunt and had hurt me deeply before she died. I don't even think she realized she did."

They seemed fine. They showed me things to get my attention. It did. The orange red face and my aunt had no problem walking across the yard. Before she passed, she fell and was totally incapacitated and needed a ventilator.

She had no problem sauntering across the yard, walking through her daughter's front door.

I realized, "Wow, she's still having to pay for hurting me. God really meant people that hurt his messenger would be punished. Eight months passed since she died."

It felt wonderful to see her. She looked fantastic. She smiled, seemed content and bright. Joy and Ken seemed peaceful and calm, just like they were when they lived. It was lovely to see them all.

Ilene played a new tune. "True Colors," by Phil Collins. I laid in bed and recalled everything that happened. No one knew she harmed me except my husband. She didn't come to our wedding, just like my Dad didn't show. It hurt me deeply.

May 26, 2020

Dream Fourteen: I stood on the beach with my husband. We rented a duplex house with two strangers. They were irritating and kept wanting to hover in our personal space with their two children. I sensed the strangers were untrustworthy and aware of the two separate rooms adjoining to ours. I left and strolled toward the beach. I saw a glimpse of the hip of my cocker spaniel, Freck. I ran toward her. I felt delighted and scooped her up and carried her back inside. I gently placed her on the couch. I sensed the how heavy she was in my arms.

I reached out my hand, "Can I have a paw?"

Freck picked up her paw and placed it in my palm. Her paw felt huge. I touched each toe and felt the fur on her paw. She looked amazing. I saw no cancer on her face, which she had when she died. She looked joyful and radiant. Freck was my lovely red and white parti-colored cocker spaniel. She had warm brown eyes and long ears, soft like a rabbit. She appeared content. It shocked me she was here. I should have taken better care of her. She visited me and I saw other dogs with her. When I saw her hip, I thought the dogs chased her and would harm her. But she played with the dogs who pursued her.

I wondered, "Does she play with other dogs in heaven? It was true."

It felt amazing to touch her paw and hold her again. I caressed her face and rubbed her ears. All the cancer gone from her being. Freck had a tumor above her eye when she lived. The cancer mass grew quickly, and I had to put her down. She died over thirty years ago. She looked delightfully happy. She missed me and came to visit. It felt remarkable to touch her again.

I woke and thanked God for letting me see, hear, and hold her again. She looked absolutely breathtaking.

May 27, 2020

Dream Fifteen: I stood in a vast, dark forest. The area appeared remote, with a modest log cabin. I spotted a small lake close by. I noticed a canopy of mature trees, dirt paths, several cars, and many inexperienced people partying by a bonfire.

I stepped closer. I am the medium viewing. I was a young girl who was an amateurish detective. We searched for a serial killer who brought us to this area.

I observed the individuals who sat by the campfire. They seemed friendly while they partied.

They laughed. "There is no one here who would do these things."

I believed there was. I trotted over to the cabin and entered. I immediately sensed *evil* inside the dwelling. The room felt heavy, thick, vile. I sensed *darkness* there. I noticed other detectives inside talking to a man. He described another man which owned the log cabin. The owner wasn't there. The agents searched and found items which led them to believe the owner was the serial killer they hunted.

When the guy showed me a picture of the serial killer. I sensed I knew him and spoke to him before frequently. The dream shifted. I had been in this cabin. I became the girl who the killer wanted to murder. I wasn't the police officer anymore. I peered down and my clothes looked different. I wore a red T-shirt with a short red skirt. Underneath the skirt, I noticed red stockings. The teenage girl panicked when she realized the guy who she thought was a friend was a serial killer.

The owner appeared in the doorway. He stood right before me. I stared at his round face. He looked repulsive and wicked. His eyes appeared slanted and black. His skin looked greasy and red. I peered closer. His skin texture looked rough and dry. His face looked wide, with a largemouth. He sneered at me. I noticed his three-inch, black, wavy hair. He looked in his late forties. The killer felt pleased he was a murderer.

He wanted to do revolting things to me, which he did to others. I backed away from this malicious man. He relished terrifying me. I felt fear because he knew I figured him out. The detectives rushed in the cabin's rear door, where I stood and arrested the guy.

He bellowed a sinister laugh while they handcuffed him. The cops led him out of the room and placed him inside the police car. The investigators looked in a different room inside the cabin. They discovered many three to four-gallon jars on a wooden shelf. When the police officer opened the jars. The objects they pulled out of the jars looked disgusting. People's legs, guts, and other parts. The killer dismembered people and kept their parts in large jars. I examined stacks of glass containers in the room. They searched and found more jars. I observed women's, men's, and young people's body parts. I felt deceived and appalled. I had been in the cabin before with this man and had sat by the campfire. I drank and laughed with these people. I assumed we all knew each other uncommonly well. This man definitely had other intentions. He was a killer. He coerced people into hanging out and became their friend. Then he slaughtered them. He placed their parts in the jars and saved them for his own enjoyment to look at later.

I woke, startled. I dreamed of *evil* again.

I asked Ilene, "Is this a man or is this evil?"

Ilene answered, "It was a man with attachments of evil. He is in darkness."

I gasped. "Wow, I am glad he is in darkness."

He felt disgusting and vile. I felt nauseated when I remembered what the killer did. I discovered he murdered over forty individuals. I was glad I woke. I struggled to erase what I went through and saw. I could not. God required me to see these occurrences to write for you.

May 29, 2020

Gabriel instructed. "Prepare the house. Your Lord will speak to you in a few days."

Gabriel added, "Your Lord will be with you today."

I prayed earlier, before I climbed out of bed, for God to be with me today. I asked because it would be emotionally trying day.

Later that evening, Noodle and I laid in "the room." I heard the song from Dad, "Precious Memories," by J.B.F. Wright.

I asked, "Dad, how are you?"

He whispered, "I love you, Beck."

I answered, "I love you too. Anything you can tell me?"

He responded, "God is going to speak with you soon. In a day or two. He has a lot to say. You must be ready, Beck."

I beamed. "I can't wait, Dad. I am excited to hear what God has to say. This week has been difficult. If God could tell me anything about the future would be outstanding."

Gabriel instructed. "Rebecca, you must pray more."

I asked Gabriel, "What should I pray for?"

Gabriel answered, "Do unto others as you would have them do unto you. You must remember to pray for those that you love. They need guidance, reassurance. Focus on what the future will bring. Remember to pray often. It will help guide thee."

I asked Ilene, "Is there anything you can add?"

Ilene added, "We love you, Rebecca. We are with you always."

I whispered, "It warms my heart knowing this. Ilene, is God pleased with what I am doing?"

Gabriel instructed. "God is pleased with your work. You must begin on book four. You must finish these things for your Lord."

I whispered, "I know, Gabriel. It's hard to work all day at the salon. I can't type all evening. Then do it all over again. I write on my day off. It's just too much. I am doing the best I can. If I didn't have to work, I could write more. But I have to work. I can't change that. I have to make money to pay for what I am writing. Few people are buying the books. It's very discouraging. You would think people would want to read something if they could hear what God had to say. They don't even seem to even care. It's terribly frustrating."

Gabriel instructed. "You must believe in yourself and do these things for God is waiting."

I replied, "I need some help. I can't work thirty hours a week and expect me to write every moment I have free and enjoy it. I am trying to balance my life. I have to live. My dog and husband need my time. I need time to rest and do tasks at home and in the yard. It's difficult. I am writing as quickly as I can. I wrote two books in a year and a half. I can't even believe I did that. We installed the pool. I help with my husband's business in communicating with his customers as well. I am doing more than I realized I can even handle. People do not understand how difficult this is. I pray more. It is hard to focus. Working, wearing a mask, dreaming of evil half the night, and waking up five times a night. It is hard."

Gabriel instructed. "Ask for what you need."

At 9:00 p.m. I posted on Facebook, "Curious, if you could know God's thoughts. Would you want to know?"

I had a few people comment, "I want to know." I took two pictures of excerpts from my book. I didn't reveal too much, but it was what God spoke.

Someone commented, "That's powerful, wow, powerful."

Gabriel announced, "God is pleased with what you have done. God has shown you the way."

The words made me cry. God was always listening.

May 30, 2020

Gabriel reminded when I woke, "Prepare the house. God will speak to you soon."

I whispered, "Thank you Gabriel, for reminding me."

June 1, 2020

I woke, Gabriel announced, "Prepare the house. The Lord will speak to you when you are ready. He will be with you today. Do not make him wait."

At 8:32 a.m. I needed to ground and pray. I had prepared the house earlier. I recited: "The LORD *is* my; shepherd; I shall not want. He maketh me to lie down in the green pastures: he leadeth me beside the still waters. He restoreth my soul: he leadeth me in the paths of righteousness for his name's sake. Yea, though I walk through the valley of death, I will fear no evil; for thou art with me; thy rod and thy staff they comfort me. Thou preparest a table before me in the presence of mine enemies: thou anointest my head with oil; my cup runneth over. Surely goodness and mercy shall follow me all the days of my life: and I will dwell in the house of the LORD for ever, Amen."

I prayed, "Lord, please surround me with the white light of the Holy Spirit. Protect me at all times while I meditate. I ask my guides, the angels, and my father to protect and guide me during the meditation. I ask these things in the name of the Father, the Son, and the Holy Spirit, in Jesus Christ, I pray, Amen."

Gabriel announced, "Your Lord is coming, Rebecca."

Ilene beamed. "He's almost here."

I immediately heard God, *"Hello, Rebecca. It is God the Almighty. I come today to help my messenger. These have been trying times for you. I have been watching, waiting, listening. My messenger is strong, diligent. I am proud of the work that you've done. There is much more to do. You must listen to your heart during these times. It will lead you. You are on the path of righteousness. You mustn't tarry in your work, for these things are God's will. You have not angered your Lord. I am a kind, loving God that knows all things. This is a difficult path I have chosen for you. You must do these things for your Lord. This is why you were born. You were Octavian in a past life, Rebecca in this life. These are God's wishes I have bestowed upon you to be my messenger. You must be diligent. Pray for your shortcomings. Dutiful, kind, loving, generous are the things my messenger needs to be. You are all of these things. You must continue on this path, God's path, the path of righteousness. I have granted to you many things because you believe in me. I hear your prayers daily for there are many. I encourage you to pray more. It will help thee, guide thee. You mustn't listen to those who doubt thee. They are not on God's path. They do not understand the things I have taught you. You must listen to your heart. I will show you the way. I will guide thee. Ask and I am there. You are weary, for you have been working hard for your Lord and Savior. I know these things for I am God the Almighty, speaks.*

You must continue on this path. I will guide thee. There will be turbulent times ahead. Pray for the ones that you love. Reassurance, guidance, understanding, patience, to help them grow with you. You mustn't tarry in your work, for God is waiting for these things to be finished. I will guide thee on this path, God's path. Remember, the truth has set you free. Do unto others as you would have them do unto you. There is much more to come for my messenger. The things you've prayed for. I've been listening. I want to do these things for you, thus saith the Lord.

You must be diligent in your work, for I am waiting. You mustn't tarry. These things will help others, thousands of people's souls from damnation. The writings must be finished so that others may read them. These are the words from your Lord and Savior, Christ the Almighty, himself. I must go now for your weary. Do you have any questions for me?"

I asked, "Lord, how long is this coronavirus going to be here? Wearing a mask at work every day is difficult. I do not enjoy it."

God answered, *"These things will come to pass. You must be diligent, vigilant. Stay on this path. The truth has set you free. Be aware of where you go. You are God's messenger. I will protect thee."*

I asked, "Lord, is there anything you can tell me about my future? The changes coming?"

God answered, *"You mustn't worry. These things will happen when you're ready. I will guide you and show you the way. Pray for the things that you need for I am listening, thus saith the Lord."*

I asked, "Lord, are you happy with the book I finished? I know I haven't published it yet."

God answered, *"Your Lord is very pleased with the work that his messenger has done. It will help others grow and believe in God the Almighty and help save their souls from eternal damnation. You have done these things for your Lord, and God is very pleased. Continue on this path. I will show you the way. Ask and I am there, says God the Almighty, himself."*

I asked, "Lord, is there anything I can pray for that will help me from this point on? You know my heart."

God answered, *"Diligence, strength, perseverance to overcome the obstacles in your heart, steadfastness, mercy for others, calmness, tranquility, these things I say to you. You must be willing to do more, and I will show you the way. I am the truth and the light. Let no man put asunder. I am your Lord and Savior, Jesus Christ, himself, the Almighty, speaks. You must remember to pray for others, for they need your guidance. It will help them to help support you on this journey. You must remember to pray for the ones that you love for I am listening, saith the Lord, God the Almighty."*

I asked, "Lord, is there anything you can tell me I should pray for the ones I love, which will help them? For you know what they need."

God answered, *"Guidance, reassurance, ask for the things that will help them grow with you on this journey. I must go now. My work here is done. My messenger has been diligent, forthcoming, dutiful, kind, and loving. I am proud of thee. You're doing God's work. You mustn't tarry for I am waiting, thus saith God the Almighty."*

I asked, "Lord, may I ask one more question?"

God answered, *"Yes, Rebecca. I am listening."*

I inquired, "You guided me to post something on Facebook about you, and I did. There were many negative comments. Why, Lord?"

God replied, *"People do not understand the knowledge I have given you. You mustn't listen to the naysayers. They try to harm thee. Evil is always waiting to harm my messenger. I must go now, for thou are weary. Listen to the things I have taught thee. I love you. Goodbye, Rebecca."*

I whispered, "Thank you, Lord, for speaking to me."

Gabriel announced, "Your Lord is gone."

I sobbed, feeling God's powerful presence. I felt humbled to hear anything from God. God spoke gentle today, but firm. I told my husband earlier, I hoped God was not angry with me.

God was listening then. I needed to proofread and felt overwhelmed. My heart tingled. My hands felt numb. My face drenched with tears. It was not sad tears, but tears of joy. I felt honored to hear from my Lord because it was him. I could not wait to see him in heaven. But I knew it will be a long time before that happens. It was 8:56 a.m.

I gasped. "Wow, twenty-four minutes. It felt as if five minutes passed. I thought I was in trouble not writing fast enough. God understood everything and wasn't mad. It made me sob all over again because I had let God down."

I must work harder and pray more.

June 2, 2020

<u>Dream Sixteen</u>: My guide, Dan, revealed himself. It felt marvelous to see him again. He showed pictures from the past of me with dark medium length hair. We smiled, laughed, and reveled in our adventures together. He gazed into my eyes. I stared at his blue eyes and his sandy blonde hair blowing around his face. We enjoyed seeing each other again.

It became difficult to recall all the details because Dan inserted himself into my regular dream and left. It felt incredible to see him, after all these years, happy. I woke and heard "Don't Stop Believin," by Journey. He loved Journey.

I whispered, "Thank you for visiting me. Thank you, God, for letting him visit me."

I climbed out of bed and heard "Blessed Assurance," song.

I beamed. "I love you, too, Dad."

I heard nothing and kissed Noodle.

Later, in the garden after work, I watered the roses and spent time with my family by the pool. I heard music.

I grinned. "Hello, Ilene."

Ilene shared, "Your flowers are beautiful, Rebecca."

I laughed. "Thank you, Ilene."

The roses looked the best I had ever grown this year. I had so much time to piddle with them during the quarantine. It paid off, and Ilene noticed. It felt awesome to hear from her.

At 8:46 p.m. I typed into my journal and heard from Ilene, "I love you, Rebecca."

I smiled and sighed. "I love you too. You are amazing."

Gabriel stated, "God is listening and is pleased with what his messenger has recorded."

I gasped. "Wow, God is always listening." I had the nag to write this down into my journal.

Gabriel stated, "God is glad you are being mindful of the writings."

I tried to be mindful after a busy, pleasant day at work. I sensed my guides and God were with me.

Gabriel reminded, "Remember to pray for the ones you love. They need your guidance, reassurance of their future." I prayed.

Gabriel announced, "God has heard your prayer and will answer in due time."

I whispered, "Thank you, God, and Gabriel for your guidance. Wow. You both are magnificent. I am blessed to hear from you both."

Ilene added, "God wants you to rest and enjoy your evening."

I replied, "I am, Ilene. It is wonderful to know God feels this way."

Noodle and I stretched out on the bed in "the room." My husband enjoyed his TV show in the adjacent room. I watched "Poldark," Season 5 directed by Mr. Selfridge. I had not seen this season and loved the entire series of "Poldark."

June 3, 2020

I played hooky because today was the first ninety-degree day. There were many changes in my schedule at the salon. I planned to spend the afternoon with my family by the pool. My husband stopped by Vito's, a local Italian restaurant. He picked up a large sausage and pepperoni pizza, and Noodle had chicken and pellets.

Noodle and I strolled toward the pool. She looked thrilled. Ilene stated, "We're excited for you, and we will be with you."

I heard music from Dad. I smiled. "I am glad you are excited and will be with me."

The afternoon was fabulous. The water looked inviting and felt delightful. I loved to feel the heat of the sun on my skin. We swam, sunned and Noodle enjoyed herself with us both at home. The two drum fans blasted to create a fake beach breeze. I thoroughly enjoyed being with my family and relished these moments.

At 3:00 p.m. Time to end our adventure, and we moved inside. The house felt cool and refreshing. My husband baked some pastries and diced some cantaloupe for a tasty treat. I scooped some chocolate ice cream into a bowl and Noodle ate a few pellets for her snack.

I worked on the writings for God after our snack. I stopped at 5:15 p.m. My husband napped in "the room." I rested on the couch until he woke. I turned on my iPad at 5:55 p.m.

I gasped. "Wow, more changes coming. I wonder what they will be?"

June 4, 2020

I woke early and could not sleep. I grounded and cleansed my aura. I envisioned my aura expanding the size of the room. I prayed for Noodle, myself, my husband, and the ones I love.

Gabriel instructed. "Remember to pray for those who have harmed you. It will strengthen your faith."

I prayed for those who harmed me. I spoke each one of their names in my prayer and asked, "Please help these people continue their life without me in it. Help them distance themselves from me, for I do not want to be a part of their life anymore. Encourage them to continue on their own journey. I ask in the name of the Father, the Son, and the Holy Spirit, in Jesus Christ, I pray, Amen."

Noodle and I enjoyed the morning together. I wondered what today would be like. Yesterday was perfect. I recalled I prayed for calmness and tranquility like God taught me. God helped me so much. I did not feel anxiety. I wasn't a calm person before. It felt wonderful to feel this peace inside my heart.

June 6, 2020

Noodle and I entered the house and took a break from lying in the sun at the pool. I diced a cantaloupe, watermelon, strawberries and arranged some chicken in the oven to bake for my husband. I waited for him to come home for lunch. I scrolled on my iPad at the news feed on Facebook. I saw another clip about Prince the Artist.

I thought, "I assumed he believed in God. I wonder if he is in heaven."

I asked Ilene, "Can I ask a question?"

Ilene answered, "Yes, you may."

I inquired, "Is Prince in heaven with you guys?"

Ilene beamed. "Yes, Rebecca. Prince is here. He says to tell you hello, and he's glad you're doing God's work. You will do more than he ever did."

I gasped. "Wow. I will write this in the book. It doesn't matter when you died yesterday, fifty years ago, several centuries, if you believe in God. You're in heaven. You should be able to see anyone from heaven. Prince can see me. How incredible is that? Wow, I haven't even thought of it that way."

I asked, "Ilene, may I ask another question?"

Ilene replied, "Yes, Rebecca. I'm listening."

I inquired, "How is Prince doing? How is he? He died suddenly. How's he doing?"

She replied, "He's with your Lord and Savior. He's never been happier. God has blessed him in many ways. He has forgiven him for his mistakes. He will see you when you're here. He's excited for you, of the things that you're going to do that you haven't experienced yet."

I blurted, "Well, he knows, just like my guides do. They know what will happen before it happens, so incredibly awesome. They are ten steps ahead of me all the time. Then when something happens, I am in shock because I don't see it coming. That's what makes it so glorious."

Later, I cooked a ribeye for dinner. I picked our first squash and zucchini out of the garden. My dinner tasted fabulous. Noodle and I settled in "the room" to watch our show.

Dad asked, "How was your dinner, Beck?"

I beamed. "Dinner was outstanding. Steak perfectly cooked. Noodle enjoyed a couple bites of my zucchini in the steak drippings. I fooled her."

He whispered, "I was watching, Beck."

I replied, "You were? I am glad, Dad. We spend more time together now than when you were alive."

He answered, "I know, Beck. It makes me sad in some ways, but I am happy I can see and talk to you anytime. God lets me. Which is almost every day."

I replied, "I have noticed, Dad. I speak to you and hear from you almost every day. I thank God all the time. It is a blessing. Our relationship really has grown. But not changed in how much we loved one another."

He whispered, "Beck, I love you more than you will ever know. I am proud of my daughter. You have been treated badly by the family. I am sorry for that. It was wrong, Beck."

I replied, "It is wrong, Dad. But they have chosen what is important to them, and it isn't me. I accept that. It hurts deeply. I forgive them and wish them well. I am honestly doing better without them in my life. There is no drama, discord, dread, uncertainty, or disdain. I don't have to deal with these problems, and I am glad. I know deep in my heart they really don't care. I know these things from the gift God gave me. I feel it. It is there. It's real."

Dad beamed. "I love you, Beck. God loves you. Ilene loves you. Dan loves you. Gabriel loves you. Your husband loves you. Noodle loves you. Your friends and clients love you. You have a lot, Beck. You should be grateful."

I whispered, "I am grateful, Dad. I could not do this without all of you who love me. It would break my heart."

Gabriel announced, "God is listening. He is proud of what his messenger is saying. For he knows these things are true."

I gasped. "Wow, tears welled in my eyes because that is true. I shook my head. God knows all things, Dad."

He answered, "I know, Beck. He is right here beside me."

I saw Dad form in my clairvoyance. I spoke to my father, "I see you beside God, floating in air. Short brown wavy hair, twenty years old, white shirt, dark brown pants, shiny black-brown shoes. You are squatting, leaning forward towards me. Your elbow on one knee. Your hand relaxed. I see you talking. God sitting behind you in the air. Light blue cloth draped, flowing over God's body. God's dark brown wavy hair touching God's shoulders and parted in the middle. Short close-cut beard, pointy nose, creamy, pale skin. God is looking at and listening to you, Dad."

Ilene added, "Your accounts are accurate."

I gasped. "Wow, thank you, Ilene."

Ilene beamed. "You're welcome, Rebecca. God is always listening. He is happy with what you are writing. It is true."

I exclaimed, "That is awesome. God and you guys are incredible. I am blessed beyond words to hear and see you."

Gabriel stated, "God is happy his messenger is happy."

I grinned. "I am Lord. I am happy, thank you."

Ilene whispered, "You must rest now and enjoy your evening."

I whispered, "Thank you, Ilene."

I loved these conversations when they happened. I never knew when they would.

June 8, 2020

I worked on writing because I wrote nothing on Sunday. Gabriel reminded me first thing this morning. God wanted me to work on the writings. I strove to get daily tasks finished in the morning. I wrote an hour and wanted to lie by the pool after lunch. The sun shone brightly in the early afternoon. Noodle and I strolled to the pool.

Gabriel stated, "God wants you to enjoy your day. He wants his messenger to be happy."

We enjoyed ourselves. I checked my phone in intervals for messages from time to time. I looked at the screen, 1:11 p.m. and glanced another time at 2:22 p.m.

I smiled. "I'm on the right path and work on balance."

I swam and Noodle enjoyed the strong breeze from the drum fans blowing her fur.

I stated, "Thank you, God, for everything. I always wanted to vacation in Florida just to swim in the blue water. Now, I have my own blue water. Thank you, Lord."

I prayed for the ones I loved and for what I needed. Today felt perfect.

My husband napped because he had a horrible night's rest. He needed to work later, and I needed to highlight my hair. I planned to write the rest of the afternoon.

At 10:15 p.m. Time for bed and I prepared for the workweek ahead. I heard the song, "Dec' 63," by The Four Seasons.

I asked Ilene, "Was this from my husband's mother? Who is playing this tune? I haven't heard the song in a while."

Ilene replied, "I am. Yes, it's from his mother."

I sauntered into the living room and shared with my husband it was wonderful to hear music from her through Ilene. I heard his mother through Ilene, "I love my son. I miss him. He could do more with his life. He needs to be more careful where he goes to protect God's messenger. I am proud of the man you are and your accomplishments. You need to pray more for what you need. You need to forgive those who have harmed you. It will help you. Be careful where you go. I love you very much and I miss you terribly. I will see you again, many years from now. I wish I could have met your wife when I was alive. You can do more, much more. You need to pray for what you need, and God will help you, guide you. I will be with you. I must go. God will not allow me to speak anymore to you."

My husband cried hearing from his mom. He loved her deeply. She popped back in for a moment. "Remember to pray for what you need. I will be by your side. Goodbye."

I felt overwhelmed, feeling her presence and personality. She felt gentle, giving, warm, soft, extremely loving, genuine. I felt her purity in her words. I shared what I felt with my husband.

He whispered, "She believed in God. She was the upmost, a strong Catholic and believed in God deeply."

I cried. "I felt her purity, softness, gentleness, the deep love she has for you."

He gazed into my eyes and whispered, "That was who she was."

I kissed him and whispered, "I hope you believe this was your mother because it was."

He replied, "Of course I believe you. Thank you."

I responded, "Don't thank me, thank God for letting her speak to you through me."

I walked into "the room," scooped up Noodle and took her outside. While I waited, I heard the song again. I stated, "I hoped he believed me."

I heard his mother, "He did." I smiled. "Does God want me to write this in the book?"

His mother beamed. "Yes, God wants you to write it."

I logged into my journal when I came back inside. It mesmerized me what I heard and experienced from Mrs. Hopkins. I had heard many times how wonderful a person she was. Her presence felt extraordinarily kind, gentle, loving, and pure. I heard the music again.

His mother responded warmly, "Thank you, Rebecca. You make my son very happy. I love you, Theresa."

Ilene beamed. "God has been listening and is proud of your work. Your husband's faith needs to be strengthened."

June 12, 2020

At 9:00 p.m. I prepared baked salmon with dill and lemon. I picked fresh yellow squash from the garden. I sliced the squash thin and seasoned with dill, salt, and lemon pepper. While my dinner baked. I mixed ranch dressing, sour cream, onion powder, dill, lemon pepper and lemon juice for a dipping sauce.

The kitchen filled with the aroma of salmon. The fish tasted fantastic with the delicious sauce. I wondered why I craved dill and lemon?

I searched online for benefits of dill while I ate. Dill loaded with vitamin C and vitamin A, which were great for your immune system. I felt immediately God wanted me to eat more of these things to strengthen my immune system with the COVID-19 rampant. New cases reported daily. Many people did not take it seriously, but some did. I sensed this was God's way of protecting me and it felt amazing. Dinner tasted scrumptious. I would cook this again. I wiped the remnants of the dipping sauce with my finger and did not waste the mouthwatering morsels.

Dad asked, "How was your dinner, Beck?"

I beamed. "It was freaking incredible, Dad. Does God want me to put this in the book?"

He smirked, "Yes, Beck."

I cleaned the dishes and thought about how wonderful today was. My guides, Dad, were with me and God. I sensed their presence in the conversations I had with clients today.

Gabriel added, "God is pleased with your work today."

I inquired, "What did I do?"

Gabriel replied, "You spoke from your heart. That is what God has taught you."

I helped clients today with problems they shared. I had spoken from my heart.

I gasped. "Wow, God is always listening."

June 13, 2020

My husband and I enjoyed the evening. I heard a new tune. "3AM," by Matchbox Twenty. I asked, "Who is playing this?" Ilene played a familiar tune then switched back to "3AM,". "Why Ilene?"

Ilene responded, "Because you 're feeling isolated, all will be fine."

My husband asked, "What is it?"

I replied, "Oh, it is Ilene, playing a new tune." She implied how my husband felt without his knowledge.

I added, "I am blessed to have clairaudience. Ilene feels like a mom, nurturing, which my soul never had."

I heard, "Blessed Assurance," song. I whispered, "Hi, Dad. I miss you. I haven't heard a lot from you lately."

Dad responded, "Beck, I love you. He is reading it now."

I asked, "The letter?" I mailed it days ago.

He replied, "Yes, Beck. They are discussing it. He doesn't understand. Wondering why not in person."

Gabriel stated, "You must believe in yourself. God knows all things. He will show you the way. Your brother has to learn. He will be with you no matter what, Rebecca. Have faith in yourself."

Dad added, "He is reading it again, Beck. He wants to understand."

God gave me the nag to write a letter to state who I was becoming. I described my abilities of my gifts, and writing was my destiny. I explained my gifts were growing, and I heard from God. This was what I wrote about to help others. I thanked him for his unconditional love. I wanted to explain the best way I could, to write it.

Our dinner cooked and ready. The sauteed fish and shrimp tasted delicious.

Gabriel announced firmly, "Do not question who you are. You are God's messenger. The ones who love you will be with you."

I whispered, "Thank you, Gabriel."

Later that evening, we discussed different topics. My husband commented about a meth addict at a clinic to get their fix.

I responded, "You must remember addiction lowers your vibration extremely. It is evils easiest way *to influence you* and get a hold of you through addiction."

He added, "I still think they're losers, users, rednecks and don't care."

I replied, "You don't know that. If you have an addiction, it doesn't matter if you're poor or a user. Evil doesn't care. It wants to control anyone it can. So, you cannot better yourself. That's evil working at its finest right there. That's what I have learned."

I walked outside to lock up Chicken. I heard music from Gabriel. It was terribly loud.

I asked, "Gabriel, did I tell my husband the correct thing?"

Gabriel answered, "Evil is vile, wicked and will torment anyone in its path."

I gasped. "Wow. To hear it from you, Gabriel, firmly. It's worse than I thought."

Gabriel announced, "Rebecca, God wants you to write these things in the book."

I whispered, "I will, Gabriel. I will."

June 14, 2020

We had a wonderful morning and afternoon together. We enjoyed delicious crispy bacon on a fried egg sandwich. Noodle could not wait to hang out by the pool. We laid out by the pool for a while and enjoyed ourselves immensely. I let Chicken and Turk out of the coop. I felt something bite me on my foot. I looked down and nothing there. We came in the house to cool off and I felt dizzy.

"What bit me?" I wondered.

I felt nauseous and thought I would puke. I laid down and my husband gave me an antihistamine. I rubbed some steroid cream on my foot because it swelled. I felt terrible. We both laid down for a nap. The sun took our energy. I still felt nauseous.

We woke at 6:30 p.m. and still daylight outside. We needed to gather our towels from the pool before the storm approached. We stacked all the pool items. I remembered Chicken and Turk were out.

I stated, "I will lock up Chicken and Turk."

I called her and heard nothing. She normally made her chirpy chicken sounds and Turk did not make her beep-beep sounds. I trimmed the weeds in the run-in today. The weeds were overgrown from the rain. Something was wrong. I stepped closer to the run-in and saw Chicken dead with her head missing. Feathers scattered throughout the run. Turk laid in the back corner of the run, dead with her head missing too. I felt devastated because I let them out. It wasn't dusk yet. An animal snuck into the coop and terrorized both birds. The animal enjoyed torturing and murdering them.

I screamed, "Something killed our birds."

He trotted over and looked inside the coop. He discovered small prints he believed were fox prints. My husband set traps, hoping to catch this vile creature. The coop stood inside a six-foot wooden fence in the garden close to the pool. My maternal instincts were to protect Noodle. This animal could attempt to harm her. Our evening ruined by this horrible news. They did not die quickly. I felt sick inside for the rest of the night.

June 15, 2020

I woke and recalled Chicken and Turk's death. I sighed and remembered I had a dream visit.

Dream Seventeen: My aunt inserted herself into my dream. Bob, who I mentioned in *Experiences Never Stop* and in *Experiences Never Stop Part 2*. Bob popped in too. He smiled standing behind his bar. I recognized his teeth. He loved owning a bar.

My aunt wore a two-piece beige pant suit. I noticed large red floral flowers embroidered on the shoulders and the waist of the jacket. The pants had flat pleats around the upper hip area. I observed her sandy blonde hair done perfectly in a set. She looked forty years old. It surprised me to see her.

I explained, "Oh, I just saw your children. I see their posts on Facebook."

She asked, "You have seen my daughter?"

That was all I heard. She disappeared. It seemed bizarre how spirits popped in. I am the medium and they try to communicate with me. I needed to figure out the puzzle.

I grounded and prayed. I slept in the middle of the bed last night. It felt more comforting since my husband slept downstairs because it was cooler. I felt mournful over what happened to our birds.

Dad whispered, "I'm sorry, Beck, what happened to your birds. A fox did it."

I mumbled, "Thank you, Dad. It was horrible to witness them attacked so viciously."

June 20, 2020

A tremendous storm raged during the night. That morning, the view felt fresh and clean. I needed to ground my energy after the hectic week at work. I listened to coronavirus discussions and wearing a mask all day felt exhausting. I sensed the turmoil of the world's energy. I was thankful to have a day off with Noodle. I felt renewed after the glorious rain.

Noodle and I went for a walk and heard music from Ilene.

I stated, "I am grateful to have you with me all the time. I love you and need you."

Ilene replied, "God has sent me to help you on your journey. I enjoy being your guide. You are a warm gentle spirit and I love you."

I whispered, "Thank you, Ilene. It's wonderful to hear that's how you think of me."

Ilene instructed. "God wants you to write this."

I replied, "I will. Could you remind me when I get back from our walk?"

Ilene responded, "I will."

I heard music, "Shout," song. I stated, "Gabriel, I'm grateful to have you as my master guide. You were with me before I even knew."

Gabriel instructed. "God wants you to pray for the ones that you love."

I prayed, "God, please protect the ones I love from this coronavirus. Help them grow with me on this journey. Give them reassurance and guidance about what their future will bring. Help them support me and love me. Give them signs of encouragement. I ask in the name of the Father, the Son, and the Holy Spirit, in Jesus Christ, I pray, Amen."

I heard "Don't Speak," song. I asked, "Dad, where have you been? I miss hearing from you. I haven't heard from you much lately."

Gabriel answered, "Your father will be with you always. He's busy doing things for God."

I smiled but missed hearing our conversations, which we had almost daily.

We arrived at the house and Noodle looked exhausted. We had not walked in days because of the rain. I needed to relieve myself. While in the bathroom, I heard music.

Dad whispered, "I love you, Beck."

I laughed while I peed. "I love you too."

He heard what I said to Gabriel. I needed to enjoy time with Noodle today. My husband worked, and I wanted to remove the run-in. This endeavor needed to end. We never caught the fox.

I worked on dismantling the run-in and missed my birds. The garden seemed quiet without them. Two hours passed. I cut and removed all the wires. We would use the empty coop to store fertilizer and yard equipment. I felt overheated and strolled inside the house.

Ilene stated, "The birds are in heaven, Rebecca. You will see them again."

I laughed because I wondered if they were. I didn't know if birds went to heaven, but so. I sought to make the area where they lived pretty and happy again. I took all the ugliness away. I needed my spirit to feel better.

Gabriel added, "God is pleased with what you have written."

I gasped. "Wow, God hears everything all the time."

June 21, 2020

Father's day, I heard music.

I whispered, "Happy Father's Day."

Dad replied, "Thank you, Beck. I love you. I wish I had been a better father."

I answered, "You were the best you could be. I love you."

He whispered, "Beck, I could have done more."

I whispered, "I am glad you're my Dad. I love you."

He replied, "I am glad you're my daughter. I am proud of you, that God has chosen you, my daughter, to do these things for God."

I sighed. "I have big shoes to fill. I hope I can make God proud."

Gabriel announced, "God is listening. God is proud of your work. You have much more to do."

I answered, "I will do my best."

June 22, 2020

Noodle and I enjoyed our morning together. I needed to accomplish a lot today. It would be over ninety degrees by lunchtime. I did not take her for a walk; it was already too hot. I wrote for two hours, then made a delicious ground beef quesadilla topped with queso cheese and sour cream.

I gathered towels and a cold drink. Noodle excited to hang by the pool. It felt like a vacation. This was the routine when on vacation and she remembered. I turned on the drum fans for the fabulous beach breeze. Umbrellas opened, ice water and oil. We settled in our spots. It felt scorching hot already. I took several dips in the pool to cool off. I poured water on Noodle's back to keep her cool. She wasn't ready yet for the big swim. We enjoyed ourselves for three hours and called it a day.

After we cooled off, I gave her a short haircut inside the house. I usually gave her a haircut on top of the hot tub. It was the perfect height for me. It was too hot for that. She did not like the different system and seemed frightened. I finished as best I could.

We returned upstairs to write. My husband came home shortly after. He needed to help a friend with plumbing issues. He looked exhausted.

He hated construction work and wished he did not have to. He obligated himself, so he must.

While he was away, Noodle and I returned to the pool. We watered the flowers and vegetables. I went for a swim. While in the water, I asked Ilene, "Did Octavian swim in the baths regularly, daily?"

Ilene answered, "Yes, Octavian enjoyed the water. He had his private bath. That is why you enjoy it so much. Your tastes for finer things. You remember."

I gasped. "Wow, I am not wealthy in this life. I was rich in my past life. I looked around the garden at the flowers in bloom. The roses, yellow lilies, mandevilla bushes, canna lilies, hostas and other Asiatic lilies blooming. I felt happy."

Ilene added, "Octavian loved his garden."

I smiled. "I love my garden too."

I dried off and heard music from Dad. He added, "Your garden is lovely, Beck."

I asked, "Do you like it Dad?"

He answered, "It is beautiful."

I stated, "I am a better gardener than you, Dad. You did not know it. Did you?"

He replied, "Beck, I was a farmer. I grew fields of plants. Your garden, Beck, is lovely."

I answered, "Thank you. I am glad you can see it."

My father never saw my garden but once when he lived. I gathered our things. Noodle and I strolled inside for dinner. My husband would be home soon.

I breathed, "What a wonderful day. I am tired, but it was perfect."

June 28, 2020

I chatted in the Zoom room from Both Sides Now TV. I enjoyed it. They wanted to learn more about the afterlife, and we shared our knowledge to help one another. I ended the chat because it was late. I heard a new tune from Ilene. "How Great Thou Art," by Carl Boberg. The song played loud. I laid in "the room" and listened to the words and thought of God's power.

Gabriel instructed. "God will speak to you soon. Prepare the house."

Ilene stated, "You have helped this man."

She meant Damien in the chat room. He talked about his wife and their problems. He needed space and was settling. He could do more with his life. I told him these things.

I realized, "They were listening."

Ilene stated, "God is pleased with your work."

I asked, "Which work?"

Ilene answered, "The man, you have helped him."

I thought, "I hoped I had. I sensed he needed to walk away from her."

I asked, "Will God speak tomorrow?"

Gabriel instructed. "God will let you know when he is ready."

I asked, "Please remind me tomorrow to sage and frankincense the house."

June 29, 2020

No work today and enjoyed spending time with Noodle at the pool. Noodle looked thrilled to go to the pool after lunch. I enjoyed watching her excitement and work weighed on my mind. Clients changed appointments and the unknown, which dangled over our heads, lingered.

At 8:00 p.m. I wondered, "Will I hear anything tonight from Dad or my guides?"

I began the new series "The Moonstone," directed by Lisa Mulcahy. The series wasn't as interesting as the other Victorian series I had finished. They tried to find the stolen moonstone was the entire plot of the series. I started playing games on my iPad and watched the series at the same time. The evening was quiet. I heard nothing eventful from my guides or my Dad.

June 30, 2020

Dream Eighteen: I looked at a scrawny man. He wore raggedy, filthy clothes. He looked in his thirties and hunted women. The guy felt vile and violent. He relished in capturing and torturing women, demeaning them. It took place in the poverty-stricken areas of the south. I observed open wheat fields. I peeked down and noticed the ground looked sandy. I felt the scorching summer sun on my skin. I saw several metal cages; the emaciated man built several yards away. He constructed the cages for women, not animals. He captured the women, shoved them into the cages to torture later. The place hidden well from town. I discovered it was a farm somewhere in the south. No one knew it existed.

I felt this man stalking me. He craved to stuff me into the cage, and he did. I looked inside the cage and escaped. I saw myself shaking in the snow on the ground, lying there. My body nude, trembling. I saw the inside part of my wrist quivering and looked bluish from the cold. The man realized I had gotten free and watched me escape. He didn't stop me. My guides protected me in the dream this way. I am the medium. This is how I saw what happened. He apprehended women in the sweltering summer, and she escaped in the winter naked and horrified.

The dream shifted to another man. He stalked women as well. I studied him. He looked thirty and had close-cut, tight-curly, blonde hair which appeared like Afro texture. The man wore black-rimmed glasses, and his eyes looked black. He appeared Caucasian, but his skin tanned by the sun. He might be biracial. He stared and gawked at me.

This man sought after rooms for rent from a homeowner. He rented a room from me in my home. I viewed his behavior as he did when he lived. This killer was a nasty, vicious man. He never kept his room clean. He wished to take care of your animals when you were away from your home. I had a gray cat. He wanted to feed it. My husband and I traveled out of town, and it would be fine. Something was weird about this guy. I sensed he was off somehow. He seemed wicked and creepy in his demeanor. I really didn't want him in my residence, but he seemed polite. We needed someone to feed our cat while we were away. I agreed.

We returned from our journey; the cat was fine. He never harmed the animals. But he had been throughout the house rummaging through our things. When the guy wasn't home. I snuck into his room and did the same.

His room disheveled and saw cat food on the floor. He didn't seem to care about anything. He had stuff scattered everywhere. He pretended to clean the outside of the home to make it look great. He showed himself to you as friendly and kind. But his belongings were unkept as he was inside his own head, a creepy dude. He wanted to harm me.

I observed a chain-link fence in a suburban area where he hunted people. He waited for a woman to go outside at night to let their pets urinate. He had won your trust by then renting from you. He stood in the yard, jumped from behind the house, and attacked the woman. He enjoyed the pounce and scaring you half to death before he murdered you. Then the crazed man fled the area immediately. He got away with many murders and never caught.

I woke, startled. I dreamed of two serial killers all night long. When I walked downstairs, I asked Ilene, "Did I dream about serial killers?"

Ilene answered, "Yes, they know who you are, and they wanted to do these things to you. They showed you what they did when they lived before. They are in *darkness*."

Gabriel announced, "God will be with you today. Do not worry. Prepare the house. God will speak to you soon."

I gasped. "Wow, what a night. I felt glad God would be with me and needed God to protect me from these *evil* beings."

July 1, 2020

I stepped into the shower and shampooed my hair. Gabriel reminded, "Prepare the house. Your Lord will speak to you soon."

I prepared the house before work. I needed to hurry and didn't want to be late.

Gabriel announced, "God is pleased."

July 2, 2020

I slept horribly and took a long, hot shower. I asked, "Am I supposed to prepare the house today? I have heard nothing."

Gabriel answered, "Prepare the house. Your Lord will speak to you this afternoon."

My afternoon appointments cancelled. I locked the gate in the driveway. Gabriel stated, "You may ask God questions today."

I struggled with what I would ask God. I asked, "What do I do?" My husband was home. It was difficult to meditate with him there. I needed the house quiet.

Gabriel stated, "God is kind and loving. He wants you to enjoy your afternoon."

Shocked. I asked, "What? When will God speak to me?"

Gabriel stated, "This afternoon when you are ready."

I replied, "I will after lunch. I will not make God wait. It seems wrong. I want to know what God will say." My husband left for work.

I walked outside. Noodle needed to relieve herself. Gabriel announced, "Your Lord will speak to you when you are ready."

At 1:05 p.m. I burned frankincense in "the room." I grounded, prayed, and began meditating. Noodle laid on the bed beside me.

Gabriel announced, "You must be prepared. Your Lord is coming. God will be with you. You must believe in yourself. Your Lord is preparing."

Ilene beamed. "God is coming, Rebecca."

Dad beamed. "He's almost here, Beck."

I heard a song, "Anticipation," by Carly Simon. From Ilene.

Gabriel announced, "The Lord is upon us. He's glad you did not make him wait."

God spoke in a firm voice, *"Hello, Rebecca, it is God. I have been watching, listening to you today. There are many things that have upset you. You have forgiven these people. You must let them go. You must continue on this journey, God's journey. The one you've been born to do. Octavian was a powerful man in his past life. You have things to learn in this life that Octavian must amend for. You must continue to pray, for you are weary. There are many obstacles in your heart. Prayer will help thee, guide thee. These things I say to you, your Lord and Savior, Jesus Christ, himself.*

I have come today to strengthen thee because these trying times weaken my messenger. You must be diligent, strong, persevere over these obstacles that you endure. You must remember to pray, for these things shall come to pass. There are many changes coming. The ones you've prayed for. There will be many changes coming that you will be pleased with. These things I have granted. You must remember who you are. You are God's messenger. There are many things I ask of thee. This journey is a difficult one. The one I have bestowed upon thee, thus saith the Lord, God the Almighty.

You must remember you are my servant, and I am your master. I come today to remind thee of these things. You have much more to do for your Lord and Savior. These things I ask of thee. This journey will humble thee because you are my servant, thus saith the Lord, God Almighty, himself.

Do unto others as you would have them do unto you. These things I say to my messenger. You must be diligent, calm during these times. Do not let others influence you. You must remember to pray. These things will come to pass. These things I say to my messenger. My messenger must be diligent, forthcoming, truthful, obedient, kind, loving, and generous. Pray for your shortcomings, thus saith the Lord.

These things will help thee overcome the obstacles that you question. You must remember to pray often. Evil is always lurking, watching, waiting to harm my messenger, thus saith the Lord.

You must be diligent in your work, for there is much more to come. These things I say to you. My messenger needs to be reminded. The future is unclear to thee. I will show you the way. You must pray for these things. Ask and I am there. I will protect thee. Remember, you are my servant, and I am your master, thus saith the Lord, God Almighty, himself.

Do unto others as you would have them do unto you. These things are required of my messenger. I say these things to you, to remind thee to stay on this journey. The path you have chosen. God's path is a righteous path. You must believe in me to have eternal life. Do not forget, you are my messenger. You must be clean, worthy of this honor. You are diligent and kind. You mustn't tarry in your studies, for I am waiting. These things are God's will. The writings will help other's souls from eternal damnation. These things I ask of thee to do for God the Almighty.

You must believe in me. Remember to pray. I hear your prayers daily for there are many. You need to pray more. These things will help thee, thus saith the Lord.

Remember to work on your studies, for I am waiting for them to be finished. Do unto others as you would have them do unto you. My messenger must be strong, diligent, and kind. Do not tarry in your work. These things will help your future. You must listen when I speak for, I am God the Almighty, himself, speaking to his messenger.

These will be trying times for you. You must remember to pray for the things you need. Pray often. Ask and I am there, thus saith the Lord God Almighty, himself.

Must be diligent, kind, and loving to those in need. Have mercy for their shortcomings, thus saith the Lord.

Pray for these people and I will help them. You must remember the power of prayer, for your many prayers have been answered by God, himself.

You mustn't tarry in the work. Must be diligent, forthcoming, vigilant, dutiful, persistent, in these things, thus saith the Lord, God Almighty, himself.

You have been diligent and kind to others. I have been watching and listening to my messenger. You must continue on this path. This path will show you the way. The truth has set you free. Remember, these are God's will. You must do these things for me. I have given thee a second chance. Do for your Lord, for I am waiting for these things. These things must come to pass. It will help thousands of people. This is the journey you have chosen. You must do these things for your Lord and Savior, Jesus Christ, himself.

You mustn't tarry in your studies. These things will affect your future. You must be diligent. Pray often it will guide thee. You must be willing to work harder for I am waiting. Time is of the essence. Are there questions you have for me? You may ask them now."

I asked, "Lord, you sound angry with me. Are you angry?"

God replied, *"No, Rebecca. You are sensing God's power. You must be earnest in your work, for these things need to be done for God the Almighty. What other questions do you have for me?"*

I asked, "I have written many down, now I can't think. What can I pray for to strengthen my marriage?"

God answered, *"Forgiveness of each other's shortcomings, patience, understanding, these things I say to my messenger."*

I asked, "Lord, what can I pray for that will help me with what you told me today?"

God answered, *"Pray for diligence, perseverance, steadfastness, calmness, tranquility, patience for those in need of it."*

I questioned, "Lord, how will I pay for what you want me to do. I know you will show me the way."

God responded, *"Do not worry, these things shall come to pass. I will provide for thee. Ask and I am there."*

I asked, "Lord, how long before this coronavirus is gone? People aren't taking it seriously."

God answered, *"There will be many months, years before it is gone, these things I say to my messenger. You must be diligent. Be careful where you go. I will protect thee."*

I questioned, "I wondered, will I have a TV show like Both Sides Now TV? Could I help people that way?"

God replied, *"These things you are not ready for. I will show you the way. You have much work to do. You must be diligent and forthcoming in your work. Your persistence will pay off. You must remember to pray for the things that you need. You are getting weary. Time is of the essence. You must work on your studies. Be diligent and kind to others. These are the things my messenger needs to be. You are these things. Continue on this path. The path of righteousness. I have granted thee many things. You must remember to pray. Ask and I am there. I will provide and show you the way. I am the truth and the light that has set you free. Remember these lessons. Do unto others as you have them do unto you. I must go now, for time is of the essence."*

I stated, "Lord, I'm sorry. I haven't been as diligent as you wanted me to be."

God replied, *"My messenger has been very busy with many things. You must remember who you are. These things are important. Do not listen to others, for they do not understand the things I ask of thee. You must remember to pray. It will guide thee, thus saith the Lord, God Almighty. Time is of the essence. I love thee, Rebecca. I will speak to you again, goodbye."*

I replied, "Thank you, Lord, for speaking with me. I'm sorry I have not done enough. I have been thinking about myself more lately. Please forgive me."

Gabriel announced, "Your Lord is gone, Rebecca."

I could hardly swallow and felt I let God down.

I cried. "I haven't been diligent enough. God sounded very firm today. I have much more to do, and I am not writing fast enough." I felt my heart pounding and swirling from sensing God's magnificent presence. I ended the meditation at 1:44 p.m.

I prayed and asked God to forgive me for my shortcomings. It has been difficult to concentrate. I must accomplish more. Wow, thirty-nine minutes passed. It felt like ten minutes. I felt sleepy and drained. I must write more.

People flustered me about COVID-19. People complained about wearing masks and our number of cases increased.

At 2:15 p.m. I drifted to sleep for thirty minutes. I woke and realized me, and Jess talked that morning about why we had many difficulties in our lives.

I told her, "We must have been a real piece of work when we lived before."

God stated I needed to amend for Octavian. He answered the question we both had. I wrote questions and forgot to bring into "the room." God answered many of these questions before I asked them. Some I did not ask. God already knew what I wrote. God is amazing.

July 3, 2020

I read what God told me yesterday. He wanted me to pray for the ones who frustrated me instead of discussing it. I prayed, "Please Lord, help those who do not understand how serious this virus is. Help them understand wearing a mask will help this virus leave. It will protect them and their family from harm. Help these people, Lord. I ask in the name of the Father, the Son, and the Holy Spirit, in Jesus Christ, I pray, Amen."

I learned a pattern in the writings. God wanted me to write as it happened. I was almost caught up and believed I could by tomorrow. I needed to publish *Experiences Never Stop Part 2*. These things would affect my future. I must do what God instructed. It was difficult and must push myself harder. I was Octavian, an emperor, now Rebecca, God's servant.

July 4, 2020

I wrote for hours until my hands ached and caught up in my notes. I walked downstairs and made lunch. I heated beef brisket and sautéed squash. Made a tiny salad on the side. Noodle had ground beef and some pellets. I noticed it looked cloudy outside.

I stated, "God, I have done my best. I just want to enjoy the afternoon by the pool. Is there any way you can make the sun come out for a few hours?"

I walked into the kitchen and finished preparing our meal.

Gabriel announced, "God is pleased with your work."

I plated the food, and the sun popped out. I smiled. "You are amazing, God, thank you."

July 6, 2020

I heard a new tune, "Holy, Holy, Holy," by Audrey Assad. Ilene liked to play music from the salon as well. I used Pandora for my music, and she played the ones I liked the most. It reassured me to know I was never alone on this journey.

Later that evening, my husband installed the wiring for the pool. I heard "Que Sera Sera," by Doris Day. I loved Ilene's sense of humor. The wiring job was terribly boring and seemed to take forever to finish. I helped as much as I could. The sun hid behind the tall pine trees. Sunset was upon us.

Gabriel warned, "You must go inside. The in-betweens are coming out."

I stated, "I must go inside. It is almost dark."

He replied, "I understand, sweetie."

I whispered, "I appreciate you doing this."

Noodle and I walked towards the house. Gabriel stated, "God is glad you are going inside. There are spirits starting to follow you."

I arrived at the front door. Gabriel warned, "There are two spirits behind you."

I closed the door and waited inside for Noodle. I opened the door, and she walked in.

I thought, "I am glad I burned sage and frankincense today in the house."

I wondered while I logged this into my journal, "I attended a wedding in the evening over a year ago. Why didn't anything harm me?"

Gabriel responded, "You were protected. It is not wise for God's messenger to be out at night. Evil will try to harm you."

I gasped. "Wow, I wasn't alone at the venue. I shrugged it off. But when I walked to my car. I knew I wasn't alone. I did not understand at the time. *How evil* would hurt me, nightmares for starters."

Gabriel added, "You are safe. Do not worry. We are with you."

Later, after relaxing with my husband in the living room. I felt weary and climbed into bed. I glanced at the clock at 11:11 p.m. I recalled earlier today. I turned on my phone and saw 1:11 p.m. It felt fabulous. I was on the right path.

July 8, 2020

At 7:29 p.m. I enjoyed the show "Million Dollar Listing Los Angeles," by Randy Barbato and Fenton Baily. I heard music from Ilene.

I asked, "Are you enjoying watching this with me?"

Ilene answered, "Yes, Rebecca, I do. It's very interesting to see how you live today."

I responded, "You lived in the Ross Castle, which is still standing today. The castle is architecturally sounder than what they're building on this show."

She replied, "This is true, but I find it interesting to watch with you."

I asked, "Does God want me to write this in the book?"

Ilene replied, "Yes, Rebecca, he does."

I inquired, "Really? God wants me to put this in the book. Why?"

She explained, "God wants others to realize that these things don't matter, objects. Material wealth stays when you die."

I gasped. "Wow, okay I will write it in my journal."

Gabriel added, "God wants you to write these things to help others understand these things are not important. They only help you enjoy life while you live. Love, forgiveness, believing in him are the only way to enter his kingdom. God wants Octavian to enjoy the things he remembers when he lived before."

I gasped. "Wow, Octavian was an emperor. I enjoy watching shows about money. I find it interesting and entertaining. I love seeing the finer things that I can never afford in this life. I know I don't need them. But I still enjoy seeing them and how others perceive them. How their egos want objects and why."

Gabriel stated, "God is pleased with what you have written. Octavian has to amend his ways."

I replied, "Oh, this is the thing Octavian has to amend? He needs to understand luxury will not help you buy your way into heaven?"

Gabriel stated, "God is glad you have written these things for they are true."

July 9, 2020

Last night, I laid in bed and prayed for protection. I begged God not to take my husband away from me. I thought about what Gabriel told me. Octavian must amend the things he has done. I wondered, "No telling what Octavian had done, and I will be punished."

Gabriel announced, "Your Lord is saddened by what you're asking."

I inquired, "What do you mean, Gabriel?"

Gabriel answered, "Your Lord has granted you many things. You are his messenger. He does not want to harm his messenger."

I sobbed. "I did not know. Can you explain these things? Please?"

I begged. "God, can you explain these things?"

God answered, *"Your Lord wants his messenger to be happy. I have granted you many things. Octavian was a good man."*

I sobbed. "Lord, can you please forgive me?" I wiped the tears flowing from my eyes. I did not understand. I thought I would be punished for Octavian's mistakes and miss deeds. I cried myself to sleep, relieved. I thought my husband would die or betray me like others had. I confused atonement with amending. I cried and drifted to sleep.

Dream Nineteen: I saw people from my past coming and going. The dream shifted to a wedding. I saw a woman, and I was her. She did not look like me. I viewed the dream as a medium. I wore a thin white blouse and a white skirt to the knees. The lining of the skirt and shirt were beige. I wore no bra or panties. But I had on beige thong panties. I was dressed properly for a lady shopping in a mall. I needed wedding attire. I spotted a man stalking me as I searched for the wedding boutique. I felt uneasy and not safe while the two men followed me.

One man grunted, "She is not wearing undergarments. That means she wants to have sex."

This was untrue. I wore undergarments. I needed these two vile men to stay away. I circled round the store to lose them. I entered a small clothing store for formal attire. Dad stood in front of me. He smiled and looked fantastic. His face looked young and healthy. He beamed with happiness. He wore a dark navy button-down shirt. His sleeves rolled up over his biceps. I peered closer, and the shirt had a tiny white pattern, a white flower. Dad had rolled the sleeves over his huge biceps. They looked full and robust. I felt relieved to see him. He protected me and I wasn't afraid anymore in the store. I forgot about the two stalkers. We smiled and talked with each other. It felt wonderful to see him again.

Noodle shook her collar and woke me. I had a visit from my father. He knew I felt heavy-hearted when I drifted to sleep. He came to me many times when I felt sad. It felt fantastic to see him again. I felt loved and cared for. He looked happy, healthy, in his thirties. His dark, thick, wavy hair brushed off his face. My Dad was thirty-seven years old when I was born. He looked younger in the dream. I took Noodle outside to pee.

I settled on the couch with coffee and investigated the meaning of amending. It meant to grow or become better by reforming oneself.

I gasped. "I had confused amend with atone. They mean different things." I felt glad I searched for the word and realized what Octavian needed to do. I had changed many of my behaviors already and needed to work on my faults.

July 13, 2020

Today looked overcast. No pool time, so I wrote for an hour. I wanted to warm up and meditate. I felt chilled working in the cold room and settled in bed with Noodle by my side. I grounded and prayed. I asked the angels, God, my spirit guides, to help me with what I needed to do in the next few days.

I heard, "Believe in yourself. God is showing you the way. You need to pray more. Pray for the ones you love."

I inquired, "Who is speaking to me."

They replied, "The angels with God." It sounded like more than one, and I felt their angelic energy.

The angels continued, "There will be trying times ahead. Be calm, centered, and grounded, will help you. God is showing you the way."

I recalled I saw 1:11p.m. today after lunch and twice on Sunday. I saw 555 twice in the last week. I drifted to sleep for a moment. Noodle woke me and wanted to snuggle. I glanced at the clock and had meditated for twenty minutes. I ended the meditation and thanked the angels. I asked for continued protection and guidance.

I heard music from Gabriel, Dad, and Ilene as I logged into my journal. They stated, "We are with you, Rebecca."

Ilene sounded the loudest of the three. I felt blessed to have guidance from heaven.

July 14, 2020

I heard a new song. "What the World Needs Now Is Love," by Jackie DeShannon, from Ilene. I asked, "Why am I hearing this song? Why did I dream about family giving me gifts all night long? I felt their guilt."

Ilene instructed. "You need to remember these are your *gifts*."

She meant I sensed their guilt through my gift.

Ilene whispered, "Believe in yourself."

Ilene was remarkable. She instructed me as a mother would. Her voice soft, firm, and loving.

July 16, 2020

I arrived home and heard, "What the World Needs Now Is Love," song. I had listened to this song for three days. The world needed love. I prayed earlier for God to send love to the world. We needed it.

I glanced at the pile of salsa tomatoes on the counter. My husband bought these tomato plants during quarantine. He did not know what kind of tomato plants they were. They appeared to look like a large Roma tomato. Only six plants but produced vast amounts of tomatoes. I wanted to make Dad's relish. He used to make it for our burgers when I was a teenager.

I diced thirty tomatoes. I turned the burner on high and grabbed a huge frying pan. I poured a generous amount of olive oil into the pan. I added salt, onion powder, black pepper, and the tomatoes. I cooked the tomatoes until they became a soft consistency.

I asked, "Dad, are you here? I am making the tomato relish. This is your recipe."

Dad spoke, "Beck, it looks good and add more salt."

I laughed. "I put a lot of salt already. You loved to salt everything heavily. I'll wait and taste it before I add some more."

I took a large black plastic spoon and smashed the tomatoes in the sauce. I did not want any sizeable chunks. I could not wait to taste the delicious relish. I scooped some out and let it cool.

I tasted, "There is enough salt, Dad."

I laughed and stirred the mixture. It looked perfect. I placed a one-quart jar on the counter and filled it. I cooked just the right amount. The jar filled to the rim. I put the relish in the fridge and texted my husband the marvelous news. He loved the relish when I made it for him in the past. He ate hamburgers a lot at lunch during the week because it was fast to prepare. He suggested I make relish yesterday and what a brilliant idea.

July 18, 2020

At 7:12 p.m. I washed and dried a load of white clothes. I walked inside the garage to fold the laundry and grabbed a bottle of red wine, too. While I folded the clothes, I heard, "What the World Needs Now Is Love" song.

I stated, "I have heard this song for four days now. It is good to hear from you, Ilene. I enjoy hearing from you. Why aren't you guys talking to me? You're silent lately."

I heard a flash of music from Dad and Gabriel. I wondered, "Am I supposed to ask things? Or wait till I hear from you?"

Dad beamed. "Yes, Beck, you need to ask."

I gasped. "Oh."

I asked about Tracy, "I spoke to her last night. She has spots on her lungs again. It does not sound good. Did it help to call her?"

He responded, "Yes, Beck, they were glad you called. They miss you."

I asked, "What can I pray for that will help, Tracy?"

Dad answered, "Pray for what you did this morning."

I gasped. "Wow, you heard me." I prayed for Tracy on my way to work. This was my prayer. "Please Lord, heal Tracy's lungs. Remove all the spots of cancer and anything that can damage her lungs. Please heal her, Lord. We need more time with her. Please send the world, love. God, we need it. I ask these things in the name of the Father, the Son, and the Holy Spirit, in Jesus Christ, I pray, Amen."

Gabriel spoke after I prayed, "God has heard your prayers. He will answer them in due time."

I thought, "I hope God answers my prayer. She might not live long. She defeated breast cancer before because God answered my prayer."

I shared in *Experiences Never Stop* and *Experiences Never Stop Part 2*. I did not know if God would give her another chance. I would continue to pray for her because God listened. I thought about her husband. Her death would utterly devastate him. I didn't know if he could handle that on his own.

I gathered the stack of fresh white towels and carried a bottle of red wine to the front door. It looked close to sunset.

I wondered, "Are there any spirits out already? The in-betweens?"

Ilene replied as I opened the front door, "It won't be long. You must not be outside. The in-betweens will try to harm you. It's not good for you."

I had not asked them questions like I previously did. It felt wonderful to know my guides and Dad were with me. I felt blessed beyond words.

I heard music from Dad, Gabriel and Ilene, "We love you, Beck. You must remember to pray often for the ones you love. They need it, Beck."

Tears swelled in my eyes because they needed it. They did not understand what happens when you die. They had many unresolved issues. I could do only so much. It was their choice.

Later after dinner, Noodle and I settled in "the room." I found on Amazon, the show "Armada: The Untold Story," Season one, Episode 1, directed by Robert Dashwood. Ilene lived during this era.

I asked, "Ilene, are you here? May I ask a question?"

Ilene replied, "Yes, Rebecca, I am here. You may."

I inquired, "The show I am watching. Do you remember Queen Elizabeth I?"

Ilene responded, "Yes, Rebecca, she was a powerful woman. Many feared her. So did I."

I asked, "Did you ever see her?"

She responded, "No, not in person. But I knew who she was and where she lived."

I asked, "Was the Queen Elizabeth I alive when you passed away?"

Ilene replied, "Yes, Rebecca, I died in 1589."

I inquired, "How did you die, Ilene? May I ask?"

She answered, "I was shot by gunfire. I felt nothing. I am with God now, with you."

I gasped. "Wow, you were shot. That is awful, Ilene."

Ilene continued, "There were many battles during those times. I am glad you want to watch when I lived before."

I whispered, "It won't upset you, will it?"

She responded, "It was difficult times, but it is okay. I want you to learn where I came from. I know you are curious. The Queen was a nasty individual. Not many liked her."

I inquired, "Is the Queen Elizabeth I in heaven?"

Ilene whispered, "Yes, Rebecca. God has forgiven her for her wrong doings. She asked for mercy."

I gasped. "Wow, that is incredible." I sighed and played the series. "Thank you, Ilene, for sharing. I hope what I watch will not bring back terrible memories."

She replied, "It will be fine, Rebecca. I am with your Lord and Savior for eternity."

I whispered, "I am glad, Ilene. I am glad you are my guide. I love you."

The show was long and drawn out and finally ended. I took Noodle outside to pee. While I waited, I stated, "The show lacked engagement. But the queen was not genuinely nice."

Ilene responded, "I remember seeing the ships pass Ireland."

I gasped. "Wow, the ships returned to Spain and crossed Scotland and Ireland."

I envisioned Ilene standing at the top of the Ross Castle watching over one hundred ships pass her view.

Noodle and I settled in bed. My husband watched TV for a while longer. I thought about what Ilene told me.

I stated, "You have been with God, four hundred and thirty-one years. Wow."

Ilene confirmed. "Yes, this is true."

I wondered, "How it felt for her to be in heaven that long. Eternity is forever."

The next day my husband and I had a lovely, quiet morning together. Noodle thrilled to go to the pool and sat by the front door in anticipation. I prepared a late breakfast. We grabbed our towels and blankets and walked to our small oasis. A perfect day in the upper 90s, not a cloud in the sky.

Ilene played music the entire time we sat by the pool. We talked and shared. Ilene played her music continuously. I sunned on my stomach and listened to "What the World Needs Now Is Love."

I stated, "I love hearing from you. Where are my dogs, Speck and Freck? Are they together?"

Ilene whispered, "Yes, they are right here beside me. They miss you."

I asked, "Please tell Speck, I am sorry for leaving her alone as much as I did. It was cruel of me."

In my twenties, I left Speck alone for hours at a time while I partied with friends.

Ilene whispered, "She understands."

I added, "I hope Freck understood why I left her briefly when Dan died. I could not keep her where I stayed temporarily."

Ilene whispered, "She understands. They are looking forward to meeting Noodle. Do not worry. You have more time with her. Remember what God told you, that he gave you more time with her."

I recalled God answered my prayer and granted me two more years with her. I smiled, remembering how it felt to receive this fantastic news. I felt in awe that my dogs could see Noodle and I from heaven.

I asked, "Ilene, will you remind me to log this into my journal when we go inside. People wonder about their pets when they die, where they go."

Ilene stated, "God wants you to write this. I will remind you."

I whispered, "Thank you, Ilene."

July 20, 2020

I watched "All at Stake" on the cooking channel, "Beat Bobby Flay."

I heard music. "Hi, Dad."

Dad whispered, "I love you, Beck. I miss talking to you."

On the show they made Salisbury steak. He added, "It looks good."

I replied, "It does."

Dad beamed. "Beck, I loved Salisbury steak."

I gasped. "I did not know this."

He added, "Your mother could not make it."

I laughed. "Not surprised. She was a horrible cook. You and I love to cook."

Dad whispered, "So true, Beck."

I asked, "Who will win?"

He replied, "Bobby, Beck."

The three judges found fault in the opponent's dish. Bobby's dish, the judges liked, but found errors in it too. They announced the winner, Chief Todd.

I gasped. "Dad, did you not know the answer beforehand?"

He beamed. "Yes, Beck, but I knew you thought Bobby would win. I wanted it to be a surprise."

I thought Bobby would win, "I love our times together."

Dad whispered, "I love you, Beck. I miss you. I am glad you're so happy with your husband."

I replied, "I am. He is a wonderful man."

He added, "I wish I had spoken to him more, Beck. I was unhappy then. He loves you, Beck, more than you realize."

I answered, "Sometimes I wonder."

Dad answered, "You will be together for a long time, Beck."

I replied, "That is great to know. I love him with all my heart."

He beamed. "He loves you more, Beck."

I asked, "Anything I could do better?"

Dad instructed. "Spend more time with him, Beck. Make him feel wanted. Men love that, Beck."

I answered, "Thanks, Dad. You know how I retreat to 'the room.' I need it. But I feel I don't spend enough time with him. I sense it. Thank you for reminding me."

Later that night, I climbed into bed early. I slept deep and had a visit from Dad, Laquilla, her mom, her husband, Willie, and their dog.

Dream Twenty: I stood in a small African Americans neighborhood. I watched people on the side of the road near their yards, cheering and laughing. They were having a marvelous time. I noticed a woman standing in the distance, facing me. She wore a black, gray dress, down to the shins, cap sleeves with a round neckline. Her hair looked gray, with a small amount of black in it. Her hair styled enormously high on top of her head. The hair teased in this fashion from a roller set. She laughed and had a stupendous time with her family and friends. They cheered for a young boy to win a race. The family watched the race with anticipation. I stepped closer to where they were and noticed a car coming towards me. The automobile looked old, not fancy, a small station wagon. Pinto entered my mind and noticed the wood paneling on the side of the car. It was challenging to make out. The car came closer. I saw Laquilla and Willie in the car. Willie drove and Laquilla sat on the passenger side. They parked the station wagon on the side of the street.

I turned around. The dream shifted. I viewed myself in the back seat of a car as it moved past the front of Willie's church. The wood lap siding on the chapel painted burgundy. The church door opened wide, and my father dashed out of the entrance. He stood firm, with his arms stretched wide to his sides. He grinned and wanted to surprise me.

Dad beamed. "Hey, Beck, it's me."

I felt shocked to see him there. He looked in his thirties and had an enormous grin on his face. His face looked youthful and beamed with happiness. Dad wore a stunning navy suit with a gray tweed mixed in the fabric. I saw one button on his tummy. The breast pocket stuffed with a white handkerchief folded neatly, straight across, horizontal. I knew instantly it was 1960.

Laquilla and Willie were easy-going and compassionate people. They were part African American and Caucasian. They were friendly to each other and to anyone they knew. I observed Laquilla far away from me. I desperately wanted to tell her I saw her mom.

I heard my husband shout, "Hey, Laquilla, you will want to hear this. Come over here."

My husband knew I had a visit from her mom. She walked closer and looked blurry. I sensed it was Laquilla standing beside me.

I explained how I saw her mom's hair and gray-black dress. I tried to convince Laquilla it was her mother. She did not seem excited because she already knew. Laquilla patiently waited while I continued to explain the details. She listened and sat across from me, smiling.

I explained, "If you showed me a picture of her. I could pick her out in the photo. There is no doubt in my mind. It was her."

Laquilla smiled. Her mom was ninety-five when she died. I met her once, sitting in the back seat of their car at my salon when she lived.

I woke and drifted to sleep. I searched for Laquilla to tell her what I learned. I needed to convince her because I was unsure if she believed me. I dressed in haste and walked down the sidewalk in Southern Pines. I saw where they were. I glanced down and realized I had on two different shoes. I heard women laughing behind me because I had on two different shoes. I stopped and turned my foot inward. I noticed a pointed black three-inch heel on one foot and a three-inch tan wedge shoe on the other. The shoes echoed differently when I walked. I strolled forward. I needed to find her and did. I explained my shoe dilemma while I faced Laquilla in her living room.

Laquilla whispered, "It doesn't matter. The heels are the same height, aren't they? How tall are you?"

I replied, "I'm five feet."

She explained, "Having on heels helps you not to be as tired, doesn't it?"

I sighed. "Yes, my shoulders don't have to work as hard to reach up higher to do someone's hair. I am short, it helps."

She continued, "Don't worry about it. It's okay."

I asked, "Do you have any pictures of your mom?" I wanted to prove to Laquilla it was her mom.

The dream shifted. Dad appeared. I strolled into a room with him. He still wore the navy gray tweed suit and looked very debonair. He stood in the room's corner and moved a gray metal chair in front of him. He put his foot in the chair and leaned over. Dad placed his elbow on his knee. I recalled my father stood like this a lot when he lived.

Dad stated, "Beck, instead of playing so many games. You should try practicing kindness and patience."

It surprised me because I had played games online. But I try to be kind and patient. He wanted me to do more. It was difficult during COVID-19. You did not go places like before. Things had changed. Dad told me this to help me.

The dream shifted. I saw individuals in the doctor's office I did not know. I observed children and men sitting in chairs waiting in a room. I explained I saw Laquilla's mother and wondered where did she go? The people looked African American. They seemed quiet, gentle, and kind to me while I stood in their space. I felt no animosity, just kindness.

A tan puppy emerged. The pup looked two years old. The breed looked like a mix of dachshund and beagle. The puppy wanted to play. I realized the dog was a boy. It made me happy to see the dog in the dream and I wondered who owned the dog? Where was the owner? I picked up the animal and tried to find the owner. I strolled into several stores and entered a dress shop. The workers seemed cheerful. I did not know the owner. I left and walked into a vet's office. I noticed medicine on the counter for the puppy. I collected the tube of medicine and struggled to read the label.

I asked an elderly African American man sitting on the couch waiting, "Have you given him the medicine yet?"

The man replied, "No."

I thought, "Well, I will not give the pup the medicine because the vet could have already given it to him. I might overdose the puppy."

I looked and saw a large sink with a sprayer. I placed the pup in the sink and gave him a bath. I grabbed the sprayer and rinsed the dog's fur. I pumped some hand soap in my hand and lathered the dog's fur. The dog enjoyed it so much. I watched the bubbles forming around his ears and face. I felt the puppy's skin soft in my hands. I rinsed off the pup and sat him on the floor. The puppy's fur magically dried.

I turned and there stood a foot away, Laquilla. She looked phenomenal and her beauty was stunning. I studied her porcelain skin, smooth and youthful. Her lips painted a shade of coral. Her black full eyebrows penciled in. She wore a dashing, stylish hat with three feathers coming from out of the top of the hat. The feathers looked grey, black, and white. She looked gorgeous and young. I stared at her. She looked in her thirties.

I had never seen her this young when she was my client. She was in her late seventies when she died. Laquilla loved to wear hats at church. She told me once, "It's the best thing to do, to wear a hat to church to look your finest."

I woke and realized I dreamed this all night long. It felt remarkable to have a visit from Dad, Laquilla, her husband, her mom, and a dog.

I asked Ilene, "Why did I dream about these things?"

She replied, "They miss you. They wanted to see you."

I asked, "Who's dog is this? It felt like it was someone's dog, even though I held it and took care of it. It wasn't mine."

Ilene replied, "It was theirs. They wanted you to see it."

I gasped. "Wow, this is incredible. The details of her so unbelievably clear and of my father. My gift must be growing. It felt wonderful to see them. I can't find the words to tell you how overjoyed they looked."

Laquilla knew the whole time it was her mother. It was her way of showing me they were all together. I believed the lesson in the dream had to do with Black Lives Matter. They knew about my book during COVID-19. They showed me how kindness and patience were vital. We needed to be kind and loving to one another. I cried writing into my journal because love was what we needed in this world.

Ilene played "What The World Needs Now Is Love," song.

I was Caucasian in the dream, in an African American part of town. They were kind and loving to me in the dream. Just as Laquilla and Willie were when they lived. They were awesome people whom I missed. My Dad never showed prejudice. He always liked all races. I recalled seeing Dad at the front of the chapel and in the rooms with these people like they were family. I felt honored to see them again. They were extremely happy and were with God.

I thought, "Wow, I am blessed to see things. She was so close. Her image burned in my memory. I can't wait to see them again."

At 8:15 p.m. I cooked dinner while my husband worked. I prepared baked salmon with lemon, dill, onion, and black pepper. I sauteed shrimp with lemon pepper and garlic. I made a cream sauce deglazed with Chardonnay for the fettuccine. I plated my meal and sat at the table alone. The meal tasted scrumptious.

I asked Ilene, "Did Octavian have any of these foods when he lived before?"

Ilene stated, "Yes, all of them, but no pasta. He ate bread instead of pasta."

I thought, "It's good. I can't seem to get the food in my mouth fast enough."

I inquired, "Do you know what Octavian's favorite meal was?"

Ilene replied, "I do not know, but I can ask God."

I panicked, "No, don't ask God. It's menial, but I am curious."

She informed, "He wants his messenger to be happy."

I logged into my journal whatever I heard from Ilene. "Fish, stews, meats of all sorts, vegetables, wine, cheese, crunchy bread, lemons, eggs, bacon, many fruits, sauces with a lemon flavor. He ate these things regularly."

I gasped. "Wow, I love all these things."

I asked, "Can you tell me what Octavian's favorite flower was? You know how I love my garden. You told me Octavian loved his garden."

Ilene responded, "Roses, Rebecca, he loved roses."

I laughed and choked on my pasta because red roses are *definitely* my favorite flower by far. If anyone wanted to give me a flower as a gift, red roses won my heart.

I stated, "Wow, thank you, Ilene. I was curious. I was an emperor in a past life. I searched tirelessly, trying to find what Octavian ate. I did not understand then. I could just ask you. You know I trust you because you're my guide in heaven with God. I grew up in the country. I never ate these types of food, fish, cream sauces, lemon sauces, and shrimp. It was too expensive to buy, nor did my parents like them. But when I eat these foods, my palate remembers them. It brings me much joy to eat these foods. I was glad God told me to eat fish, and it was good for me. I listened because God knew before I did that was what Octavian loved. I am enjoying salmon now with creamy fettuccine. I love crunchy bread as well. I tried not to eat it too often because it makes me fat. Crunchy bread dipped in sauce, oils, or stews, yummy. Fresh vegetables, fruits. I love them all. Thank you, Ilene."

I heard music from Dad and asked, "I haven't heard from you all day. Do you have anything to add? It was fabulous seeing you again in my dream. Can you talk to me?"

Dad beamed. "Beck, I love you. You're a beautiful daughter. I'm so happy you're learning about Octavian. This is who you are, Beck. I am honored to have you as my daughter. God has blessed me to have an emperor as a daughter that is God's servant."

I whispered, "You're right. I'm honored to have a second chance. I will do whatever I need to as God's servant. To write the things I am learning from you in heaven with God. I just hope others want to read it. It breaks my heart. I struggle and people closest to me don't seem to care. They are not interested because they don't believe me. I do not lie and never have. I might stretch the truth to make a story more thought-provoking. But I never lie. That is just not who I am."

My phone rang while I talked to Dad. I answered, "Hello."

My husband whispered, "Hello, how are you?"

I added, "Good, I'm eating dinner."

He asked, "How was it?"

I replied, "It was excellent."

He continued, "I'm done bagging over thirty dozen Yum Yums and coming home."

I stated, "We might be in 'the room'."

He whispered, "That's okay. See you in fifteen minutes."

I beamed. "We can't wait for you to come home. We love you, miss you."

He whispered, "I love you, goodbye."

I whispered, "Bye."

I sighed. "Wow, what just happened. I heard what I ate in a past life. My Dad and God listening all the while. Wow."

July 26, 2020

I dreamed all night about family, people from my past I had distanced myself from. They had returned to my life unannounced. They wanted their place in my life like before, wanting things and time from me. I did not allow it and it shocked them.

I woke, "Why did I dream this?" Ilene played "Piece of My Heart," by Janis Joplin.

I asked, "What does this mean?"

Ilene replied, "Your heart is remembering the pain these people have caused you. You must let them go."

I gasped. "Wow. I realized during the dream how I felt and the pain they caused. They seemed not to notice or care. Only wanting for themselves."

She played the song all day, reminding me to let them go.

July 27, 2020

I dreamed all night long of family and people that I have distanced myself from. I asked, "Why am I still dreaming these things?"

Ilene replied, "Remember who you are. God has asked you to let them go, *permanently.*"

I sighed. "I remember."

I needed to further remove contact from these individuals. I had unfollowed them on Facebook and had not let them go completely. I grounded, prayed, made coffee, and opened Facebook. I googled how to not allow certain people to see my posts. I followed the instructions and restricted these people from future posts. I did not want them as a part of my life. It was difficult to cut off ties completely. A tiny part of me needed to have some form of contact if they became ill. I did not want them to know about my daily business. I certainly did not want them to see my new upcoming book published. They did not care. I needed people in my life that supported me on this journey for God. This would help me stay positive. God told me his messenger needed to be kind, loving, generous, strong, and to show mercy. I wanted to unfriend them, but I felt this would be what God wanted his messenger to do.

Ilene played "Hold On," by Wilson Phillips. I googled the song and read the words. It was how I felt. Change was difficult, but necessary. I needed to continue to grow without them.

July 28, 2020

I swam while my husband mowed the yard. Noodle found a frog and was content chasing it. I enjoyed the water cascading around my body.

I asked Ilene, "Why did I feel tingles in my heart today at the salon? Or was it the new obsidian crystal I wore my husband gave me?"

Gabriel answered, "God was with you. He watched you reading his words."

I asked, "Does God want me to put this in the book?"

Ilene replied, "Yes, he does, Rebecca."

I had a break at the salon. I filled the pedicure bath and soaked my feet until my next client arrived. I read only the parts of what God spoke to me in succession in *Experiences Never Stop*. I felt tingles in my heart, like when God talked to me. I noticed it, but I did not ask. Ilene played her music while I read. God talked about the changes coming I had experienced. It was difficult to endure these changes, and some were remarkable. I did not understand at the time. A year and a half had passed. My life enriched by the changes. I am the happiest I have ever been. My soul felt awesome inside. God, my guides, and Dad showed me the way… There was more to come. I sensed God watched me while I read. Gabriel confirmed it. It felt amazing to hear validations.

July 31, 2020

At 8:21 p.m. I ate my homemade enchilada with fresh tomatoes over white rice. I cooked the tomato relish in the enchilada sauce I made. It tasted scrumptious. I watched an episode of "Million Dollar Listing Los Angeles." I finished cleaning the kitchen and heard a flash of "Don't Speak," song.

I asked, "Dad, where have you been? I haven't heard from you." I heard "Santa Claus Is Coming to Town," song from Ilene.

I laughed. "I haven't heard you play this song in a while."

I filled my glass with water and Ilene instructed. "Prepare the house. God will speak to you in a few days."

I choked on the water. It surprised me because I wondered if God would speak soon.

I replied, "Wow, I cannot wait. Let me write this down."

Today was Friday, so it will probably be Monday when I heard from God. It was usually three days of preparing the house, then it happened. My guides would let me know.

I thought, "Wow, I have been writing and doing everything God has asked me to do. I wonder what he is gonna say?"

I felt the nervousness in my belly of anticipation. God watched me all the time, hearing what I say to people. I tried to be kind, generous, loving, and show mercy. It was difficult listening and seeing the ignorance said and done by people. I really wanted to say what an ignorant remark you made. But I must not. It would make me a better person. I hoped God was pleased with everything I did. I felt blessed to have God give me this knowledge.

Ilene played "Anticipation." I sighed. "Wow, she knows how I feel."

August 1, 2020

I woke and Ilene played "Love Will Keep Us Together," by Captain & Tennille. I heard the chorus repeatedly.

Later, Saturday morning, I scheduled a client for a facial at 9:00 a.m. During the service, I heard music.

I stated through my thoughts, "Hello, Dad." He liked to watch me work. I heard music from my father a lot while I gave facials.

He replied, "You're doing good work, Beck."

I thought, "I give a wonderful facial."

I finished early and drove to the grocery store. I needed wine, a few insignificant items and Noodle a rotisserie chicken for lunch. I arrived home, brought in the bags, and placed them on the counter.

Dad asked, "What are you gonna have for lunch, Beck?"

I answered, "I will have a grilled pimento cheese sandwich and maybe a little chicken too."

He stated, "I haven't had that kind."

I answered, "This brand, 'Palmento Cheese,' is awesome. I haven't eaten it in a while."

I made lunch and Noodle waited patiently for us to eat together. She had chicken and pellets. I heard nothing else from Dad.

We finished eating and strolled to the pool. I swam and heard music from Dan. I smiled and whispered, "Hello."

Dan beamed. "You're beautiful."

I replied, "Thank you." I swam around in the water, enjoying our conversation.

He added, "You were the love of my life."

I smiled and laughed. "You didn't live very long. But it makes me feel special to know. It was horrific losing you. My life turned upside down, and I ended up on the wrong path. It has taken some time to get on the right path."

I thought of the past, which happened over thirty years ago. I had to experience great turmoil then, to understand where I am today. I would hear from God, in a few days, how blessed I was.

Gabriel reminded, "You must remember to pray for those that you love. They need your guidance."

I prayed, "Lord, please guide the people I love. Help them make positive decisions in their lives. Help them grow with me on this journey. Protect us all from the coronavirus. Give them guidance, strength, diligence, steadfastness during these difficult times. I pray for Tracy and Maria. Please remove the cancer from her breast and her lungs. Heal them Lord. I ask these things in the name of the Father, the Son, and the Holy Spirit, in Jesus Christ, I pray, Amen." I crossed myself as a Catholic.

Ilene beamed. "God is excited about speaking with you soon. He has much to say. You must be ready. Prepare the house tomorrow. Be ready when your Lord comes to you."

I gasped. "Wow, God is excited about speaking to me and has a lot to say? Wow."

I felt anxious, but I can't wait to hear what God had to say. It always helped me understand what I needed to work on. I prepared the house this morning before I went to work. I could still smell the sage and frankincense when I came home for lunch.

August 2, 2020

At 10:16 p.m. I brushed my teeth and heard "Santa Claus Is Coming To Town," from Ilene.

Ilene announced, "Your Lord will speak to you tomorrow. You must be ready."

I carried Noodle down the steps to pee outside. She was hesitant the last few days walking up the stairs. While I waited, Ilene stated, "Your Lord is anticipating speaking to you tomorrow."

I inquired, "What do I do? When Ilene?"

Ilene answered, "When you're ready."

I kissed my husband good night and carried Noodle to bed with me. He wanted to watch TV for a while. I needed a good night's sleep and wanted to feel rested in the morning when I heard from God.

August 3, 2020

I woke and heard from Ilene, "We Three Kings of Orient Are," by Mario Lanza. I heard the second verse. I heard a different song when I made my coffee. "Can't Feel My Face," by Weekend.

Gabriel announced, "Your Lord is ready to speak to you. When you are ready."

It was 8:10 a.m. I needed to hurry. I gulped coffee, showered, and dressed. I burned sage and frankincense. Noodle and I settled in "the room." I placed selenite, labradorite and amethyst crystals around my body.

Gabriel announced, "Your Lord is waiting."

I grounded and prayed, "Lord, I ask for protection during this meditation. Surround me with the white light of the Holy Spirit. Keep all demonic spirits and earthbound spirits away from me. Protect me while I listen to you, Lord. Keep my guides close, to protect me. I ask these things in the name of the Father, the Son, and the Holy Spirit, in Jesus Christ, I pray, Amen."

Gabriel announced, "Your Lord is coming."

Dad beamed. "He's almost here, Beck."

God spoke in a gentle voice, *"Hello, Rebecca, it is God. You've been busy working on your studies like I have asked you to do. You must continue on this path. You are on the path of righteousness with your Lord and Savior.*

These things will bring you much joy in your future. You must remember to pray for the ones that you love. They need guidance, strength, and perseverance. They are weak and are not humbled in God's presence. Remember to pray for these individuals, for they need much guidance. You must prepare for the upcoming changes. These things I have granted. The ones you've asked for. There will be many changes in your life in the next few months. You must be ready. Count your blessings, for there are many. Your Lord has granted many things to you. You must remember to be grateful in your heart. Remember to pray often. It will strengthen thee. There are many things I will ask my messenger to do. Must pray for guidance, strength, perseverance to overcome obstacles that will be presented to you. You must remember to pray for the things you need, and I will grant them. I am very pleased with the work that you have done. You have much more to do. I will provide for thee. Do not worry, these things will happen in due time. Many things must occur before the second book, 'Experiences Never Stop Part 2' is published. You must be patient and wait for these things to happen. I will show you the way. The Lord is by your side. I am here to comfort thee. Your heart is heavy. I know your thoughts and I hear your prayers, for there are many. You must pray more. It will strengthen your being. Ask and I am there. Do you have any questions? You may ask them now."

I asked, "Lord, what changes are coming? I feel the heaviness out there lingering... what does this mean?"

God replied, *"You are sensing evil wanting to frighten you. Evil has great power. The Lord overcomes all things. Evil never wins when you believe in me."*

I asked, "Lord, what can I do to prepare for the changes you have granted? I don't know what they are. I asked for many things."

God replied, *"Pray for protection. Pray for the ones you love. Ask for guidance. Pray for what you need, thus saith the Lord."*

I stated, "I'm nervous, Lord. My heart is swirling. It's hard to focus."

God spoke, *"Do not be afraid. I am a kind, loving God. You are sensing my power. What other questions do you have?"*

I asked, "Lord, what is wrong with my baby Noodle? She doesn't want to walk up the stairs. Has she hurt herself? Can you help her?"

God answered, *"She will be better in time. She is getting older. She has overdone things. I will protect her. I know that you love her deeply. She will be better in a few days."*

I stated, "Thank you, Lord, for telling me these things. Can you continue to guide me with what I need to do? Meeting new people and distancing myself from those who don't care about me, parts of the family. I must let go. It is difficult, Lord. Can you guide me?"

God answered, *"Yes, Rebecca, I have been guiding you. These things must be done. These people harm thee. They do you no good. You must let them go, for time is of the essence. You must work on your studies. Focus on your future, not your past. I know these things are difficult for you, but I am showing you the way. You must listen to your Lord when he speaks. I am God the Almighty. I have much power to do many things. You are my messenger, I love. I am showing you the way, on the path of righteousness. These people that you love are not on God's path. They believe in me, but they do not live by God's word. God knows all things. You must distance yourself. Move forward. Focus on your future. I will show you the way. The truth has set you free. Remember to pray for what you need, and I will grant it to you."*

I asked, "Lord, can you tell me why Tracy has distanced herself from me? I feel different things. Can you explain?"

God answered, *"She doesn't understand the changes that you were going through. It frightens her. You must remain calm, centered, steadfast. These things I say to you, your Lord and Savior. I must go now, for time is of the essence."*

I begged. "Lord, please don't leave. Is there anything else you can tell me about my future? What to do? This coronavirus is still lingering. Can you please tell me any guidance of what I need, Lord?"

God answered, *"You must remain calm, centered, and grounded. Pray for these things. These difficult times will linger for some time. They will pass. You must remain calm, show mercy for those who need it. Ask and I am there. I will help thee. You must remember to pray often. It will strengthen thee. It will help guide you during these difficult times. Ask and I am there, your Lord and Savior, Jesus Christ the Almighty, himself."*

I begged. "Lord, is there anything else you can tell me about my husband or my family meaning him, me and Noodle?"

God answered, *"Your love is growing. You are learning to put your family first above all things. These things have been instilled in you, but your family has changed. You must remember who your new family is. It will strengthen your marriage. I will help guide thee. You must remember this journey will not be easy. This is the one you have chosen to be my messenger. You have great strength from your past life. This is why I have granted these things. Not many can do the things that you were able to do. This is why I have chosen you to be my messenger, says Christ Lord, God Almighty, himself.*

Do unto others as you have them do unto you. You must remain calm and centered during these times. It will be difficult for you because I have given you knowledge of the future. Ask and I am there. God is the truth of the way, the light to eternity. You must believe in me to enter my kingdom.

Rebecca, you are my messenger. I only speak to thee. You must write only what I say to help others understand God is real. I know you believe in me. You have great faith. You have shown mercy to others like I have taught thee. I must go now, for time is of the essence. I do not want to harm my messenger. God's power is great. It will harm thee if I stay too long. I do not want to harm thee."

I pleaded. "Lord, please don't leave. I'm honored to hear from you. I am humbled by your presence. I am blessed for you to speak to me. Thank you for showing me the way. It has been difficult, but I am happy. I know if I stay on this path you will continue to bless my life more."

God replied, *"Rebecca, I must go now. You are welcome for the things I have granted. I know they bring you much pleasure. I see you, watch you daily, I hear your prayers. Your Lord is very pleased with his messenger's work. Goodbye, Rebecca, I love thee, your Lord and Savior, Jesus Christ, himself has spoken to you."*

I sobbed. "Thank you, God."

Gabriel announced, "Your Lord is getting ready to leave."

I begged. "God, is there anything else you could tell me before you go to help me, my business, the writing of the book, anything?"

God answered, *"You must remember to pray for what you need. I will grant these things to you, Rebecca. I will show you the way. Ask and I am there. I love thee, goodbye."*

Gabriel announced, "Your Lord is gone, Rebecca."

I sobbed uncontrollably. God's presence felt so powerful, and I wanted to be with him. I wanted to be where God was and did not want him to leave. It overwhelmed me, and I sobbed more uncontrollably. My head felt dizzy, and my heart swirled with love. I could barely speak and needed to end the meditation.

I prayed, "Please, God, continue to protect me throughout the day. I pray for calmness and tranquility. Protect me from all evil and surround me with the white light of the Holy Spirit. Guide me, Lord, and show me the way. I ask in the name of the Father, the Son, and the Holy Spirit, in Jesus Christ, I pray, Amen."

I looked at the clock, 8:59 a.m.

I gasped. "Wow, it felt like ten minutes passed. I can't stop crying."

Gabriel announced, "God has spoken to you. You must do these things for your Lord and Savior, Christ the Almighty."

Ilene beamed. "Your Lord loves you, Rebecca."

Dad beamed. "Beck, God is awesome. I am with him right now."

I sobbed more, to know my father was beside God. I knew he was and tried to envision Dad there with God.

I heard for a second, God say, *"You must remember to pray for what you need, Rebecca."*

I stated, "Lord, I need strength, diligence, and perseverance to overcome these things in my heart. So, I can walk away from these people that I love. They don't care about me. I want it gone. Please help me. I ask these things in the name of the Father, the Son, and the Holy Spirit, in Jesus Christ, I pray, Amen."

Gabriel reminded, "You must pray for the ones that you love."

I prayed, "Lord, I pray for those I love, and you know who they are. Please guide them, help them make positive decisions for themselves and their family. Give them strength and perseverance to overcome their uncertainties of the future. Please guide them, Lord. Show them the way. I ask these things in the name of the Father, the Son, and the Holy Spirit, in Jesus Christ, I pray, Amen."

I gasped. "Wow, I finished editing. I did not know what I would hear from God. God knew everything in my heart, all of it. I will do what God has instructed. My heart feels full of God's love, swirling round and round."

August 4, 2020

Dream Twenty-One: I woke at 5:30 a.m. I had a visit from my ex again. We were getting married at 5:00 p.m. at a hotel. I gathered my wedding attire and belongings to prepare. I wandered outside and my car disappeared. I searched in *darkness* and spotted the front of the hotel. I noticed the valets waiting to give the keys to your car. I searched frantically for my automobile. It was not there. I sensed panic rising in my chest. I felt scared and unsettled. What was I to do? I begged a valet to give me a ride to the hotel for the wedding.

The dream shifted. I felt starved. I asked the valet to stop at Mc Donald's on the way to grab some food. My stomach felt famished. I entered the dwelling. The place looked nasty. No one seemed to care about anything. I tried to ask for help because I was in a hurry. I noticed no one wore masks. I felt unsafe inside this place and struggled to control my fear. I needed to relieve myself and spotted a restroom. The stalls appeared occupied. I sensed the individuals there were vile and rude. The restaurant and bathroom looked filthy. No seats were available to sit and eat. I glanced around the small eatery and saw lots of different people. They glared at me while they ate with disdain. I finally was next in line at the register. No one took my money for my food ordered. I checked the restroom at the back of the building, still no toilets available. I watched people waiting in line. I tried to pay for the hamburger and chips, no fries were available. The dark-skinned lady behind the counter glared at me.

She smirked, "No, this is the one that's bad. Somebody spit in it."

I had the bag in my hand, and she snatched it from me. I felt angry, hungry, and left. The valet dropped me in front of the hotel. 5:45 p.m. I was late and missed the ceremony. The hotel staff led me to a corner nook where the servants gathered coffee and dishes for the tables in the dining room. I must dress here for the wedding. I made the best of it. I pulled out the wedding dress and slipped into it. I spotted a small mirror in the nook. I struggled to apply makeup and lipstick quickly. The pink-reddish lipstick smeared on my lips over to my cheeks. I looked like a cheap whore. I saw no family or friends there to help me. I plugged in the curling iron and attempted to curl my hair. My hair looked black, not blonde like it was today. While I dressed, I saw a lady who managed the hotel in the mirror behind me staring. The lady looked in her eighties. She wore a satin mint green dress. She seemed appalled I was late and disrupted her schedule.

Staff behind me made callus comments, "Wow, she must be broke to get ready back here with us."

They stood a few inches away and glared, snickered, and gawked at me while I got ready. I felt humiliated and thrown together. I only had ten minutes to dress. It wasn't wise to leave my wallet and all my things unattended. I had no jewelry on. I forgot in my haste. I opened a drawer in my luggage where I packed my jewelry. The jewelry looked tacky, ugly, and not mine.

Mildred appeared over my shoulder and lied, "Oh, that piece would look fine."

I peeked in the top drawer, found long pearl earrings, and put them on. It was not my taste in jewelry, but it was all I had. I searched frantically through the drawers and discovered a purse appropriate for a wedding. I took all my cash and my wallet and shoved it into the purse. These characters were not trustworthy. They would steal everything I had as soon as I left.

I walked toward the lady in the mint dress and followed her. The wedding would happen here since I was late. The back of my dress not zipped and felt vulnerable. No one helped me and heard them laughing behind me. They made rude comments about my dress unzipped. I entered a room. It contained a bar, dining room, and a stage where people performed. I passed Bob on the way. He glared and kept walking past me. I turned and watched him. He wore a white suit and a white top hat. I noticed on the back of the suit, adorned with pink velvet tassels. They hung from the bottom of his suit and dragged the floor. It was weird to see him there. He looked distressed and miserable. I saw no family, just people who worked there. One servant would be my bridesmaid. The ladies looked African American, and they laughed at me. Their hair not styled, and they wore their maid uniforms. The uniforms looked like maroon dresses with short sleeves with a black apron tied at the waist. They wanted to watch what would happen.

They did not care and shoved me to the side. They sneered, "Wait here since you were late. You'll have to do your ceremony vows another time."

I waited in a line. The men in the wedding led, and I followed. I heard the groom laughing at the bar, drunk. He had no intentions of marrying me. This entire event was a joke played on me. The groom wanted me to feel his humiliation. I made him feel when I left him because I was unhappy in our relationship.

I woke and gasped. "Wow, I have been dreaming this all night. Today is our anniversary. We have been married for ten years. My ex still strives to hurt me."

I asked, "Why would he do this?"

Ilene replied, "He still tries to hurt you from *darkness*. But he cannot. We protect you."

I slept a while longer. I woke and walked downstairs. I opened my phone to call my spouse. I received a provocative message of how much he loved me and wished me a Happy Anniversary. He was amazing and a fantastic husband. My ex never came close to being like the man I married. I felt blessed and the happiest I have ever been. I saw parts of *darkness* with my ex still playing the victim. Just like he did when he lived. I felt awful while I recalled the dream. I was thrilled I would never see my ex again when I died.

Later, on my drive to work. I stated, "Wow, *evil is always watching me... it knew* when my anniversary was. My ex is in *darkness*. Coincidence? Nope, this happened on purpose, to hurt me."

I moved my schedule around because I had two cancellations that morning. So, I could come home early to spend the afternoon together. I texted him to let him know about my recent changes.

My husband beamed. "Awesome. I'll see you at 2:00."

On my way home, I pulled behind a black pickup truck. The license had 333 in it. I smiled and signed his card in the car when I stopped to buy a small fuzzy toy for Noodle. She loved special occasions.

I pulled into the garage and walked towards the house. My husband smiled and stood on the deck above me.

He grinned. "Go look at the pool."

I wondered why. I strolled into the garden, scanned the pool. He bought a load of white Sahara beach sand. We discussed a few days earlier about buying sand instead of pouring concrete. He surprised me for our anniversary. Shocked because he had spread half the sand around the pool already.

I gave him an enormous hug and beamed. "I love it. Thank you so much."

He added, "You have to reset up the chairs and stuff."

I answered, "Oh, I don't mind. I'll do it after I come inside and change clothes."

I entered the house. My husband bought two white orchids and a lovely card arranged on the dining table.

I glowed, "Oh, honey, you bought me flowers too? I love them. They are beautiful."

I opened it. He always found the perfect card and shared his deepest thoughts of how he loved me. I handed him his card and Noodle her prize. Grateful God sent him to me. We both held each other tight and whispered, "I love you."

I changed clothes and could not wait to set up the chairs by the pool. I rearranged the umbrellas and two throw rugs. I turned the drum fans on high and walked inside. I filled a large glass of ice water for Noodle and me. My husband grabbed the towels and his drink. We were off to the "beach." That was what we called it now. We enjoyed the afternoon together. My husband continued to spread more sand. He wanted it thick. We enjoyed swimming, talking, and gazing into each other's eyes; loving one another. Noodle decided it was her first time to get in the water. He held her and slowly let her get used to the water. A few minutes later, she wanted back in the water. She relaxed in his arms in the water and liked it. At 5:00 p.m. We took a break from our wonderful day together as husband and wife. I strolled towards the house, following Noodle.

I whispered, "Thank you, Lord, for a wonderful day. Thank you for all that you do for me and my family."

I turned on my phone and it was 4:44 p.m. I laughed and knew God had shown him the way… and the angels were with us.

Later that evening, before I went to bed, I heard "Dec. 63," by The Four Seasons, from my husband's mother. This was the song she played on rare occasions.

His mom spoke warmly, "Thank you for making my son so happy."

I beamed. "Thank you... for giving birth to a wonderful man that makes me extremely happy."

August 5, 2020

I talked with a client about her trip to the beach. She missed her mom, who passed a few months ago. They planned the trip in honor of her mother and did things there in her memory. She entered a photo contest for the best sunset. She hoped it would win also in honor of her mother. She continued, "I hope mom is proud of me."

I heard music from Dad and sensed he would give a message. I rinsed the color bowls and her mother replied, "I am proud of her. She needs to focus on herself and her future."

I relayed the information. She cried. I explained, "You have been talking about your past. You are still grieving. Your mother wants you to focus on yourself and your future. That is what you must do."

She wiped tears from her eyes, "I was hoping I would hear from her."

I replied, "That's when they come through. She knows you're grieving. God knows you are grieving. They love you. They were listening to everything you said."

She added, "I have been reading your book. I have changed the way I pray."

Shocked, I asked, "Why? What did you read that made you want to pray differently?"

She beamed. "In a Baptist church, we always prayed in Jesus' name. But now I say all of it like you did."

I looked into her eyes, "Do you say in the name of the Father, the Son and the Holy Spirit, in Jesus Christ, I pray?"

She beamed. "Yes, that is what I say now."

I added, "I was told this shows respect to God and to your faith. I do it every time I pray, and I cross myself as a Catholic. It shows respect, and it feels right. I was raised in a Methodist church and was taught like you were. I feel it's not enough and lacking not to say it all."

I thought, "Wow, I am thrilled what I wrote helped her. This is the whole point."

I added, "You can pray for yourself. What do you pray for? You must pray for yourself first, then pray for others. Pray for what you need, not what you want. It is difficult. It will make you cry when you pray for what you need. My guides and God have instructed me to pray this way."

Her hair color looked perfect. She seemed happier hearing from her mom. It gave her lots to think about. We told each other goodbye. I cleaned the salon and wiped down everything because of COVID-19.

Gabriel interjected. "Pray for those you love."

I asked, "Should I say their name?"

Gabriel answered, "Yes, it is wise."

I gasped. "Wow, I thought saying their name meant more. I had gotten lazy lately. I just prayed for those that I love."

I prayed and mentioned each person's name and asked for specific things I knew they needed. I remembered God told me on Monday they were weak and needed guidance, perseverance, and strength.

Gabriel replied, "God heard your prayers and is pleased with what you have asked for."

I gasped. "Wow, I am glad I said their names. It really makes you think about the individual and what they need. I am an empath. You can't hide your feelings from me, not all of them, maybe some, if you're good."

Later, in bed, I woke at 5:00 a.m. Noodle needed to pee. It was a restless night. I laid there for over an hour before I drifted to sleep after taking her outside. I woke again and heard music, "Dec. 63" from my husband's mom, Theresa.

Theresa whispered, "Your husband misses you."

I drifted to sleep. I woke at 8:00 a.m. and heard music from Theresa. I asked Ilene, "Why am I hearing from my husband's mom without me asking?"

Ilene replied, "God is allowing her to."

Theresa whispered, "Please tell my son I miss and love him. He must do more. He can do more. These things will help you."

I made coffee and logged into my journal. Gabriel announced, "His mother misses her son. God is allowing her to speak to you. Give him the message."

I called immediately and shared what happened. The message touched his heart. But it made him anxious. I explained, "They know you can do more than we realize. I have heard this many times. God has told me to do more."

August 7, 2020

Today started as a wonderful day. I noticed my car hesitated, cranking. I pushed the thoughts aside and drove to work. Later that morning, my husband called. Maria had surgery to remove her breast because of cancer. Unfortunately, the doctors found cancer in her lymph nodes under her armpit. They removed the lymph in that area as well. This was horrible news for Maria and my husband. She would be fine. Her surgery went well. The unexpected news of cancer in her lymph nodes surprised me.

I locked the salon and drove to Lowes Foods grocery. The deli had the best chicken salad in town. I craved it and bought some. I walked back to my car, and it would not crank. I knew immediately my battery died. It felt steamy in the eighty-five-degree weather. The sweltering heat did not take long to overcome me. I opened my door and rolled up the windows just in case I needed to leave my car there. I called my husband. He sounded sad, and my car troubles did not make him happier from all the bad news he heard.

He whispered, "I will be there in a few."

I hated to even ask him to come to my rescue. I did not know what to do. I called my 1:00 appointment and told her I might have to reschedule. I ate my lunch in the sweltering heat. Sweat poured down my back. I lost my appetite and ate in frustration. I carried jumper cables in my trunk because this happened before and left me stranded.

My husband pulled beside my car. He hooked the jumper cables to the battery, and my car started. I could have asked a stranger to help, but during COVID-19 I hesitated. No one came out of the store, which parked close to my car. I called Jason's Auto and asked if they could replace my battery.

Stanley told me, "We are booked today. I cannot promise I can get to your car."

I panicked and drove my car there in hopes they had time. I drove a convertible. To reach the battery, you must remove the tire and other parts. This was not a simple task. I needed to work on Saturday and hoped they worked me in. I left my car and my husband drove me to work. I noticed 666 on a license plate in front of us. The angel number 666 meant to balance your thoughts and emotions. I felt dreadful inside.

I stated, "You know, this really puts things in perspective. I really don't have anyone I could call but you."

Tears welled in my eyes, knowing these things were true. I had friends, but you hoped family in times of stress would help. I did not have a family I would call anymore.

My husband whispered, "You are my wife, and I will always be there for you."

We hugged and whispered, "I love you."

I thanked my husband again for rescuing me. I texted my last client if she minded dropping me off at the auto store after her appointment. She had no problem helping me. I felt humbled to ask for help because I was so independent.

She dropped me off, and I thanked her. I waited another hour and a half for them to fix my car. They were behind but made time to repair it.

I told the owner, Jason, and Stanly who worked behind the front counter, "I truly appreciate you guys taking care of me. I was desperate."

They both smiled. It felt wonderful to be inside my car again and in control. I drove home relieved and thankful. My husband and Noodle waited for me on the deck. It felt wonderful to see their cheerful faces.

Later, my husband drove to the bakery for his Saturday morning rush. I drank a glass of red wine and enjoyed watching TV while I decided what to cook for dinner. I craved two ground beef quesadillas with chips and dip. I waited for the hamburger to thaw. I scrolled on Facebook and saw where someone posted a question about angels. He wanted to know did anyone hear from angels. I smiled when I read this and answered the question. I heard from my master guide, an angel, and heard from angels when I meditated.

I scrolled down to read the other answers to his question. A lady responded if you think you heard from angels, they were not. They were demons. There were many comments telling her she had the right to her own opinion, but they heard from angels, not demons. I questioned what I heard for a split second. Could this be true? Shocked, I knew this was not true. Why did I think this even for a moment? I felt sick inside and immediately apologized to God for even considering these things. I knew they were untrue.

Gabriel instructed. "You need to ask for forgiveness from your Lord and Savior."

I prayed and asked for forgiveness. Evil tried to trick me.

Gabriel replied, "Your Lord has forgiven you. You must pray for the people that you love."

I asked, "Can you tell me their names?" I heard names from Gabriel and prayed for each of them.

I cooked my dinner and still kept hearing a voice in my head, making me think about what I read.

Ilene instructed. "Stop thinking about these things. They are not helping you."

I struggled and prayed for God to remove the evil thought. Evil tried to still convince me I heard from demons, not angels. I asked God to help me.

God whispered, *"I am with thee, your Lord and Savior."*

It softened my thoughts, but they still came. I ate dinner and walked into the bathroom. I burned sage and frankincense. I moved the smoke around my aura. Evil hated frankincense. The thoughts immediately ceased, and I felt relieved.

I watched the series "A Place To Call Home," directed by Mark Joffe, Lynn-Maree, and Catherine Miller. I was on Season four. This series played on the Acorn channel. It was a wonderful series, and I thoroughly enjoyed it. It was late, and I had a client at 9:30 a.m. My husband came home from the bakery after 11:00 p.m. I turned off the TV and took Noodle outside. I gave him an enormous hug and kiss.

I whispered in his ear, "I'm sorry you had a horrible day and learning such terrible news about a family member."

He hugged me tighter and said nothing other than I love you. He still felt worried about her.

I whispered, "Gabriel told me earlier, we must pray for a full recovery, daily."

He held me tighter and kissed me goodnight. I picked up Noodle to let him kiss her, too. I carried her upstairs because she hurt her hind leg a few days ago. I placed her on the bed and the lights were off. I walked around the bed and turned on my bedside lamp. I looked at the bed and saw my two-inch rose quartz crystal laying in the center of the bed. Shocked, I leaned down and touched it. It felt cold, and I did not put it there.

I asked, "Who did this?"

Dad answered, "I did it, Beck. You need it to heal."

I grabbed the crystal and hurried downstairs to tell my husband. I explained what happened, and he looked baffled.

I whispered in his ear, "Dad did it."

I gave him another hug and kiss. I marched upstairs and climbed into bed. I needed to pray. I held the crystal in my hand and my other hand on Noodle. I looked at the rose quartz, and tears flowed from my eyes.

I whispered, "It's wonderful to see you move something from heaven. Knowing you can move an object is incredible."

I cried and grabbed the other crystals out of the glass dish. I slept with selenite, labradorite, amethyst and obsidian every night as Ilene instructed.

I asked, "Why did you put it on the bed?"

Dad replied, "Beck, you have much to heal. Will help you. You need to pray for the ones that you love."

It surprised me because I had already prayed for the ones I loved earlier in the evening. Dad did not tell me these things. Ilene and Gabriel did.

I asked Dad, "Can you give me a list of who I need to pray for? Maybe that will help me."

He stated the names of the ones who harmed me and my brother. It shocked me. I sobbed. "I cannot pray for these people in the manner you are asking. They do not care about me."

Dad continued, "They love you in their own way."

My mind raced; it did not feel right to pray for the ones who harmed me. My brother did not harm me.

I stated, "God told me himself, Dad, these people do me no good. They do not care about thee. Walk away. I cannot pray for these people. I cannot. It's wrong. It's too painful. It feels wrong." I sobbed as I explained.

Gabriel instructed. "You need to pray for these people."

I stated to Gabriel and Dad, "I cannot." My instincts told me no. It was too painful. I thought about what God told me.

I stated, "These people do not care about me. They do me no good. I cannot pray for them in this manner."

Gabriel announced, "You have been tested by God. Evil is always around."

Dad whispered and sounded hurt, "I'm sorry, Beck. God told me to say these things to you."

Gabriel answered, "God will answer your prayer. One of your prayers will be answered."

I cried. "God, I hope it is Maria."

I prayed earlier for God to heal her and for a full recovery from her cancer. I laid in bed and sobbed. I prayed for protection for the night.

I asked Ilene, "Please don't let me oversleep."

Ilene replied, "I will wake you. Do not worry."

I closed my eyes and desperately tried to relax and finally drifted to sleep.

August 10, 2020

I wrote for hours and felt weary. I did not sleep well last night and laid on the bed with Noodle to nap. I slept for an hour and realized I forgot to prepare the house. I came downstairs and made Noodle's dinner. She ate while I prepared the house. I finished and walked to the garage to put the clothes in the dryer.

Gabriel announced, "God is pleased. You remembered to protect yourself."

I replied, "I almost forgot. I usually do it after I pay bills on Monday mornings." I smiled, knowing God watched me prepare the house.

Later, in bed, I woke at 3:33 a.m. I laid there for three hours, tossing, and turning. I felt frustrated and finally drifted to sleep. The alarm woke me at 7:30 a.m. I felt exhausted and my brain swirled with thoughts of demands of the day. I climbed out of bed and walked downstairs. I heard the song, "Dec' 63," from my husband's mother. I felt out of it and could not understand what she said. I took Noodle outside to pee and brought her back in.

I asked, Ilene, "What did she say?"

Ilene replied, "She wants you to call her son and tell him that she loves him, misses him. He can do better."

I made my coffee and called. I explained to him what his mother said in his message.

My husband replied, "I love and miss her too." The call dropped.

Theresa whispered, "Thank you, Rebecca. He needs to help you more. God wants him to help his messenger more."

I replied, "I wish he would. I feel like I have to beg sometimes for him to help me with anything. I know that doesn't work either. He must want to help me on his own accord."

Later in the afternoon, I glanced at the clock, 5:55 p.m. I thought, "More changes coming. What would they be?"

August 12, 2020

I left work early. Noodle and I had plans to hang at the pool. While we enjoyed ourselves by the pool, soaking in the heat. I poured water on her back to keep her cool. Noodle appeared content, enjoying the wind from the fans blowing. I walked over and kissed the top of her head. I noticed most of the tumor had fallen off. I always felt it when I rubbed her head. She had another tumor between her brows, and it felt smaller.

I whispered as I kissed her, "Thank you, God."

August 13, 2020

At 6:00 p.m. I sat on the couch beside my husband. He still looked groggy from his nap. I heard, "Dec' 63," song. I tuned in to what she said.

His mother spoke, "Pray for one another. It will help you support one another."

Theresa added, "Speak to Maria, more. I love my family very much. Pray for her full recovery, support, and guidance. God will grant these things. He's waiting to hear your prayers. He's not ready for her."

I shared the message. I struggled to hear anything else. She sounded far away.

Theresa whispered, "Please tell my son that I love him. I miss him. I miss all of my family. I love them very much."

I asked him to turn off the TV. It was difficult to hear her. I held my husband's hand while I heard again from his mom.

She continued, "Maria does not believe in mediums."

My husband hissed, "I could have told you that."

I explained, "I am letting you know what I am hearing from your mom. That's why she wants you to call her more often, because I can't tell her directly what I am hearing. She wouldn't understand."

Gabriel announced, "God has given you a great gift. Do these things that his mother has asked you to do." I explained.

Dad added, "God is awesome, Beck."

Theresa whispered, "Tell my son I love him." She sounded closer, and she spoke in a hurry. Then I heard nothing more.

I gasped. "Wow, I don't hear things from spirits directly. I hear things from my guides or Dad." I thought, "This is a gift I hoped for. God's listening to help guide his family to pray for things they need."

Later in the evening, Both Sides Now TV had a chat room open after Kellee White's show online. On Thursday's show, people could ask questions of Kellee online. The questions were spiritual. She was a medium and teacher. Kellee looked in her late fifties. Her blond hair long and wavy. Her spirit felt bubbly, sincere, and generous.

At 10:30 p.m. I needed to end the chat room and call it a night. John the mediator returned to the discussion after eating his dinner. He looked in his thirties, handsome, an empath and extremely kind-hearted. His voice sounded soft and patient. He mentioned he shared today with a coworker at James Van Prague's office about his mother coming through in our last chat room. I received a message from his mom during a Zoom chat. His mom loved her son and would help him on this journey. I had shared this information with John. It surprised me he talked about it today to someone. He commented tonight on how upset I was when it happened.

I replied, "Her energy was strong. I felt it when she spoke."

I explained to the group about my husband's mother came through earlier. I added how their motherly energies felt similar. Their mother's energy felt kind, loving, and how they knew what was going on in their son's lives. They wanted to help their son's because they loved them both so much.

Gabriel stated to me about John, "God has plans for you."

I told John immediately and explained how important it was to hear this information. When my master guide spoke anything, I must listen. He was an angel. I did not disclose my knowledge of Gabriel. God told me not to until I printed the book.

People on chat revealed to John how he could have his own show. I agreed. He laughed.

I added, "It's because we love you so much."

John sighed. "I can't because I am just an empath."

I giggled. "Oh no, it was just confirmed by my master guide. You have much more to do. You don't know what exactly that means. But it is coming."

Everyone in chat laughed, and they agreed. I told them goodnight. I prepared for bed and recalled I heard from God on my way to the salon. I had asked God to speak to me. I needed to know where my life was headed.

God had whispered, *"You must have patience for these things to unfold."*

My patience felt tattered. The unknowing wore on me. What I heard tonight made me wonder about plans God had for John. What did it have to do with me? I felt a connection. I must wait for the unfolding to happen.

I logged into my journal the next morning. Gabriel announced, "God is please that I have written these things."

I gasped. "Wow, they're always watching and listening to everything I do."

I took the morning off. Noodle and I went for a walk. She ran up the driveway, so happy. It had been days since her last walk. The heat felt oppressive. We returned and cooled off. I sat her on top of the hot tub for a haircut. The hot tub was the perfect height. She looked like a puppy again. I gave her cheese for a treat for sitting still during her puppy spa time.

It appeared it would rain. I strolled into the garden and spread nitrogen to the flowers and roses. The garden looked weary from the heat. Fall approached. I wanted to bring back any life I could to our garden, my happy place. I walked inside and it was 11:11 a.m. I giggled and loved it when my guides gave me signs of encouragement.

August 16, 2020

I woke in the middle of the night and felt tingles on my lower lip. I felt a dreaded cold sore formed. I snuck downstairs and grabbed the bottle of Lysine and swallowed two pills. I climbed back into bed and worried, "I am stressed more than I realized and have not felt rested in days. The doom and gloom of COVID-19 hovered over us." I drifted to sleep.

Dream Twenty-Two: The dream horrified me. I viewed myself in a familiar place. I remembered I was shown this ghastly place before in another dream. The area looked black, massive, archaic, dreary, a mansion of sorts. I realized parts of this place *evil lived*. I did not belong here. I entered this dwelling because of my gifts. I crossed the threshold of a chamber that seemed above the many lower rooms below. I felt anxious, nervous, timid, and terrified.

The dream I had before I was shown a door to where evil lived. *I sensed evil behind the huge, locked door.* That time I could not enter, nor did I want to.

I reached toward the enormous, ancient, dark wooden door. It creaked as it opened. I crept inside the room. The black space looked vast and dead silent. My heart pounded as I sensed immense danger standing in *its space*. I immediately realized I should not be here. I spun around and the room looked black and filled with moving dark shadows. I felt extremely unsafe and snuck towards a staircase in the dark. I crouched down, trying to hide. I glanced above and observed an old, black, oak, wooden railing that led upstairs to *its bedroom, where evil lived.* I tiptoed forward, up the steps. The battered old steps creaked and made a sharp noise. I stopped and turned towards the balcony. I held my breath and peeked over the banister. I saw the dark black bedposts of the immense bed and grimy bedding. I noticed a few old, dirty, tattered pillows scattered on the bed. It looked ancient and filthy. I sensed imminent danger again and my heart thumped with fear. *I sensed evil coming towards me.* Evil heard the creak of the steps. I wanted to bolt out of there, but it was too late. EVIL KNEW WHO I WAS, *God's messenger.* I felt shielded by God, but my stomach dropped to my feet. I sensed evil creeping slowly towards the bed. I spotted a gigantic shadow as it slinked closer. *It relished smelling my fear.* I thought I would pass out. My head spun off what to do. My heart palpitated, and I grabbed my mouth not to scream. *I KNEW it would show itself. I sensed IT wanted me to see it.* I saw the frightening, powerful entity inching closer. My heart pounded and my eyes wide open, glaring at the railing and bed. Frozen, I stood there waiting. The edge of an enormous face met the railing. *IT KEPT COMING. The entire ginormous face hovered at the top of the railing in its lair. I gawked at the gigantic, blasphemous, midnight blue eyes the size of two moons.* The depths of its eyes seemed endless. *Evil scowled and glared at me*, knowing who I was, disgusted *I* was in its space. The edges of its face appeared as misty, gray smoke. The grayish smoke moved and formed its face. I noticed evil changed its expression by moving the mist. *The grayish smoke never stopped moving.*

I freaked out. EVIL DID NOT WANT ME IN ITS LAIR. I pissed it off, and I did not belong here. *It surprised me and retreated towards the bed.* IT wanted me to see it. I woke. I thought I would puke and could not breathe. I felt petrified, but I recognized God protected me.

I realized, "*What had I SEEN?* EVIL'S LAIR."

Shocked and horrified, I climbed out of bed and came downstairs. My husband sat on the couch drinking coffee. My chest pounded. I excused myself to "the room" to log this dream into my journal.

I thought, "Evil looked right through me with those *terrifying, enormous, moon eyes.*"

Gabriel announced, "God wants you to write these things. This is where evil resides."

Shaken, I logged into my journal. Evil didn't have a body, just ginormous, malicious, smoky face. When evil formed, I saw it sneer and frown at me. The gray smoke formed into the shape of eyebrows. EVIL had GLARED AT ME. I had the image burned into my memory. *IT looked massive.* I realized then; God told me evil was powerful. But God trumped all things. It looked gigantic compared to me. I did not tell my husband about this. It felt difficult to swallow and breathe. It paralyzed me to SEE IT. My stomach knotted writing this down. I saw some rooms below its lair in other dreams. I sensed evil watched over everything. I felt relieved I wasn't there. I wanted to bolt out of there. But I could not until it showed itself. I sensed I would puke to have seen something so vile and disgusting. *It tormented and shifted shapes of whatever it wanted to be.*

I recalled part of the dream. I noticed after evil retreated away from me. I spotted evil's servants at the top of the stairs. They appeared as black shadows, observing me. *It* had many followers that did everything for the revolting, vile entity. *I sensed it.* These servants protected evil and its lair. Shocked by what I observed, it scared me half to death. I took a few deep breaths and felt rattled to the core of my being. It shook me to write this down. I relaxed some after I took a few more deep breaths.

God wanted me to write these things for you to understand evil is real. *God is real.* Glad God was on my side. God protected me. God kept me safe with his enormous glory and power. God was much more powerful than evil. I remembered God warned me evil comes in many forms. *Well, I saw that firsthand.*

Gabriel announced, "God is pleased with what you have written. God wants you to enjoy your day. He is with you and protects his messenger."

I took a deep breath and opened the door. I struggled to hide the shock on my face from my husband. He did not even seem to notice my distress. I made a cup of coffee and thanked Gabriel for reminding me God was with me.

I sat on the couch and pretended everything was great. My mind churned, remembering the images I saw in the dream. I hated evil, and it's disgusting ways. The memories of the dream spun in my mind. I desperately tried to forget what had happened.

August 18, 2020

I had IBS symptoms. My stress level was at an all-time high. As the day progressed, the symptoms worsened, and by the evening, the pain felt unbearable. I laid in bed with Noodle. I took all the antacids in the medicine cabinet. I sipped on plain chicken broth for dinner and woke many times in pain during the night. I finally passed out and slept.

In the morning I felt relieved my tummy felt better and heard music from Theresa.

I asked Ilene, "Is the music I am hearing from his mother or you?"

Ilene answered, "It is his mother."

Theresa whispered, "I'm glad you're feeling better. My son needs to help you more."

I thought, "How do I get a man to help me more?"

I heard, "I'll Fly Away," by Albert E. Brumley, from Dad and it made me smile. I had not heard from him in days.

Dad whispered, "I love you, Beck. Be careful what you eat today."

Gabriel announced, "God is with you. Remember to pray."

I prayed and grounded. The stress came from the anniversary two years ago when that horrible spirit followed me home with a demonic attachment. It was the most terrifying, horrific experience in my life. My body expected there was more to come. I remembered the dream I wrote about yesterday. *Evil wanted to terrify me, and it did.* I struggled to get the thoughts out of my mind.

I heard, "I'll Be There," by Four Tops song from Ilene. I smiled. "I miss you and glad I have you with me. It is difficult being God's messenger but an honor."

I climbed out of bed and thought about what Dad suggested. I heated chicken broth in a cup instead of coffee. I needed to buy more antacids, too. My intestines needed several days to rest. They felt swollen, inflamed, and bloated from the stress I endured.

August 21, 2020

I drove to work and whispered prayers. I asked God, "Please guide me today of how I can help my clients."

My first client arrived. I mentioned her in *Experiences Never Stop.* She was a wonderful woman in her early seventies. Her hair styled short and blonde. She looked much younger than she was. I loved her gentle spirit, forgiving, kind and loving. I sensed she had tremendous faith in God and looked forward to her appointment.

I applied the blonde hair color and while it processed, we enjoyed our conversation with one another. She looked distressed because someone robbed her car last night and stole her walking cane. She made a quick call to her lunch date. I excused myself and walked to the restroom while she was on the phone. I entered the bathroom and heard "I'll Fly Away," song.

I chuckled. "Hello, Dad."

I immediately sensed he would give me a message for her. I washed my hands and returned to the other room. She continued the call. The music played.

She shared she needed to buy a new cane at lunch. I interrupted. "I have been hearing things."

She smiled and stopped talking. Dad beamed. "Irving has a message for his wife."

I placed my hand on her shoulder and listened to my Dad. He spoke for her husband. I shared what I heard.

Dad whispered, "Please tell my lovely wife, I love her and miss her."

She burst into tears. I listened, "I will see her soon." I reminded, "There is no time on the other side. Don't worry about seeing him soon."

Dad whispered for Irving, "She needs to pray more. I am with her every day. That is all, Beck."

I explained, "He is gone. That was his message for you. Wow, his lovely wife. I was not expecting this today." She sobbed. I did not look at her expression until I finished. It was difficult to hear Dad.

I explained, "I could hear his masculinity in his voice as he spoke through Dad. He spoke softly, sounded soft, like whispering." She cried more.

She added, "That is how my husband spoke, softly."

I beamed. "That is exactly how he sounded."

She added, "He always referred to me as his lovely wife."

I gasped. "Wow, I did not know. That's what they do sometimes. Spirits say certain things that only you know."

She confessed, "I had hoped to hear from him today. I asked if I could before I arrived. I didn't want to ask you and put you in an awkward situation. But I really hoped that I would hear from him today. Monday will be the anniversary of his passing. It will be two years."

I grinned. "Well, that's why he came through. You asked, and it's almost the anniversary of his death. He wants to let you know he's okay and is waiting for you. He will see you again. But you have more to do. Do you need a tissue?"

She replied, "No."

I beamed. "Let those tears of joy run down your cheeks because you heard from your husband today. You asked and God has given you this blessing."

I felt wonderful to hear these things from a kind, gentle, loving man for his wife. She needed encouragement. We finished our session. My next client had already arrived. We wanted to hug each other but did not because of COVID-19. We laughed about it. I helped her out the door because she had no cane to help her steady her balance. I told her goodbye.

My next client came in for a nail treatment. She was a client for over thirty years and knew me well. We shared many private matters. We trusted each other and always wanted the best for one another. She looked younger than she was, but in her early seventies too. She devoted more of her life now to God. She strived to be a better person, as I did. She wanted to learn more and grow spiritually, just like me. I wondered what would happen because I still heard music. God allowed Dad to give messages at the salon. I sensed his excitement.

I started the appointment and listened to what had been going on since the last appointment three weeks ago. The more she talked, the louder the music played. I could not listen to them both.

Dad interjected. "Her mother is in transition, Beck. She's amending for what she's done wrong to her daughter."

I asked, "Will she be with God?"

Dad answered, "She is still in transition. She's amending for what she's done wrong to her daughter."

I asked, "Am I supposed to tell her this?" Her mother passed years ago.

He replied, "Yes, Beck, God wants you to tell her these things."

I interrupted. "I am hearing things from my father. He is telling me God wants me to tell you these things. Are you ready?" This would not be easy to hear.

She looked shocked, "Yes, I am ready." She gently touched my arm, and I felt her anticipation.

I repeated what Dad said, "Your mother is in transition, amending for what she has done to you."

She replied, "I always wonder how my mother could be such a Christian and do such unchristian things. I always wondered why these things happened, especially after she died."

I responded, "You must remember you do not get away with the things you have done wrong. Transition is your life review, the good and the bad. You must own everything you did when you were alive. That is why it is better to amend anything you can, any unfinished business with your loved ones before you die. When you 're alive you can call, drive, physically do things. When you 're dead you cannot do those things. It is harder for you to amend. You must amend. You won't get away with anything. God will not let you."

I asked, "How long has your mom passed?"

She whispered, "Eighteen years."

I gasped. "Wow, that is a long time." I said it without thinking.

I whispered, "Remember, there is no time on the other side. You have been here forty-five minutes, which can be a moment there. I don't know what your mother did, and you don't have to explain. She is answering for these things."

Dad instructed. "Beck, she's amending through Christ. These things will be difficult for her." I relayed the information.

She explained, "There was something online this morning that I couldn't read. It would not open. The article was about this and maybe that's why she came through."

I reminded, "I cannot hear or see a spirit in transition. They cannot see me either. Dad gave this message." I sensed her mother did many terrible things, not only to her. She would amend for some time.

I explained, "My guide Ilene shared with me what happens in transition. Some spirits are in transition for a day and other spirits for a few days. Your mother has issues she must resolve, and it will take some time."

Dad added, "These things will be difficult for her. But she will do them."

I replied, "I hope this did not upset you. But this is true. You don't get away with things. You don't."

She seemed shocked in processing what she heard. I added, "I have never lied to you. I have always been honest. There is a reason this happened. God wanted you to know. You must remember this."

Dad beamed. "God told me to tell you this. There's a reason why God wanted her to know these things. It's to help her and only she knows what it is." I shared the message.

She whispered, "Well, she used to grab me by my hair and drag me across the floor. She did awful things to my siblings too."

I sighed. "Well, she is amending for hurting all of you. She has been in transition for eighteen years. That is a lot to amend for. She will go to heaven when she is finished. Then I can hear from her."

We talked about other things and her appointment ended. We told each other goodbye. I cleaned up before lunch and felt starved.

I asked Ilene, "Does God want me to put this in the book?"

Ilene beamed. "Yes, Rebecca, God wants you to write these things."

I asked, "Can you please remind me of everything said, so I don't forget the details? I have to work before I can log into my journal."

Ilene replied, "You will remember, and I will help you."

I grabbed lunch and received a message from my first client. She texted. "I was telling my friend Barbara about your message from Irv. She didn't hesitate but to say, you heard from God. You are a blessing."

I texted. "That's exactly where my father and your husband are, with God. Tell her about my books if you think she would be interested."

She texted. "Will do. Blessings." I texted three heart emojis.

At 7:01 p.m. I remembered everything and felt fantastic helping these women. They were both caring, kind, loving, wonderful, giving individuals. I loved them both. I logged into my journal. I asked God for help to guide me today and he answered my prayer. God was incredible.

Later that evening, I watched trash TV before my husband came home. We texted how much we loved one another. I texted my loved ones how much I loved them. They responded quickly, and I sensed their love. My salmon baked. I bought gorgeous green lettuce and diced it. I added scallions and fresh tomatoes. My dinner looked fabulous and tasted perfect. I enjoyed my wonderful dinner alone. I checked messages and played backgammon. Octavian loved dice games. I texted my husband several times during dinner.

I held Noodle and whispered, "Do you want to go outside and pee?"

I put her on the floor, and she ran to the door. She heard me. I prayed for days regarding improving her hearing. I picked her up and carried her down the thirteen steps to the yard. I lifted her when she finished and came inside. We carried her as much as we could now, up and down the steps we have in our home. Noodle was getting older, and we felt it would help her as she aged. I turned off the TV in the living room and sauntered towards "the room." She waited by the stool beside the bed. I collected her and placed her on the furry blanket. I clicked on the fan and settled on the blanket with her. I turned on the heating pad behind my back and watched her on the bed, happy. I kissed her on the head and snuggled close.

I whispered in her ear, "I love you. You're the best friend ever. I love you more than anything in this entire world." She enjoyed my hugs and kisses. She heard me.

Ilene beamed. "She loves you more that you know." With Ilene's encouragement, I leaned down and kissed her some more. She raised her paw, and I kissed her paw, too.

I told her, "You're an awesome friend and love you so much. I hope you understand how much I love you." I caressed her head and kissed her face. She glanced at me with her eyes gazing into mine.

I thought, "You could hear me." I smiled and held her tight.

I whispered in her ear, "You must remember I will always do what's best for you, always. I love you more than you could ever imagine." I kissed her on her head and rubbed her body. She enjoyed it immensely. I nestled my face into her back.

Gabriel announced, "God has blessed you."

Tears flowed because God had blessed me. Noodle was healthy because of God. Today she heard me. I whispered, "Thank you, God, for everything. I know you did it. Thank you."

Noodle still enjoyed the attention. I kissed her a few more times and asked Gabriel, "Does God want me to write this down?"

Gabriel announced, "Yes, God wants you to write these things."

I logged into my journal at 9:48 p.m. and thought, "I am blessed. Thank you, Lord, for all that you've given me. Thank you for what you do for me and my new family."

I received a text from my husband. He expressed how much he loved me through emojis, which we often do when he worked. He finished baking and would be home soon.

At 12:00 p.m. I felt excited I didn't have to work in the morning. Tired, I lifted Noodle and carried her outside. I wandered down the steps holding her and wondered if any spirits watched me. I gently placed her on the green grass and glanced around the yard. It felt calm and cooler than it had been in several days. I sensed I wasn't alone and heard music from Ilene.

Ilene warned, "There are a lot of spirits out. You need to go inside. Spirits are starting to gather."

I scooped up Noodle and rushed up the steps to the front door. Glad she warned me. I opened the door and hurriedly stepped inside. It made me quiver to know spirits watched and gathered towards me.

August 22, 2020

On our walk, I recalled I woke and smelled cigarettes, an ashtray. I sniffed the air, and it left. I smelled cigarettes at the salon yesterday for a moment.

I asked Gabriel, "Why did I smell cigarette smoke at the salon and in bed last night?"

Gabriel answered, "Your abilities are growing. God is allowing them to. You must protect yourself more because of these things."

I asked, "Was the smoke from my father? He smoked when he lived."

Gabriel answered, "Yes."

I felt the cool white sand under my feet. I needed grounding. Noodle enjoyed herself marking and smelling the special spots left from other animals. It was seventy-eight degrees, and it felt wonderful. I hoped today would be sunny. I wanted to enjoy lying by the pool. I treasured each quiet moment on our walk. I am an Empath and desperately need quiet time to recharge.

August 26, 2020

I played hooky. Today was the first sunny day in the nineties. It had rained for days. I needed a break from the doom and gloom. I wanted to spend the day with Noodle by the pool. I wasn't sure if my husband would be on board with our adventure.

I opened the front door and heard a new song from Ilene, "I Can See Clearly Now," by Johnny Nash. I chuckled and called my husband. I explained what happened. He laughed too. I loved Ilene's sense of humor.

I took Noodle for a walk. The breeze felt wonderful on my skin. The morning air felt pleasant and refreshing. We enjoyed our walk together and heard, "Jesus Loves Me," a song from Dad.

I smiled. "Wow, hearing from you makes the day even better."

We came inside. I needed to log what happened into my journal. Ilene played the song I mentioned earlier throughout our walk.

Gabriel announced during the walk, "God wants you to enjoy your day, today, with your family. He wants his messenger to be happy."

I replied, "Thank you. I want to be happy. I already feel great today just knowing it's going to be a wonderful day." I enjoyed the wind blowing through my hair and felt fabulous inside, knowing they were with me. I had changed things in my life, which made me a happier person.

My husband arrived home. I prepared a delicious barbecue sandwich with slaw and spicy sauce. I sliced fresh green bell peppers from the garden. Noodle had chicken and pellets. We laughed and enjoyed our time together.

He wanted to take a nap instead of hanging by the pool. I gathered our towels and water and strolled to the pool with Noodle. She looked at me, excited we were together. I thoroughly enjoyed lying in the sun with the drum fans blowing full blast. I absorbed the heat of the sun on my face and the water was the perfect temperature. I grounded and meditated for a while.

Gabriel instructed. "Pray for those you love."

I asked, "Which ones?" Gabriel named my husband, and two other people close to me.

I asked, "What do I need to pray for? Is it guidance?"

Gabriel instructed. "Guidance, knowledge for the truth."

I finished meditating and prayed for those three individuals. I heard, "Knock Three Times," by Tony Orlando and Dawn, a song from Dan.

I questioned Dan, "What is knowledge for the truth mean?"

He whispered, "It will help them grow with you."

I gulped, "Oh."

I logged into my journal when I came inside. My husband was awake, sitting on the couch. I leaned down and gave him a kiss.

I stated, "What a glorious day."

He smiled. "Good." I patted Noodle on the head, and we hung out till dinner.

August 28, 2020

I waited for my 3:00 nail appointment to arrive. I met her at the door. She looked tall, in her late fifties, a lovely lady with short blonde hair, and a bubbly personality.

She explained, "I've got something to tell you." While she chose a nail polish. I knew immediately what she was excited to share.

A few months ago, my client asked me to help her. A family member died, and they could not find the key to open a safe. She asked if I could hear any information about where the key was located. Ilene had told me, "It is in the garage, under a cabinet." I had shared this information with her. The garage filled with the family's belongings. They had not dispersed the items to the family members. I wondered every nail appointment if they found the key.

She sat at the manicure table. She explained her husband's relative came over to clear out her things from the garage. It took most of the day. When she finished.

She proudly announced, "I found the key."

My client inquired, "Where was the key?"

She replied, "In the foyer."

My client asked, "Were in the foyer?"

She replied, "In a drawer."

My client and her husband knew she lied because they had searched the foyer many times, no key. They searched the entire house for the key except for the garage.

I smiled. "Well, my guide never lies. That is what Ilene said. The lady you are speaking about is lying to you. She knew where the key was the whole time."

My client laughed. "Well, we believe you way more than we believe her."

I grinned. "Thank you. It means a lot to hear you say these things. I have no reason to lie. I have no emotional attachment to your things. That was what I heard."

I heard, "I'll Fly Away," song, and sensed there was a message coming. I buffed her nails and listened to her and Dad at the same time. I finally interrupted.

I explained. "I am hearing things from my father. It's hard to hear." I paused my work and listened.

Dad explained, "Her father is tall and skinny, Beck. He is standing right beside me."

He continued. "He wants to tell his daughter how much he loves her and misses her. He wants her to think about her future. Listen to her heart when she makes decisions."

The sound of her father's voice was quiet at first. He got more excited as I heard more words from him through my Dad.

I relayed the message and asked, "Was your dad soft-spoken?"

She grinned. "My Dad never raised his voice. He was always soft-spoken."

I added, "I've learned that's when it's hard to hear what they are saying. They speak softly."

Dad added, "That's all, Beck."

I added, "He's gone."

I explained my father loved to give messages and God allows him. My Dad sounded excited to do this for you.

I asked, "Are you going to retire soon? I feel like this message was about you retiring."

She answered, "Yes, I am going to retire in two years."

I asked, "Have you been thinking about retiring lately?"

She answered, "I have, but we've decided to wait so we both will have health insurance." Retirement was what her father meant.

I stated, "Remember, your father is with God. Your loved ones always know what is best for you. When you make these decisions. Listen to your heart and make sure it's the right thing for your future, not anyone else's but yours. You always put everyone else first in your life. Your father is telling you to listen to your heart and make these decisions for your future."

She smiled. "I loved my father. He was a wonderful man. I miss him too."

I explained, "He is listening right now. He has been listening to what you been thinking about, retiring. That is what they do."

I finished applying her red gel on her nails and needed to prepare for the next client. She waited in the parking area. I needed to clean for COVID-19 and heard music from Dad still as I cleaned. I wondered what I would hear about my next client and sensed a message coming. She entered the salon. Her medium brown hair looked long and in her early forties. She had a teenage son. Her mother passed several months ago. I had heard from her mom before. I mentioned in my previous book.

I removed the gel from her nails. She shared what had happened in the last three weeks since I saw her last.

Dad beamed. "Her mother has a message for her, Beck."

I interrupted. "I have a message for you from your mother. I am hearing things from my father." I felt tired, and it was difficult to hear sometimes when I felt this way.

I sensed her voice, feminine, soft, joking, loving. Dad gave the message, "She's working too hard. She needs to take better care of herself. I love her and miss her terribly. I wish I were there. My grandson is growing fast. I miss and love my husband. I am glad our dog is doing better. God is not ready for him yet. Your husband will be with us soon." Dad added, "That is all, Beck." I gave her the message.

She explained how much her son grew in the last few months. He was five foot nine inches tall. He wasn't that tall when her mother passed. Her Dad's dog was sick the last time I saw her for her nail appointment two weeks ago.

She clarified the dog was much better and her father took great care of him. He made sure the food was prepared a certain way for the dog to eat easier.

I commented, "Your mother mentioned your husband. He would be with them soon."

He had work to do on the other side. I sensed it because of the way he died suddenly. I had heard nothing about him until now. My client wanted desperately to hear from her husband.

I reminded her, "If he will be with your mother soon, I can hear from him."

She beamed. "That would be great."

I knew hearing these things could overwhelm someone sometimes. My client kept her emotions buried deep.

I asked God that morning to guide me on how I could help my clients today. These messages were answering my prayer. My Dad loved giving the messages. He beamed with excitement and joy. I finished applying her dark red gel. I told her goodbye and enjoy her weekend.

She stated, "Well, I'm going to pick up dinner and put on my pajamas. Gonna put my feet up and I am not gonna do anything."

I replied, "Great, that's exactly what your mom wants you to do. Take better care of yourself."

I asked Ilene after she left, "Does God want me to write this in the book?"

Ilene replied, "Yes, God wants you to write these things." I realized how exhausted I was. When I received messages, it drained me, plus the day was long as well.

I asked, "Will you help me remember the details when I get home?"

Ilene whispered, "Yes, I will."

I locked the salon and looked forward to seeing my family. I sighed and strolled to my car. It was ninety-six out, and thought, "Wow, today was good." I slid into the car seat and drove home.

September 1, 2020

I booked a massage at 2:30 p.m. with my second therapist. She was a friend in her late forties. She had alluring, long, dark hair. My friend was independent, considerate, and caring. Her specialty was Swedish massage.

I undressed and laid on the massage table, face down. She began my massage on my right leg, calf, and foot. I heard, "I'll Fly Away," song and tuned in.

Dad beamed. "She has a lot of family members with us, Beck. They are standing beside me."

I tried to concentrate and relax. I relayed the message to my friend. She read my first two books and knew I was a medium.

Dad continued, "Her grandfather wants to tell her he loves and misses her. He is proud of her."

The grandfather spoke happily through Dad, "She's, my girl. I miss her." I relayed the message.

She replied, "I've been thinking about my grandfather lately. His birthday is in September."

I chuckled. "That's what spirits do. That's why he is coming through. You have been thinking about him and I am here with you."

She continued to massage the other leg.

I asked Ilene, "Is her grandfather with God?"

Ilene replied. "Yes, he is with us."

Dad beamed. "Her grandmother wants to say hello." I relayed the message.

She asked, "Which one?"

Dad replied, "On her father's side." I relayed the message.

She inquired, "I don't know her."

I explained, "It doesn't matter. They want what is best for you and they see you."

I heard her grandmother say through my father. She spoke in a loving, warm voice, "She's a lovely woman." I relayed the message.

My friend chuckled, and I sensed it surprised her. I heard her sniffle and did not know if I made her cry. I thought about what happened. How I sensed her grandfather. His spirit felt the strongest.

I asked, "Was your grandfather soft-spoken, kind and gentle? That's how he sounded."

She whispered, "Yes, he was a very gentle man."

Dad continued for her grandfather in a gentle but firm voice, "She needs to pray more. She needs to ask God to help her. She's, my girl. I miss her." I relayed the message.

I asked, "Is your grandfather a religious man?" Which I felt sounded weird since I just asked Ilene was, he with God.

She replied, "Yes, he was."

I added, "He spoke firmly about you praying and asking for what you need from God."

I heard her take a deep breath and whispered, "He's missed very much."

Dad announced, "God is glad you have given this message. Her faith has weakened. Her faith needs to be strengthened for her to grow with you."

I asked, "Has your faith weakened?"

She answered, "Sometimes."

I explained, "This is why your grandfather has come through today."

I prayed for my friends to grow with me on this journey daily, as Gabriel instructed.

Dad replied, "That is all, Beck." The message ended.

I enjoyed my massage and stopped talking. She thanked me afterward, and I drove home.

September 3, 2020

I saw 11:11 a.m. and 777 on a license plate today. I woke at 5:55 a.m. as well. I searched for 777 online. I forgot what it meant. I understood it meant spiritual changes and seeing 777 meant doubt, lack of faith. I struggled to have faith in the new changes coming. I felt drained, but glad my guides reminded me of these things.

September 4, 2020

I enjoyed being home while my husband worked. I watched "Million Dollar Listings Los Angeles," by Randy Barbato and Fenton Bailey. It was the last episode of the season. I diced redskin potatoes to bake. I tossed the potatoes in olive oil, onion powder, dill, garlic, celery salt and black pepper. I would add one tablespoon of mayonnaise after the potatoes cooked. I baked salmon and olives in a different pan. The salmon seasoned with dill, lemon, and black pepper. I remembered I washed our huge king-size, cream fuzzy blanket for the bed that morning. The blanket was in the dryer, in the garage. I trotted downstairs to check if it was dry. The comforter had some wet spots. I shook and placed it back into the dryer for ten minutes. I ran inside and set the timer.

The potatoes and salmon were almost ready. The timer sounded at 7:47 p.m., not long before sunset. My guides did not like me outside at sunset because the in-betweens came out then. I dashed downstairs again. I reached for the doorknob and heard music.

Dad whispered, "We are with you, Beck. Do not be afraid." I sighed and opened the door.

I replied, "Thank you, Dad. I am glad you are with me."

I opened the dryer, and the blanket still damp in places. I grabbed the ginormous comforter. It smelled fresh from the bleach.

I thought, "I can't wait to put it on the bed. It will have to do."

I stepped out of the garage and headed up the stairs towards the front door.

Dad beamed. "God is glad you're learning to do these things because you're God's messenger."

I sighed. "I'm trying. I don't wanna be outside by myself at night. I know it's dangerous for me."

I came inside, Noodle asleep on the couch. I threw the vast blanket on the railing of the stairs to finish drying. I logged what happened in my journal. My fish rested, and the potatoes done. I tossed the potatoes in the mayo. The creamy potatoes tasted great with the dry salmon. I noticed my husband called. I needed to relax and enjoy the evening.

Ilene announced, "God is glad you have written these things."

I sat at the dinner table and texted my husband, "I left our bedding in the dryer and had to get it before dark. Can't wait to enjoy my dinner. I love you and miss you."

Dinner tasted scrumptious. Salmon cooked to perfection with crispy skin and the creamy potatoes, perfect.

Later that evening, I climbed into bed with Noodle and needed to prepare for work earlier in the morning than usual. My husband still worked.

I whispered, "Lord, please protect me and my family while we sleep. Surround us with the white light of the Holy Spirit and protect us. Keep all evil, demonic spirits and earthbound spirits away from us. I ask these things in the name of the Father, the Son, and the Holy Spirit, in Jesus Christ, I pray, Amen."

I heard, "What Child Is This," by Burl Ives, song. I could hear Ilene singing the lyrics. She sounded excellent. I asked, "Where is Gabriel? I haven't heard from him today."

Gabriel announced, "God has heard your prayer. Your Lord will speak to you soon. Prepare the house."

I gasped. "Wow, I thought I heard Ilene say something about God would speak to me yesterday. But I wasn't sure. It was hard for me to hear when I was exhausted."

I asked Gabriel, "Will you please remind me in the morning, so I won't forget. Remind me of what we said to each other so I can write it down."

I asked Ilene, "Would you please wake me a few minutes before seven? I must ground and pray. I do not want to oversleep. Will you help me?"

Ilene whispered, "I will, Rebecca. You need to rest. Your body needs to heal."

I had a reaction to my regular prescription a couple of days before. My lips and the side of my face swollen from the allergic reaction. It scared me. I worried about the changes in my body since I will not take the medicine anymore.

At 6:50 a.m. I woke and thanked Ilene for waking me. I came downstairs and made coffee.

Gabriel instructed. "Prepare the house."

I gasped. "Wow, thank you both."

I sent a text to my husband while Noodle peed outside. I recalled my husband's mother popped in, in the middle of the night and wanted me to tell her son she loved him. I sent him a text message.

He texted. "Thank you for the message." It contained lots of heart emojis. I took a shower and burned sage and frankincense throughout the house.

Thrilled it was Saturday. I could spend time with my family. The weather would be perfect today. Noodle and I needed much time at the pool before fall arrived.

September 6, 2020

I woke, grounded, and prayed. Gabriel instructed. "Remember to pray for the ones you love." I did.

Ilene instructed. "Prepare the house. Your Lord will speak to you tomorrow."

I asked, "Will you remind me? Don't let me forget."

Ilene replied, "I will, Rebecca."

I edited today and prepared the house afterward.

My hubby napped. I prepared salmon for dinner and heard, "Don't Speak," song.

I questioned, "Hi, Dad, you never ate salmon cooked this way, did you?"

Dad chuckled. "Once, but I did not like it."

I laughed. "I gotta write this down."

Ilene added, "God is listening, and laughed too, Rebecca. He is eager to speak with you tomorrow. Do not make your Lord wait."

I whispered, "I won't Ilene, right after coffee. I will prepare the house, ground, pray and meditate."

I thought, "Well, God is coming to see me tomorrow. How magnificent and lucky I am."

Ilene beamed. "God is smiling, Rebecca, and is pleased."

Later that evening, I climbed into bed, prayed for protection.

Ilene reminded, "Prepare the house in the morning. Your Lord will speak to you when you are ready."

I sighed. "I can't wait to hear what God has to say. Can you tell me anything?"

She warned, "No, you must wait, have patience."

I whispered, "I know, Ilene." She added, "Your Lord is eager to speak to you."

I thought, "How lovely, *God* is eager to speak *to me.*" I drifted to sleep.

September 7, 2020

It was 8:00 a.m. I needed to prepare the house after I guzzled my coffee. Noodle and I settled in "the room." At 8:39 a.m. I placed labradorite, amethyst, selenite crystals around and on me.

Ilene stated, "God is waiting."

I grounded and prayed. "Lord, I ask for you to protect me during this meditation. Keep all evil, earthbound spirits, and demonic spirits away from me. Surround me with the white light of the Holy Spirit. I ask my guides, angels, and my father to protect me while I listen to my Lord and Savior. I ask these things in the name of the Father, the Son, and the Holy Spirit, in Jesus Christ, I pray, Amen."

Ilene instructed. "Your Lord is preparing. He will be with you soon."

Dad announced, "He's coming, Beck. Your Lord and Savior is almost here."

God spoke immediately in a soft tone, *"Hello, Rebecca, it is God. You have been very busy. You must remember to pray more. These things I say to you, God the Almighty, himself.*

There will be difficult times ahead, many weeks, months to come. I urge you to pray more. It will help thee. My messenger is strong and diligent. I have been watching, listening, observing. You have listened to your Lord and Savior. You have not tarried in your work. This makes God very pleased. You must focus on your future. There are many changes coming. These things will please my messenger. I have granted many things to thee. Remember to be grateful, as I will grant thee more. I listen to your prayers daily, for there are many. These things will be done by your Lord and Savior.

You must remember to pray for the ones you love. They need guidance, structure, diligence, calmness, centeredness, and grounding. These things I say to you. Pray for these things. It will help those who you love. Your husband has been diligent in his work. He must continue. It will affect your future. He mustn't doubt these things. I will protect you from all evil, as you have requested. You mustn't worry about the changes coming. I have granted these changes to you. They will help you grow to be who Octavian needs to be. You must remember to pray more. It will help guide thee. I am waiting to hear your prayers. You must listen when I speak to thee, for I am God the Almighty, himself, speaking to you.

You must remember I am always with thee, my messenger. I have granted and bestowed these blessings upon thee. Not many people receive this honor from their Lord. You must remain calm, centered, grounded during these difficult times. They soon will pass. They will be trying times for everyone you know. Pray for these people and I will help them. You have been listening to your Lord, for his messenger is strong. You must continue on this journey. The changes ahead will change your life to help you grow and become the person you need to be. I have granted these things to my messenger because of your diligence, perseverance, steadfastness, and strength. You have prayed for these things, and I have given that to you. My messenger has learned many things from your Lord and Savior.

It will help others believe in me. I sobbed. *Your Lord is with thee. Do not be frightened of me. I am a loving, kind God. I show mercy when it is needed. People must believe in me to enter my kingdom where I reside. It is full of love. I am a powerful God. You will want for nothing in my kingdom. If you do not believe in me, you will perish in eternal darkness. These things I say to my messenger, Christ the Almighty, himself.*

You must listen when I speak, for I am God the Almighty. Let no man put asunder. These are God's will. I am pleased with my messenger's work. You have much more to do. These things will happen in time. You must remember to pray, and I will help thee. I have granted many blessings upon thee. Remember to pray for the people you love. They need it. I will be waiting to help thee. I must go now, for time is of the essence. Do you have any questions for your Lord, the Almighty? You may ask them now."

I wailed, "God, I'm overwhelmed and happy to hear from you. I cannot think. I have not published the third book. Can you tell me when it will happen so I can prepare for it?"

God answered, *"These things will happen in due time. I will show you the way. Now is not the time for these things to happen. You must continue with your studies like I have taught you."*

I asked, "Lord, is there anything you can tell me to pray for that will help me during these upcoming difficult times?"

God replied quickly, *"Steadfastness, endurance, tranquility, grounding, centeredness, calmness, strength, guidance for your future, these things I say to you, God the Almighty."*

I asked, "Lord, is there anything I can pray for, Noodle, to help her as long as you allow me to have her? You granted me two more years with her."

God answered quickly, *"Pray for endurance, overall better health, strength, longevity, more time with her, these things I say to you, your Lord and Savior. I must go now, for you are weary."*

I begged. "Oh, God, please don't leave. Is there anything else you can tell me about my marriage, my future, job?"

God answered hurriedly, *"I have granted many things to thee. You must ask for guidance, and I will help thee on this journey. You are on the path of righteousness. This journey will be difficult, but I am by your side, my messenger. I will help thee. Ask and I am there, thus saith the Lord."*

I blurted, "Lord, I am glad you're pleased with my work. I tried hard to be diligent."

God replied swiftly, *"You must remember to pray for guidance. These things will help thee, thus saith the Lord, God the Almighty, himself. I must go now, for time is of the essence. I will speak to you again. Do not worry, for I am always here. Ask and I am there, says Christ the Almighty. I love you. Goodbye, Rebecca. Do these things I've asked of thee, says your Lord and Savior. I love thee."*

I sobbed. "Oh, God, I will do these things for you. I will."

Gabriel announced, "Your Lord is leaving."

I sobbed uncontrollably. My cheeks soaked with joyful tears. God's glorious presence felt so powerful. It was overwhelming. When God spoke, I wanted his words to never end. God sounded calm, reassuring, loving, and kind. I wished to be where God was and needed to end the meditation. I glanced at the clock, 9:08 a.m. I felt overwhelmed. I did not know what God would say and felt honored. I had prayed for God to speak to me and missed him terribly. I could not stop crying. I sobbed tears of joy. The feeling of God's presence, love, and kindness overcame me. I felt nothing like it before. I took a deep breath to calm the bawling.

Gabriel explained, "You are feeling God's love."

Dad beamed. "Beck, God loves you. I love you. We love you."

I sobbed hysterically all over again.

I felt blessed beyond words. People did not know what I heard. It was true. I took deep breaths and struggled to calm myself.

Ilene stated, "Your Lord has spoken to you, Rebecca. You must write these things for our Lord and Savior, Christ the Almighty."

I sobbed. "I will write these things, Ilene. I don't care what anybody thinks. I know it is true."

Gabriel announced, "Your Lord is with thee. You are feeling his love and grace, Rebecca. That's why you are crying."

I shared, "Oh, Gabriel, my heart feels full of love. I'm having a hard time swallowing. I feel the swirling around my heart, full of love. Tears of happiness flowing from my eyes. I know in my heart this is only a portion of what heaven feels like. It is too much for my pathetic body to take and feel."

Noodle had no comprehension of what happened. She looked calm, lying on the bed with me while I meditated. My body felt overwhelmed, sensing everything. I took a few more deep breaths to calm down. Tears still flowed down my cheeks. My face tingled and my heart swirled with enormous love. I had a difficult time swallowing. I felt like my best friend had left me. I bawled all over again. I needed to proofread what I recorded. God warned me before to only write what he spoke. I will write what I heard exactly, word for word.

At 9:18 a.m. I finally felt like I got myself together and finished proofreading at 10:04 a.m. I prayed for the ones I love, for myself, and Noodle like God instructed. I will ask for these things daily until I hear from God again.

September 10, 2020

My last appointment, and I heard a message. My client, a lovely lady, she looked in her thirties, but she was older. Her skin appeared creamy and youthful. She finished reading one of my books and she knew I was a medium.

I applied the brown-red color to the roots of her hair. While she processed under the dryer, she shared a story.

She beamed. "I had a spiritual experience since I saw you last."

I inquired, "Oh, tell me about it."

She explained, "I had a dream visit from my ex's mother."

I watched her while she spoke and noticed tears in her eyes. The visit touched her.

I assured, "Oh, it was her. It is easy for spirits to visit while you dream. Your mind is open."

She continued, "Someone called me the next morning to tell me my ex died. He was an alcoholic and had many problems. I had the dream right before he died."

I stopped listening because I heard music from Dad and sensed a message coming.

Dad beamed. "He is with us."

I asked, "Is it her ex-boyfriend?"

He reassured, "Yes, he is fine. God has forgiven him."

I explained, "I am hearing a message from my Dad. Your ex is with God. He is fine. God has forgiven him."

She sighed. "He found God before he died from his liver problems. I hoped he was in heaven."

I reaffirmed, "God forgave him. He is there."

I touched her shoulder as I lifted the dryer hood. "He is fine, don't worry. Tell your friend about this. It might help her."

She whispered, "Thank you." I shampooed her hair and finished her appointment.

Later, on the drive home, I asked Ilene, "Does God want me to put this in the book?"

Ilene instructed. "Yes, Rebecca, God wants you to write these things."

I stopped by the grocery store and asked Ilene to help me remember the details. Later, when I logged into my journal. Ilene whispered about what happened earlier.

September 13, 2020

Sunday morning, the weather sixty-seven degrees, felt perfect. I took Noodle for a quick walk. I anticipated how the cool white sand would feel under my feet. The weather would change in the upper eighties later today and heard music from Dad.

I beamed. "Can you speak to me?"

Ilene answered, "Your father is busy this morning doing work for God."

I asked, "Ilene, what can you tell me?"

She replied, "God wants you to enjoy your day with your husband. These things will make you closer."

Gabriel announced, "God is glad you are staying grounded and centered."

I sighed. "It feels fantastic. I want it to continue." I heard music from Dan.

I asked, "Is there anything you can tell me?"

Dan whispered, "I love you and miss you."

I smiled. "I love and miss you. It's funny how our love has changed. I had to continue living without you. But you were an inspiration, that there is more. When I was with you, you motivated me to seek more. You helped me understand that when I was young."

Gabriel announced, "God is pleased with what he has heard." I heard music from Ilene.

I asked, "Should I put this in the book?"

Ilene replied, "It is up to you."

I thought, "I will write these things down. To have these wonderful conversations with my Dad, my guides. Hearing what God thinks while it happens."

I wanted to share this with you and glanced at the clock, 2:22 p.m.

I laughed. "Work on balance. My guides reminding me."

September 15, 2020

My client at 1:00 p.m. arrived for her nail appointment. I received new gel polish for the fall. I showed her the new products while we talked. I heard music and felt a message was coming. I tuned her out so I could hear what my father had to say.

Dad beamed. "He is standing right beside me, Beck."

I asked, "Is it her son?"

He replied, "Yes, he's right here with me."

I listened to her. I struggled to tune her out again. It became difficult to hear my father's voice. Suddenly, I heard through my Dad a child's voice, which sounded excited, youthful.

I heard, "Tell my mommy that I love her." I relayed the message. I explained I needed to quiet myself to hear. Her son was in his forties, autistic and in a wheelchair at the time he died.

I heard, "I miss my mommy. She needs to take better care of herself. Stop worrying so much." I relayed the message.

I inquired, "Did your son call you mommy?"

She whispered, "Yes, he called me mommy."

I described, "He sounds childlike." She sighed.

She added, "I have been worried about upcoming things."

She worried about the election and other things. I tried to tune her out again to listen to Dad. The music continued.

Dad beamed. "He's jumping up and down right beside me, Beck. He's excited that he's talking to his mom." I relayed the message and reminded, "He was in a wheelchair when he lived, correct?"

She nodded her head and whispered, "Yes."

I explained, "You must realize in heaven he is perfectly fine. He's actually jumping up and down in his excitement speaking to you."

Dad added, "God has allowed him to speak to her today because he wanted to terribly. He misses her."

I heard a child-like boy's voice, "I miss my mommy. I miss my daddy." I shared this with her, and she absorbed what transpired. I felt surprised to hear from her son. I had a dream visit I mentioned in my first book, *Living Life as an Empath and Medium*.

I explained, "God is amazing. God is giving me updates on my 'characters' in my first book, which will be in this book." I shook my head and smiled, realizing what unfolded.

She leaned back in the chair and sighed. "I was just with my husband and my other son today. Maybe that is why he came through."

I added, "It could be. Was there anything that happened special in September?"

She explained, "I can't think of anything."

I added, "It doesn't matter. Sometimes spirit comes through on birthdays, the day they passed, or a holiday because you need it. Your son wants you to take better care of yourself. He wants you not to worry so much. He sees you from heaven. How exceptional is that?"

She absorbed what I explained. I mentioned, "I really would love for you to read *Experiences Never Stop.*"

She responded, "I wanted to read it, but have been busy."

I replied, "I did not say this to you to buy the book. I really would love for you to read it."

It would help her. We ended her appointment. My next client pulled into the parking area. She loved the new mauve gel color and walked with her to the door.

September 17, 2020

Today was Dad's birthday. I heard, "I'll Fly Away," song.

I beamed. "Happy birthday, Dad."

He whispered, "Thank you, I love you."

At the salon, my nail appointment arrived. At her last appointment, Dad spoke about her mom. She was in transition, doing her life review. I felt a message coming.

Dad added while I worked, "Her mother will be with us soon. She is trying hard to do what God wants her to do." I relayed the message.

She looked surprised, "I have been thinking a lot about her lately."

I explained, "Our last visit, Dad said she was in transition. I asked Ilene a while ago about this. She explained, your mother must have done many terrible things to be in transition this long. You don't get away with what you did wrong after you die. The spirit must review their life and understand and feel what they did to you or anyone else."

She whispered, "She hurt my siblings, too. She used to drag me across the floor by my hair."

I replied, "These things she must atone for before she crosses. She believed in God. She will cross, but not before she does the work. Have you forgiven her?"

She whispered, "Yes, I did on her deathbed. I held her hand and told her I forgive you." I sensed she had not truly forgiven her for everything.

I explained, "My book you bought explains how God taught me how to forgive and why you should. I want you to write about all the things your mom did to you. Such as neglect, abuse, whatever resonates with you of how she has harmed you. I want you to say out loud to God. I forgive my mother for the neglect when I was a child and so on. I know this will help you. Is there anything in your heart you have not forgiven her? When you feel forgiveness, it can make you cry. When you're done, your heart will heal. This is not for your mom. It is for you. I also feel it will help her when she transitions to heaven. This is important for you while you're still alive. You have more to experience. I want you to re-read the part in the book and do these things. My father is letting you know these things about your mom. It is important for you both."

I finished the appointment. My client and friend, I hoped, would follow through with my advice. I had a couple more appointments and drove home.

Later in the evening, we had Zoom chat with the group, "Both Sides Now TV." Dad and Ilene came through with a message for the mediator, John. He talked about technical issues he worked on, and decisions about his future he needed to make. I walked out of the room to hear my guides better. Many people in Zoom chatted. I wanted to make sure I heard the correct information.

Dad added, "He's on the right path. He will figure it out soon. He must do these things. He will figure it out. It won't be long."

I walked back into "the room" and told John what my Dad advised. He listened and kept the group chat going.

I wondered, "How would his decisions affect me? I sensed they would."

September 18, 2020

My husband left for the bakery. I watched "The Young and The Restless," and enjoyed the evening with Noodle. I opened the front door to let fresh air in. It felt much cooler today. Fall approached. While I watched the show. Noodle's battery powered mouse moved near my foot. It startled me. I had not used the remote to move her toy.

I asked, "Why did the mouse move?"

Ilene replied, "It was me."

She reminded me to close the door. It was after sunset. I sent a text to my husband about what happened. The mouse moved twice when he was home alone, too. Ilene told me it was his guides trying to get his attention. It did. I walked into the bathroom to relieve myself.

Gabriel announced, "It was your guides. Do not be afraid. They are letting you know they are there. You must remember you asked for these things. God has answered your prayers."

I recalled I prayed for my guides to speak and be with me more. That was exactly what they did.

I prepared a T-Bone for dinner with mushrooms and a baked potato. I felt hungry and had not eaten a steak in weeks. I waited for the potato to bake.

I sat on the couch and told Dad, Gabriel, Dan, Ilene, "I love you guys. I am glad you're always with me. It feels wonderful not to be alone."

I plated my dinner and thought about opening a new chat room.

Gabriel announced, "You must let these things unfold. These things must happen in time. There are things that must happen for your future changes."

I chuckled because I attempted to force the issue. Octavian was impatient, and Gabriel reminded not to do it. Noodle scratched at the door. I put my fork down and carried her down the steps to the grass. It was dark and cool outside. I sensed my guides and God protected me.

Gabriel announced, "We are always with you, protecting you. You are God's messenger."

It felt remarkable to hear these things from Gabriel. I carried Noodle inside. I knew the in-betweens were out and did not want to linger.

Gabriel added, "God is listening and is pleased with what you have written."

When you think God is not listening. He *IS* listening, and I was delighted.

September 26, 2020

Last night I misinterpreted what I needed to pray for to help myself grow. I prayed for God to bring new individuals into my life to encourage me on this journey. Those events happened. I met new, wonderful, inspiring people. These people were supportive. They were empaths, mediums, and had psychic abilities. I believed they would help me in areas I required the most help with, along with love and encouragement. Now, I must pray more specifically to receive the exact help I needed.

I prayed, "Lord, help guide me in the knowledge which I need to know to help understand the technical problems I face. Help me have endurance and strength to produce videos and online marketing. So, people will discover my work."

I would ask until I figured it out. Octavian needed to understand where I needed to grow. God told me this a few days earlier. I could do these tasks. I needed to find a niche. The online group I joined earlier maybe closing because of personal reasons. I missed talking with them and enjoyed connecting with others about these topics. I needed to shift and change my prayers, thoughts, and energy.

I saw 555 three times on the computer screen, phone, and TV. I woke last night at 5:55 a.m. I researched material to help me. I must prepare before beginning the live broadcasts. I wanted to look and sound professional. I represented God, the angels, and my guides from heaven.

At 7:00 p.m. I walked downstairs to take the bedding out of the dryer. I heard "I'll Fly Away," song as I opened the front door.

I sighed. "Dad, where have you been? I haven't heard from you in days." The music sounded louder than usual.

He beamed. "I've been busy, Beck. I love you." I walked in the grass towards the laundry room in the garage.

I answered, "I love you too. Help me with this tech thing. I struggled for two hours. What am I to do?"

He instructed. "These things take time, Beck. You're on the right path."

Frustrated, I blurted, "Is God having a good time with me trying to understand this?"

Dad replied, "God is glad you are understanding."

I grabbed the blankets. Ilene played music and Dad shared nothing. I sighed and felt God tested me on patience. Octavian had no patience in his past life. God tested me on patience often to help Octavian, me grow.

September 27, 2020

I woke and wondered, "What should I share on the live shows?" I wrote the messages in my journal. I laid there for hours, hearing the words popping in and out of my mind. I could not sleep.

Gabriel announced, "God is showing you the way, Rebecca."

I grinned and realized it was true. I prayed for days for God to show me the way how to market my book. How would people learn what I heard from my Lord and Savior if they did not read it? I felt the excitement building in my chest and looked forward to my new adventure.

Noodle and I laid down to rest in the afternoon. I felt exhausted. I watched a movie and meditated because my eyes burned.

I asked the angels, my guides and God to speak to me during the meditation. I pleaded. "What can I know about Noodle?"

The angels instructed. "Pray for God to heal her sight and more time with her."

I asked, "What am I allowed to know about the online stuff I will work on?"

The angels instructed. "You must believe in yourself. God is showing you the way. Pray for diligence and strength. He is answering your prayers."

Shocked, I thought I heard God's voice fluent, firm, and soft. I inquired, "Is this God? It sounds like you."

God responded, *"Yes, the many changes I spoke to you about are coming. These things will change your life. I will show you the way."*

I beamed. "Thank you, God, for speaking to me." God's voice sounded soothing, warm, gentle, and loving.

I logged into my journal and smiled at how spectacular God was. I glanced at the clock at 3:33 p.m. Awesome.

September 28, 2020

I made a test video to check sound and lighting for my live videos online page. I reviewed it. At the end of the video, I stated I wanted to be a teacher. I saw a small flicker of light form in front of my cheek. The orb looked irregular, translucent, goldish tint, round, no bigger than my thumb. It moved quickly from my cheek, up through the center of my forehead and out the top of my head. It disappeared into the ceiling. I watched the part of the video over fifteen times. It was visible. The orb moved fast, within a second it disappeared. I showed this to my husband.

He gasped. "It is definitely there." We looked at each other in amazement.

I explained, "I burned sage and frankincense in the house this morning. This cannot be anything bad."

I walked into "the room" and asked Gabriel, "What was the gold light that flickered in front of my face and ascended through my head towards the ceiling?"

Gabriel replied, "It was your guardian angel. She was delivering a message to God of what you said."

I gasped. "I said I wanted to teach. Wow, my guardian angel." I watched the video many times, mesmerized, I caught my guardian angel on video.

September 29, 2020

I asked Ilene, "What was the light in the video? Gabriel told me it was my guardian angel."

Ilene explained, "You have many angels that guard you. You are God's messenger."

I stood on the landing of the deck watching Noodle and absorbed the information.

I thought, "I have many angels that protect me. How remarkable, and I saw one. I really need this protection. I need their support and guidance while I do these live videos. Wow, they are there with me."

Noodle had an appointment with the vet at 9:30 a.m. Her eyes looked infected. I felt everything was okay and had prayed for her daily. Noodle was fourteen. It saddened me to see her having problems. She was my best friend and loved her deeply.

My husband took Noodle to the appointment. He called soon after I arrived at work. He shared because of her age, she needed eyedrops for dry eyes. We both felt relieved hearing the good news. My friend was healthy.

Later, after lunch, I shared with two clients about my new adventure going live on Facebook.

Gabriel announced, "Your Lord is pleased you are excited. This will be a pivoting point that will change your life."

Shocked. I beamed. "Wow, I am excited and looking forward to engaging with others. I need guidance on how."

Later that evening, I learned the group I joined closed. The group wanted to get together, to continue sharing Zoom. I missed it and gathered the people's names in the group. I shared invites to become friends on Facebook. I would start a new group. I explained what I had in mind and sent the invites. They seemed receptive and accepted my invitation.

I watched "The Young and the Restless," and prepared dinner.

Gabriel stated, "God is glad you were understanding what you need to do."

This surprised me. I need people to find my work. This was the hardest part, marketing. I did not want to seem pushy and forward. I sensed God showed me the way.

I recalled I saw 555 again tonight and asked, "Is there anything you want to add, Gabriel?"

Ilene answered, "Your Lord is listening, Rebecca, and is pleased with your thoughts. This journey will be difficult for you. These are things that you must do to help your Lord and Savior. He is showing you the way."

I gasped. "Wow, I felt like God was showing me the way. I have prayed for it. I hoped my friends were receptive, and I did not appear to look like an idiot online."

Gabriel stated, "Your Lord has advised to take things slow. He is showing you the way. Be patient and kind to others in this process."

I asked, "What do you mean, Gabriel? Does God want me to do this immediately?"

Gabriel reminded, "You must remember you are God's messenger. Things need to evolve. Remember to pray for help, guidance, and he will help thee."

I thought, "Again, I am being tested of patience. In my heart, I know I am not ready. When I go live, I need to look professional. I am giving messages from heaven."

Gabriel instructed. "You are ready. You must share things slowly. These things take time. You are on the right path. Your Lord is showing you the way."

I sighed because this was true. Part of me always got excited when I started new adventures. That was who I am. I needed to be calculated how I shared what they were ready to hear for the audience to grow.

September 30, 2020

Dream Twenty-Three: Dan, my guide, visited me. I appeared as a teenager with dark hair. We dated when I was in my late teens. I saw I lived in a house with other people like I did when I grew up. I wanted to be independent and dated different people. They weren't right for me. They wanted more from me than I wanted to give.

Dan appeared. He stood at the large window and peered inside. Embarrassed that he saw me dating someone else. I hid under the window. He looked down at me.

Dan asked, "What are you doing on the floor? I'm here."

I stood up and walked to the front door and opened it. Dan walked in. I panicked, "What am I to tell the man in the other room?" Dan strolled by me.

I peeked down the narrow hallway and saw Dan sit on the green sofa. He waited for me to return. The man I dated entered the room. He knew what was going on. Dan confronted him and made him angry. The man left in a hurry.

Dan stretched out on the sofa and put his feet up. I joined him and felt a flurry of happiness in my heart to see him. I sensed he came to reassure and protect me. I looked closer at his face and noticed his sandy-blonde hair. He smiled. His beard looked sparse. Dan never could grow a full beard when he lived. He wore an expensive white linen shirt with fine-black horizontal stripes. He wore silky, dark magenta pants with a two-inch cuff. The outfit looked in the eighties. I had forgotten how handsome he really was. I laid my head on his chest, and he held me in his arms. It felt wonderful for him to visit me.

I woke at 7:30 a.m. I overslept ten minutes. I recalled the warmth, kindness, and how he protected me. Dan reminded they were protecting me. He was my guide. When he died in 1989, I felt abandoned and lost. I had to live without him. I felt guilty when I dated after he died. He showed me he was still there, helping me.

I whispered, "Thank you, God, for letting me see him."

I asked Ilene, "Why did I have a visit from Dan?"

Ilene explained, "He misses you and knows you are struggling with all the ideas you were working on. God wanted him to remind you how powerful he is. You will see him again, but you have much to do. He wanted to remind you, we are with you, helping you, right by your side. God is showing you the way."

I whispered, "Thank you, Ilene, that is exactly how it felt; comforting, protecting, showing me love and compassion."

That was what I felt when I touched his body. I forgot what he felt like. It was over thirty years since he died. Part of me felt guilty because I am married. But my love for Dan was different now. I loved my husband way more on a deeper level. Dan felt warm, caring, like a friend who stopped by to help me. I recalled the texture of his white linen shirt, rough to the touch. It was good to see him.

October 5, 2020

Last night I flip-flopped in bed. I felt hot, then cold, and aggravated. I threw off the top blanket to the center of the bed, close to Noodle. My husband went downstairs where it was cooler. I woke several hours later, and I had been *covered with the blanket I tossed aside.* The blanket I threw aside was neatly placed around me, all the way to my feet, spread out neatly. The top three inches of the blanket neatly folded down near my belly. It shocked me. I did not move the cover.

Gabriel announced, "I covered you. God wants you to be rested for tomorrow. These changes will change your life. This is the beginning."

I listened to Gabriel and sensed a guide moved the blanket. Glad Gabriel explained why.

I looked down at my feet under the blanket, "Wow, this is a big blanket."

I slept for several hours without waking and woke rested. I grounded and prayed for the day. I stared at the blanket as Noodle, and I climbed out of bed. The cover vertically placed where I laid. The blanket wasn't square, but rectangle in shape. It became disheveled through my sleep, but I observed where Gabriel moved it.

I thought, "How wonderful for Gabriel to do this. I feel loved and nurtured."

I did my first live video online on Facebook. It would be the first of many. This video was about "How to Raise Your Vibration." Why it was crucial to connect with your higher self. Why one must distance themselves from the ego. I prayed earlier that morning for God to be by my side during the recording. I needed God's guidance on how much to say. God taught me people must be ready to receive information, or it will not help them. God would be with me.

The live video went well and hoped people would watch it later. Time would tell.

October 6, 2020

I thought about the live video. One step was to be grateful daily. I spoke out loud about what I felt grateful for.

I whispered to God, "I am thankful for all the things you've done for Noodle, all the blessings. Thank you for healing her eyes, removing the tumors, and making her healthier. Thank you for letting me have more time with her. Thank you for the two extra years you have given me with Noodle. I cried. I am thankful for my husband loving me, new friends, customers who care for and support me. I am thankful for this new journey and for you showing me the way. I am grateful there are no toxic people in my life. I am grateful I am healthy and not pregnant. I am grateful for all the blessings you have given me, Lord. I am grateful for hearing from Dad, Ilene, Dan, and Gabriel. I am grateful for the beautiful sunny, warm day today. I am grateful for all these things, Lord, thank you." I sobbed.

Gabriel announced, "Your Lord is pleased with what he is hearing. He has granted many things. There are more to come."

This made me bawl even more because I was happy. There was more to come. That was why it was important to count your blessings because God listened. Gratitude raised your vibration immediately.

I asked, "Does God want me to write this in the book?"

Gabriel instructed. "Yes, God wants you to write these things to show others how to be grateful."

I smiled and logged what happened into my journal.

October 8, 2020

My client arrived, and I started her nail appointment. She shared what happened in the last three weeks. I heard, "I'll Fly Away," song.

Dad beamed. "Her mother is with us, Beck. She misses her daughter and loves her."

I sensed her mom smiling and her loving presence through Dad's words.

He continued, "She understands now. She did many bad things, and it was very wrong of her."

I relayed the information. It shocked her, and she looked relieved.

She stated, "I did the things you told me. I have forgiven her."

I asked, "Did you say out loud to God what you were forgiving her for, each one?"

She answered, "I said it out loud to God like you instructed, and hoped it helped her."

I whispered, "I am glad you forgave her because now it will help you heal. It takes time to heal. Your mom did not get away with how she mistreated you or anyone else. She had to own what she did, seeing how it affected you and others."

Dad added, "God has forgiven her."

I sensed her mom felt happy and content. She knew what she did was wrong and atoned for her misdeeds. It took eighteen years.

October 10, 2020

My husband and I discussed business and marketing strategies during dinner. He ate baked flounder, green veggies, and shrimp. I complemented him on choosing high vibrational foods. I prepared baked salmon and red potatoes for myself. Our lifestyle changed years ago because our schedules constantly shifted.

He stated, "It took me ten years for my business to be where it is today."

I shot a glance, "That is totally unacceptable for me. I cannot wait ten years for this to happen. I cannot continue to do hair for ten more years and can't fathom thinking about doing hair for that long."

He walked outside, and I checked on my fish. It looked perfect. I plated the food and heard, "I'll Fly Away." The music seemed louder than usual.

I smiled. "Do you have anything to add?"

Dad beamed. "Beck, these things take time. You're on the right path." I took two deep breaths.

He added, "You need to ask for more help, Beck. God will help you."

I grabbed my plate and sat at the table. I explained to my husband about Rachel. Ilene told me, "She was sent to you by God to help inspire you of what you need to do." I already knew what, but how, I wasn't sure. I knew in my heart I must do much more to achieve the goal. I needed to write for God. I prayed and asked God to help me before I ate. I logged what happened in my journal.

Gabriel announced, "Your Lord is pleased with what you have written. You must have perseverance to do these things. Your Lord will help you. Just ask and he is there."

I remembered earlier today. I had prayed daily for a full recovery for my husband's sister, who has breast cancer. I heard, "Dec.'63," by The Four Seasons, driving to work. I asked, "Ilene, is this you or my husband's mom?"

Ilene answered, "It is me. She is right beside me."

I heard his mom, "You need to continue doing these things for God. Thank you for praying for my daughter. God is listening."

I cried while driving. God listened, but I did not think about his mom listening. She validated it, and I had more to do. Sometimes I did not know where to begin. Octavian had no patience in his past life. God tested me. I learned God prepared me for the trials and things that could happen. I needed strength to do these things.

While I drove, God spoke, *"Do unto others as you would have them do unto you, thus saith the Lord."*

I asked, "God, is that you? It sounds like you."

Gabriel announced, "Your Lord has spoken, Rebecca."

I gasped. "Wow, it was fast."

Ilene added, "Yes, Rebecca, it was your Lord and Savior. He is with you, beside you, every step of the way. Just like you asked in your prayers."

I gasped. "Wow, I did not know God would speak in the car." I felt blessed and protected.

Later that evening, I downloaded pictures from my iPad to my Windows 10. I loaded many pictures over a ten-year period of Noodle, my husband and myself. We had shared amazing times together. It broke my heart to think it might end. I knew God blessed me with more time with her.

I whispered, "Thank you for being in my corner, Lord, and showing me the way. I love you."

October 12, 2020

Last night, Rachel called me, and we had an enjoyable conversation. She wanted to know more about her grandfather. She asked, "Are you tired? How's your energy level?"

I mentioned to Rachel before if I was tired it was difficult to hear from the other side.

I replied, "I am a little tired but fine."

I closed my eyes and asked my guides, "What am I allowed to know about her grandfather today? Is he with God?"

Gabriel stated, "He is here with us. He is a lovely man with dark brown eyes, chiseled face, and a hairy chest. He dressed well and was tall in stature. He loved his family very much. He wants her to do more. He wants her to believe in herself more."

I shared the information. She stated, "I've been asking for these things. If he is okay. Was my daughter, okay?"

Gabriel stated, "Her daughter wanted to say, 'I love you mommy.'"

Rachel miscarried late in her term. It devastated her life. Her daughter and grandfather are together in heaven.

I emphasized, "This message came from my master guide, who is an angel with God. Do you realize how significant that is?"

She beamed. "I do, thank you."

We talked a while longer and told each other goodnight.

The next morning on my walk with Noodle. I asked Ilene, "Does God want me to write this in the book?"

Ilene answered, "Yes, God wants you to put this in the book. He wanted her to know these things because she's been asking. She needs validation."

I thought, "How wonderful, God hears everything."

October 14, 2020

Today at the salon, Rose came in for a haircut. She looked in her late sixties and loved her dark brown hair cut super short. I mentioned Rose and her husband, Jo, in my other books. While I cut her hair, Rose talked about Jo.

Gabriel stated for Joe, "He is here beside me. He wants to tell his wife hello. He wants her to give the kitties a hug for him. He wants to tell his lovely wife he misses her and loves her. When she thinks of things they talked about, he is with her."

I relayed the message. She seemed surprised.

She stated, "I love you too, Jo, wherever you are." A part of me wondered if she believed in God. This was why Jo came through today.

I asked, "Did Jo refer to the cats as kitties?"

Rose answered, "Yes, he referred to them as kitties. Two of them he hasn't met."

I replied, "He wants you to give them a hug for him. So please do when you get home. Remember what he said."

She changed the subject and talked about other things. I noticed this was people's behavior when it made them uncomfortable, did not believe me or did not know what to say. Those scenarios ran through her mind. I finished her haircut. She appeared happy and bright when she left the salon. I shut the door and waved goodbye. It felt great to hear from Jo. I missed him as well. He was a wonderful, intelligent, caring man.

Later in the afternoon, I meditated before my massage appointment. I soaked my feet in scorching water with lavender essential oils. I enjoyed the thirty minutes of serenity. I asked God and the angels what I needed to pray for while I meditated.

The angels answered, "Pray for rest, strength and guidance."

I spoke, "I need rest. I haven't rested well in the last few weeks."

The angels reminded, "Be kind and loving. You are God's messenger. That is what God's messenger should be, always kind and loving."

I stated, "I need to remind myself of these things."

I thanked my guides, the angels, God, and ended my meditation. I turned everything off and drove to Ginna's workplace. I looked forward to her deep tissue massage. She knew exactly what my body needed without me saying a word.

As Ginna gave the massage, I realized how stressed my body was. While she massaged my left leg on the front side, I heard music.

Dad stated, "Beck, she does really good work. Your aura is already brighter. This is why God sent you to her. God knows what you need. God knows all things."

I listened to Dad while she massaged my leg. She worked out the knots, and it felt painful, but I needed it. I remembered the message, "God knows exactly what I need, and this is what my body needs, really deep work. I am doing a lot of tasks, juggling salon, writing, online videos, marketing, home, and family. It is a bunch of work for anyone. I have learned I must take self-care time to recharge and let my body rest."

Ginna finished and instructed. "You need to soak in the hot tub to let your muscles relax more. It was bad today. You were tight." I examined the concern on her face and knew she was right.

She added, "I am almost finished with your book. I have twenty pages left."

I asked, "What do you think? Did you enjoy what you read?"

Ginna pondered, "I realize I need to pray more, and I am enjoying it."

I stated, "Thank you for taking care of my body. I would be a wreck without you."

Ginna laughed. "I am glad to help you. I always look forward to seeing you."

I added, "So do I."

I paid and left. My muscles felt numb from the toxins released. I looked forward to soaking in the hot tub and seeing my husband and Noodle.

October 24, 2020

While I worked four hours on a marketing software, I heard music from Ilene. "Total Eclipse of the Heart," by Bonnie Tyler. I wondered what the lyrics meant. I felt a mess inside trying to market.

I took a break from the software. I noticed I had over one hundred followers on my Facebook page, "Experiences Never Stop by Rebecca Walters Hopkins." Shocked, I met my goal. I posted diligently for the last two weeks. I read everything I could find to help improve my page. I prayed for guidance; knowledge that would help me understand what to do to grow. Two clients offered information to help on Instagram. The other was this software to enhance videos. I worked for days on this project. Exhausted, my husband walked in the house from work. I saved my work and went downstairs to greet him.

We spent hours together and shared what happened today. I prepared salmon, broccoli, and squash for dinner. The food smelled delicious, and it tasted delightful.

Dad interjected. "Beck, God is glad you are realizing and doing these things. He is showing you the way."

I smiled and felt God's guidance, "Thank you, Dad for telling me. Do I write this in the book?"

He beamed. "Yes, Beck, God wants you to write these things for others."

Gabriel announced after I wrote in my journal, "God is pleased with what you have written."

I took two bites of my crispy salmon skin and thought, "God has led me in many ways. It has helped my life in more ways than I could imagine."

Dan added, "I am glad you told me about God, Rebecca. Heaven is wonderful. I can't wait to see you again."

I thought, "Wow, I am excited to see you too, Dan. It has been a long time."

My husband watched TV. I glanced at him, relaxing from his strenuous day. His baked goods sold out. I prayed this morning for God to provide for him. God had. Nothing felt better than to know God was in my corner.

October 25, 2020

I watched two series of "Beat Bobby Flay." Bobby lost twice. I blurted to Noodle, "Bobby lost again. I wanted him to win."

I heard Noodle's toy playing in "the room." Shaken, I crept into "the room" where the toy dog dressed in a Mexican hat and outfit laid on the floor beside the toy box. The toy was for a kid. You needed to press the paw for the toy to play. Noodle loved toys that moved. That was why we bought it for her. I listened to the song, "la la bum ba, la la bum ba." I felt chills on my arms and back for several moments. I walked out of the room after the toy stopped moving.

I inquired, "Ilene, who turned on the toy?"

Ilene replied, "It was me."

I asked, "Why?"

She answered, "I wanted Bobby to win too." Bobby cooked a Mexican style chocolate cake on the last show. It startled me, hearing the toy play in the empty room.

I greeted my husband and explained what happened. Noodle looked excited to see her daddy. I recalled while my husband was in the bathroom washing his hands. How Ilene had added two new eggs to the egg carton when there was only one egg left. She turned the broken shells in the carton into fresh eggs. I was positive there was only one egg in the carton and the rest of the eggs were cracked. I left the shells in the carton for the garden. I forgot to buy eggs at the grocery that day and wrote about this experience in my book. Ilene had showed me how powerful my guides were, and they were with God.

I wondered, "Was she reminding me of this? She was."

Ilene watched things with me and knew me well. I typed in my journal, "Is this correct?"

Ilene replied, "Yes, it is."

Later, we played with Noodle's rat remote control toy, her favorite.

Dad joked, "It was Ilene, Beck, she is learning from me."

November 1, 2020

The first rain after the time change. Noodle and I walked outside after the rain subsided. The yard looked like fall. The red pine straw and yellow-golden leaves coated the ground. She ran up the driveway, excited from boredom inside the house. I needed to ground and desired a walk. I thought about my new friends I made online.

I asked Ilene, "What can you tell me today that will help me?"

Ilene answered, "Stay grounded and centered. Remember, you are God's messenger."

Gabriel reminded, "Stay grounded, calm during these times. God is showing you the way. You are branching off this path, but still on the path of righteousness, God's path. He is showing you the way. Remember your family comes first, friends second."

I sighed. "I thought I put my family first. I have been spending a lot of extra time talking with friends. My husband and Noodle are everything to me."

I took another deep breath. I needed to shift my focus back to writing for God and my family. The online group took my extra time. My guides warned several days ago to distance myself from one individual in the group. I sensed her energy was off the first time I heard her speak. But I continued to listen to her. My instincts told me not to trust her. Everyone missed talking and sharing with Zoom. So did I, except this one person. I opened a new group temporarily, and never should have asked her to join. But I did. I tried not to judge and went against my instincts. The second Zoom chat, she was the only person in the room. Not being rude, I listened. It felt awkward, and I ended the Zoom an hour later.

Ilene warned, "Distance yourself from this energy."

I asked, "Why?"

Ilene warned, "She has evil forces around her, from her practices."

It shocked me, "What do you mean evil forces?" Her tone scared me, and I sensed danger.

Ilene warned, "She has three demonic attachments. Distance yourself from this type of energy. It will try to harm you. You are God's messenger, remember to protect yourself."

I immediately recalled Ilene's tone as the same when she warned me of the earthbound spirit in Florida, which had a demonic attachment. This happened at the vacation house we rented. The earthbound spirit had followed me home. I would not go through that again. My family and I were too important.

John opened a new online group to hold space for one another to share. He was the group's original creator. I felt jubilant to see it unfold. I could not be a part of the group if she entered the meetings. She always joined, never adding, or helping anyone. She claimed she was a witch. I sensed through her energy; she did not believe in God. I will miss the rest of the group. I made several new friends and enjoyed speaking to them outside the group on chat.

I strolled back to the house with Noodle and realized, "God knows all things. I must trust the path he is leading me on. I need to focus on my family and work more."

We spent the whole rainy day being lazy with one another and rested. It felt right.

I asked Ilene, "Does God want me to put this in the book?"

She whispered, "Yes, God wants others to understand this is real."

November 2, 2020

Dream Twenty-Four: I had a multitude of dreams last night. Two dreams stood out the most.

A married couple from New York. I sensed the woman in her thirties, wearing a dress made in the 1940s. I noticed her husband on my right. He wore a navy suit, white shirt, and dark tie. His body looked skinny and his hair black. He looked in his forties. The group felt uneasy where we were headed. I felt like a child leading them into the unknown. We wandered forward. I glanced down at my legs and feet. We stood on top of dark water. It shocked me. The murky water looked deep, with no end to its depths.

The man stated, "The water freezes on top at home." He meant in New York.

The water wasn't frozen. Something unseen pulled us quickly forward on top of the water so we did not sink. It felt like a sled under me in the snow. There was nothing under me. I watched my bare feet blasting through the top of the dirty, dark water as we moved forward. Debris on the water hit me in the face and body.

The wife asked, "Where are we? I don't like it. Is this a lake?"

It was a lake. I did not understand where we were and where we were headed. I woke.

I asked Ilene, "What was the dream of the dirty lake? Where was I?"

She answered, "This place is the *in-between.*"

I questioned, "Why was I there?"

Ilene explained, "This is where souls go that have no faith. They are not evil. They just have no faith. They must learn where to go. *They are lost souls.*"

I realized then why Ilene did not want me outside after dark, because in-betweens saw me.

Dream Twenty-Five: I drifted to sleep and dreamed of a different encounter. I saw a building built in the late 1940s. People gathered here to share food and talk. The place looked simple in decor. I looked inside a little wooden closet and saw a few wire hangers inside. I glanced around and noticed two twin beds with a small nightstand in between them. The beds looked hard, old, and covered with thin, light blue blankets. I saw two small bags with toiletries taped to the headboards. I walked out of the bedroom towards people, laughing and talking. I entered a dining area and saw a round, light-colored wooden table in the center of the room. The walls looked a light beige color. I observed a few small wooden chairs against the walls. People placed food on the table, and everyone walked around to choose what they wanted to eat. You sat wherever you wanted. I spotted a lamp and a large dresser at the head of the table against the wall. The light looked antique. I touched it and looked at the plug at the bottom of the lamp. You plugged things in there to turn on the lamp. It looked like a fire hazard. I tried to insert the plug into the lamp. The style of the light looked in the 1940s. The area needed light. I glanced to my left and Dad stood there leaning on the wall in a hallway outside this room. He looked in his twenties. His dark, wavy hair brushed off his face. He smiled and watched me. He wore a casual, white, short-sleeve shirt and dark pants. I wondered why he stood there. The time seemed like *The Andy Griffith Show* by Sheldon Leonard, but in color, not black and white. Everything looked simple and not froufrou.

Dad whispered, "Beck, I miss these things."

I wondered, "Why, the stuff is old. There's not much and technology is much better now."

I watched the individuals share conversations with each other while they ate.

I woke confused. I asked Ilene, "Why was Dad here? Dad is in heaven. Why did he miss these things? I thought God took care of everything you needed?"

Ilene explained, "God does. Your Dad was showing you he misses the simple things. That is what people miss sometimes. How important the simple things are. He showed you these things to help you. Simple things are hugs, sharing, spending time with one another."

I understood immediately. We could not do these things during COVID-19 and how important it was. Last night I watched a movie, and the people were interacting, touching, hugging. It affected me watching these interactions. It had been a year where I had not touched and interacted with people in this manner, except my husband. I felt glad to see Dad again. He seemed calm, watching me, reassuring me in his tone. He missed the gathering with the people he loved, the simple things.

I gasped. "Wow, what a dream. The in-betweens part felt scary."

I felt lost. Where was I going? I sensed I might drown but didn't. I felt relieved I wasn't in this dark, lonely place. I felt confused and isolated. The dream with Dad felt inspiring. I observed these places, people, and things from the other side for you to read.

November 6, 2020

Overwhelmed, I attempted my best in marketing to grow my base. There was a roadblock at every corner. Frustrated, I wondered, "What am I to do?" I sat on the couch alone and heard music from Ilene.

I begged. "Can you help me?"

God interjected calmly. *"You must remain calm and centered. These things will pass, says Christ the Lord."*

I sobbed. "God, is this you speaking? It sounds like you."

Ilene whispered, "God is speaking to you, Rebecca."

I pleaded. "What am I to do? Nothing is working. It is slow."

Ilene instructed. "You are on the right path. These things take time."

I asked, "Is this a test of my patience again?"

Gabriel announced, "Your Lord wants you to pray for what you need."

I sobbed. "Lord, please help me with these things. I am trying my best and feel it is not enough. I am weary, Lord. Please show me the way. I need followers on my business page to find my work for you. I need people to want to read my work. I am frustrated, Lord. I pray for strength, perseverance to overcome these obstacles. I need guidance, knowledge of technology to do these things. I need to hear from you, Lord. I miss your love and guidance in your words. I feel worn down. Please show me the way. I beg you. I am doing my best and need encouragement, Lord. I need strength and answers. I need fulfillment and happiness in doing these things for you. I need joy in my life. Please help me, Lord. I know you will. I need you to show me the way and be by my side. I ask these things in the name of the Father, the Son, and the Holy Spirit, in Jesus Christ, I pray, Amen."

Gabriel announced, "Your Lord is listening. He will grant these things to you, Rebecca."

I broke down, "Thank you, Lord. Thank you." I took a deep breath and knew everything would be fine.

November 7, 2020

I woke rested and renewed. I worked a few hours at the salon and the stress I felt had disappeared. I felt peaceful and tranquil inside. I found new ways to advertise on Facebook, which was there the entire time. I did not see it. I worked on my next video, "How Prayer Raises Your Vibration." I shared the video online and, to my surprise, people responded. I knew deep in my heart God gave me peace and showed me the way. The video was my best work. The words flowed, and I did not feel anxious about going live.

I whispered, "Thank you, God, for everything."

November 9, 2020

At 5:00 p.m. Noodle and I napped in bed. She knew it was time for dinner and smelled her daddy come home. She jumped off the bed. Noodle ran towards the railing and down the stairs before I could grab her. We carried her up and down the stairs now because of her age. I heard her slip halfway down the steps. I saw her barrel roll down the last five steps and hit the bottom.

I panicked. She stood up, and I knew she was hurt. My husband heard her fall and came into the room.

He looked frantic, "You got to be careful, honey, with her."

I blurted, "She ran ahead of me, excited to see you. I didn't have time to grab her."

Noodle wobbled and fell over. I picked her up and laid her on the rug, thinking she might have hurt her spine or broken a leg. I held her head still and examined her body. She peed herself. She needed to go out when we woke. The incident scared her. My stomach dropped and my innards terrified.

I thought, "I hope we don't have to go to the emergency room. I chipped my front tooth yesterday. What else is going to happen?"

My husband stated, "Let me take her outside."

He collected her and held her close. He sat on the grass holding her. I noticed the worry on his face. I walked back inside and grabbed a towel and blotted the urine. I trotted outside to see how she was doing. He placed her in the grass. Noodle pooped and still looked unsteady on her feet. He scooped her up and placed her on pillows in the window on a platform we built behind the couch. This was her favorite spot to view outside.

I asked, "Would you get her dinner ready?"

I snuggled close to her while he walked into the kitchen. I prayed, "God, please heal my baby Noodle. Please heal her."

He placed her chicken and pellets in front of her. She wasn't interested. I recalled she got scared easily when she was hurt in the past. I hand fed her bites of chicken. A few minutes later, she ate on her own. I could breathe again and searched online for mesh gates. I ordered two and it would arrive on Thursday.

At 9:00 p.m. I carried Noodle to bed and prayed again for God to heal our baby. My husband stayed up for a while longer. I held her close and drifted to sleep.

Later, in the middle of the night, Noodle needed to pee. I carried her outside and placed her in the grass. It felt creepy outside. I sensed something behind me, watching while I waited. I glanced in that direction and saw nothing. I felt it, though. I scooped her up and trotted inside. I locked the front door. I heard music from Ilene.

Worried, I asked, "Are there in-betweens out tonight?"

Ilene explained, "Yes, there were several behind you, watching you."

Relieved I was safe inside. I carried Noodle back to bed and drifted to sleep. Noodle woke this morning and seemed like nothing was wrong. She rubbed her back on the blankets, which she loved to do. She looked happy and rested. I collected her and carried her down the steps. I dug out an old baby gate from the shed last night. We had years ago when Speck, our cocker spaniel, needed when she was blind. I walked into the kitchen and prepared coffee. I heard a song from Dad, "Nearer, My God, to Thee," by Sarah Flower Adams.

I whispered, "Good morning, Dad." I heard music from my guides, "Good morning, Ilene, Gabriel and Dan."

November 16, 2020

I enjoyed my delicious medium rare sirloin steak with sauteed mushrooms and baked red potatoes. The potatoes seasoned with dill, mayo, onion powder, garlic, salt, and pepper. I thought of chatting with my friend Ned from the group. I had not joined the Zoom group in a while because the woman with attachments was always there.

I thought, "That is what attachments do, take."

Gabriel instructed. "God wants you to speak to those that you love."

It surprised me. I loved my new friends and prayed for them every day. I would reach out after dinner if Ned were free. I missed sharing with him about spiritual topics and wondered if he was doing better from my prayers.

Gabriel stated, "God wants you to do these things."

I thought, "As soon as I finish dinner I will call."

I asked, "Is there anything you can tell me that will help Ned?"

Gabriel answered, "You must call first. God will guide you."

I prayed for God to help me with Ned and felt excited. He was a spiritual man and his energy felt humble. I sensed he struggled in his past and wondered what the conversation would be.

Gabriel added, "Your Lord will be with you, Rebecca. Remember, you are God's messenger. He will need guidance."

I replied, "Wow, I hope I can help, Ned."

I called, and we talked for over an hour about spiritual topics. It felt great sharing, laughing, and listening to one another. Ned needed more clients to pay his bills. We talked about how COVID-19 had hurt his business.

I asked, "How's work going? Any new clients?"

Ned beamed. "Yes, I got nineteen new clients. I hope it continues."

I replied, "Remember to ask for referrals. Don't be shy. I have been praying for you a lot lately. Now I know God answered my prayers for you."

Ned smiled. "Thank you for praying for me."

I beamed. "Glad to."

We told each other goodnight. We both encouraged each other to continue with our work. I had helped Ned through my prayers. God's grace felt glorious in helping my new friend.

November 20, 2020

I dreamed of different places and people. Most of my frustrations I had endured listening to clients complaining about their life came out in my dreams. I had not felt grounded and centered like I should. It was difficult to hear complaints for hours. I felt aggravated with one client in particular. His know-it-all attitude was infuriating. I read trash magazines while I waited in between appointments hoping to center myself.

Dream Twenty-Six: I woke and realized I dreamed of my aunt. I saw myself inside a grocery store. I took off my mouth mask temporarily because no one was around. I studied the pictures in my trash magazine. My aunt sauntered over without a mask. She leaned down close to my face. I felt uncomfortable.

She inquired, "Do you have any *Southern Living* magazines?

I thought, "You don't have a mask on, get away from me."

When I looked at her, she had extremely blonde hair pushed off her face. She appeared in her thirties. Her skin looked smooth and vibrant. She smiled. I saw a light brown mink stole wrapped around her shoulders. She sauntered past me and looked at a few cans of soup. I got the impression she was buying food to cook a fabulous meal. My aunt was an excellent cook when she lived. The magazine she requested would have been her favorite, since she was southern, loved cooking and decorating.

I needed to return to my client waiting and walked away. I didn't realize until this morning my aunt popped in to visit. It was the first time she spoke. She was a few inches from my face. She seemed tickled, vibrant, young, and at ease. I remembered the dream and realized she knew about my frustrations at work. She saw me reading the magazines from heaven. She sought to comfort me. She knew I did not have any *Southern Living* magazines, either. It felt funny how spirits showed me things and wonderful to see my favorite aunt again.

I asked Ilene, "Why did my aunt visit me after all this time?"

Ilene explained, "She learned what she did was wrong and wanted to be there for you."

I smiled and smeared on coral lipstick, "She wasn't there for me in my past. It hurt deeply she wasn't there for me but attended gatherings for the rest of the family."

I dressed for work and gave Noodle kisses. I drove to our locked gate and stepped out of the car to unlock it. I heard the song from my husband's mom.

I asked Ilene, "Is this you or my husband's mom?"

Ilene replied, "It is me. But she's right beside me and she wants to talk to you."

I unlocked the black iron gate. I asked, "What do you want to say?"

His mother whispered, "I need you to help your husband with his anger issues. It's not good for his spiritual growth."

I pulled the huge gate open and stated, "It doesn't surprise me. His anger gets the best of him often. I try to help him. There is not much I can do. What do you want me to do?"

His mother whispered, "Tell my son I love him, miss him terribly. He has much more he needs to do, helping you with these things."

I replied, "I will try my best, but I need help with that."

I sat in the car and closed the door. I asked his mother, "Is there anything else you want me to do? Do you want me to call him?"

Ilene replied, "Yes, she wants you to call him and talk to him."

I grabbed my phone and dialed his cell. I drove quickly up our dirt road, late for work. While the phone rang, I stated to his mother, "Please talk to me while I am talking to your son. So, I can tell him what you want him to know."

My husband answered. I heard the music playing from his mother. I stated, "I am hearing from your mom, and she has a lot to say. Do you wanna know?" I sensed this surprised him.

He answered, "Yes, I do."

I explained, "I talked with your mom while I opened the gate. She told me you need to work on your anger issues. It doesn't help you grow spiritually."

He laughed. "Well, I got a lot of problems in that area."

I retorted, "Yeah, you do. Your mom is telling me you need to work on it, be aware of it, and stop doing it."

I heard, "Please tell my son I love him." I relayed the message.

He whispered, "I love her dearly and miss her every day." He sounded heartsick.

I added, "Well, she is listening to you. She knows what you are doing, and she is not happy with you being angry about stuff. So, you got to work on that."

I reminded him we had a lot of changes going on in our private life. She knew about them. Then my dream of my aunt supporting me, and his mom did the same thing. I relayed this revelation to him. I told him how incredible this was. But I needed to finish my prayers. We both whispered, "I love you."

I logged what happened into my journal at 9:16 p.m. Gabriel played the "Shout" song.

I asked, "What do you have to say, Gabriel? I haven't heard from you."

Gabriel announced, "God is pleased with what you have written. This is what your gift is for, to help others." I smiled and listened to his warm words.

Later that evening, I laid my head on the pillow. Ilene announced, "God will speak to you in the morning. Prepare the house."

Shocked, I stated, "I haven't prepared the house for three days. Will that be, okay?"

Ilene answered, "God knows all things. Sage and frankincense the house heavier, shower with salt. Do not make your Lord wait."

I ran downstairs and told my husband, "God is going to speak to me in the morning." I cried. "I miss him so much. I will not call you in the morning. I must be ready for God to speak to me."

He gazed into my eyes, "That is okay."

He kissed and hugged me. My husband understood the magnitude of what I went through.

November 21, 2020

I woke and remembered God would speak this morning. I needed to prepare the house and made a quick cup of coffee at 8:00 a.m. I felt excitement building in my chest and anticipated what I would hear from God. I chugged coffee and took a quick shower. I scrubbed my body with baking soda like Ilene instructed. I burned sage, frankincense through the entire house, garage, and laundry room. Ilene instructed me to sage there too, heavily.

Gabriel instructed while I burned sage. "Your Lord is waiting."

I needed to ground and pray for protection.

Gabriel announced, "Your Lord is preparing. Your Lord is coming."

God spoke gently, *"Hello, Rebecca, it is God. You have been busy doing God's work. I have been watching, observing you doing these tasks. I hear your prayers, for there are many. You have listened to your Lord. I have taught you many things, thus saith the Lord.*

There will be difficult times ahead. You must prepare. These things will soon pass. Pray for the things that you need, and I will grant them to you. You must remember to pray for the ones that you love. They need guidance, structure, discipline, diligence, unwavering faith. These things I say to you, your Lord and Savior, Christ the Lord.

I come to you, for you are weary. My messenger needs to be strong, diligent. You must remember to pray for the things you need, and I will help thee, thus saith the Lord.

Do unto others as you have them do unto you. Remember these things I have taught you. These things are important. This will help you. My messenger must be kind and generous to others, for they know not what I speak to thee. You mustn't let these things bother thee, walk away. Be generous, show mercy for their shortcomings. These things I say to you, says Christ the Lord, the Almighty, himself.

Do unto others as you would have them do unto you. You must be diligent in your work. There's much more to come. You have been working hard on the things I've asked of thee. Time is of the essence. Many changes are coming that I have granted through your prayers. Remember, God knows all things. These things will help my messenger be the person that you need to be. My messenger must be strong, diligent, forthcoming, dutiful. These things I say to you.

Do unto others as you would have them do unto you. Pray for those that need guidance. Pray for strength and understanding of their shortcomings, these things I say to you.

You must remember to pray for what you need, and I will grant it. My messenger has been trying hard. I know these things. That is why I come to you today, to help thee. I am with thee. Can you feel my presence?

I sobbed. "Yes, Lord, I can feel you. Your love is filling my heart. I have missed you."

God continued, *"My messenger must be strong, not weak, thus saith the Lord.*

These things I ask of you are difficult for you. These things will help you grow and learn what Octavian needs to be, thus saith the Lord.

Ask and I am there. I am with you every step of the way. Remember these things. I have granted many blessings to you, my messenger. You know these things are true. Do not doubt your work. You have much more to do. I have been guiding you. My messenger knows these things.

Continue on this path, God's path, the path of righteousness and you will be rewarded in heaven, thus saith the Lord, God Almighty, himself.

Time is of the essence. You must remember to pray for those you love, for they are weak, not dutiful in their faith. Pray for strength, dutifulness, unwavering faith, diligence, and I will help them. You must show mercy to those that do not understand these things. These things I say to my messenger, says Christ the Lord, himself. Do unto others as you would have them do unto you. I must go now, for you are weary."

I begged. "Please don't leave, Lord. Can you tell me what is going to happen in the future? It is going to be difficult. What am I supposed to prepare for?"

God answered quickly, *"You must pray for what you need, and I will help thee. You need to be diligent, forthcoming in your work."*

I asked, "Lord, when am I expected to publish the third book?"

God answered, *"Now is not the time. I will show you the way. Continue on this path, the path of righteousness, and I will help thee. You must be strong and diligent, my messenger. Use your gift that I have given you, wisely."*

I asked, "Lord, is there anything that you could tell me about my husband and my family?"

God answered, *"Spend more time together. Strengthen your bond. I have been helping thee with these things."*

I whispered, "I know you have, Lord. I've been asking for help."

God continued, *"You must continue to do these things, will help your marriage."*

I asked, "What do I pray for to help Noodle, Lord?"

God answered swiftly, *"Longevity, endurance, more time with her, overall better health, strength, endurance, these things will help her. She is getting older. Do these things daily."*

I whispered, "I will, Lord. I will."

God asked, *"Is there anything else my messenger, I can help you with?*

I asked, "Lord, what does my future hold? What am I to do about my job? I don't know what to do?"

God answered, *"You must be patient for these things to unfold, says Christ the Lord, God the Almighty. I am showing you the way. It requires great strength, diligent work to make these things happen. Pray for these things and I will help thee."*

I asked, "Do I need to save more money, Lord? This coronavirus lingering, is there anything you can tell me?"

God answered, *"You must prepare for the changes that are coming. I will provide for thee, ask, and I will help thee. Do not worry. I will take care of thee. I must go now, for my messenger is weary. It takes from thee when I speak to thee."*

I begged. "Please don't leave. Can I see you, Lord? Please let me see you."

God answered, *"You are not strong enough, my messenger. It's too much for thee. I will speak to thee again. I must go now. Time is of the essence. Pray for what you need, and I will help thee."*

Gabriel announced, "Your Lord is leaving." I sobbed uncontrollably. I wanted God to stay with me. My face soaked with tears. God's presence felt powerful and strong. I didn't want him to go. I forgot to write about the time. It was close to 8:30 a.m. when I meditated. I rushed to get ready and forgot to log it into my journal. Oh, how I missed hearing God's warm, kind voice. God knew everything. He felt incredibly kind and loving. I was weary and work had been difficult. I had not been dutiful and did not show mercy to all the people who drove me crazy at the salon. I needed help.

I ended the meditation and prayed, "Lord, I pray for strength, diligence, dutifulness, mercy for people's shortcomings. Help me with these things, Lord. I pray for guidance. Surround me with the white light of the Holy Spirit and protect me at all times. Keep evil away from me, Lord. Continue to guide me, please. I beg of thee. I ask these things in the name of the Father, the Son and the Holy Spirit, in Jesus Christ, I pray, Amen."

I glanced at the clock at 9:06 a.m. Thirty-five minutes had passed. My heart tingled with God's love. I bawled again. "Lord, I am grateful you spoke to me. It has been a couple of months since I heard from you. I missed you."

I proofread and realized I had not done enough. I recalled how God taught me before about the mercy of shortcomings. I forgot. I disappointed God in doing so. It was difficult being kind to people who were infuriating. But I knew in my heart when I could, it made my heart soar with joy. I must show mercy to those who show ignorance about things they do not understand.

I whispered, "Thank you, Lord, for reminding me of what you expect of your messenger. I will do these things for you."

Later in the evening, I prepared salmon for dinner. I cut open the package and pulled the salmon out to drain. Dad played music.

I laughed. "Hello, what is own your mind?"

Dad asked, "Hey Beck, I love you. How did it feel to talk to God today?"

I smiled. "It was utterly incredible. Knowing God is with me every day."

Dad beamed. "I can't wait for you to meet him."

Gabriel announced, "Your Lord is pleased with your work today."

I wrote about what took place today and the dream of my aunt. It took three hours to write. It felt fabulous to know it pleased God. I sensed God watched as I wrote.

Dad continued, "God is smiling, Beck. He is pleased with his messenger. He is glad you talked to your husband today, what God spoke to you."

I grinned, while I seasoned the fish. I made God smile. I put the salmon and the red seasoned potatoes in the oven to bake. I listened to music from Dad and Dan played "If This Is It," by Huey Lewis.

I smiled. "Yes, this is love, and I am feeling it."

Dad whispered, "I miss you, Beck. I love you. I am proud of the daughter you're becoming."

I confided, "I am trying, Dad to change and grow. God wants Octavian to learn and grow. You encourage me a lot." I took a sip of red wine.

Gabriel reminded, "You must remember to pray like your Lord taught you today."

I whispered, "I know, Gabriel. Please remind me when I need to."

Dad added, "God is glad you're eating fish, Beck. It is good for you."

I grinned. "I am loving salmon now. I crave it. It feels good in my belly when I eat it."

He added, "Your brother misses you, Beck."

I inquired, "Which one?"

He replied, "Your younger brother."

I beamed. "That is great to know. I am glad someone in the family misses me."

Dad added, "The family doesn't understand, Beck."

I mumbled, "It is sad, Dad. But I get it. I am moving forward without them. I must do these things for God."

Ilene interjected. "God is pleased you have learned these things."

I loved these conversations. It happened when I cooked often.

November 24, 2020

Tonight, my front tooth pounded with pain where I chipped it. I tried online to establish an appointment with a walk-in dentist. They informed me they would look at it and reschedule to mend it another time. The same response as the current dentist I went to two weeks ago. I must wait until December 21, 2020, for their next opening. I cancelled the online appointment. I had already paid one hundred and eighty dollars for the other dentist to *look* at the tooth. I cried as I closed my iPad. I felt devastated and frustrated. I laid on the bed in "the room" and meditated. I asked my guides, the angels and God, to help me.

I asked the angels, "Is there anything you can tell me to help me? This tooth is aching."

The angels whispered, "Pray for God to heal this area. Pray for God to remove the pain."

I ended the meditation and prayed, "God, please heal my tooth. Remove the pain from this area until I can repair it. Lord, it hurts. Please help me. I ask in the name of the Father, the Son, and the Holy Spirit, in Jesus Christ, I pray, Amen."

Gabriel announced, "God has heard your prayer and he will help thee. Do not think about this pain and it will soften."

I whispered, "Thank you for helping me. I know in my heart it will ease off and go away completely. I did not think to ask God for help earlier. The thought of enduring pain for four weeks felt unbearable."

It saddened me a dentist will delay this long to repair a tooth to generate more money. I heard music.

I asked, "Is there anything you can tell me about my tooth?"

Dad answered, "It will get better soon, Beck. Your Lord will help you."

I sobbed. "I hope so."

I thought, "I am trying. It is hard to focus on anything with my tooth aching. Thanksgiving is in a couple of days. I don't enjoy eating food. I will not think about it like Gabriel instructed."

November 25, 2020

I laid in bed and prayed for guidance on the subject for the next live video. I begged to hear from God.

Ilene responded, "Your Lord is busy. You mustn't ask things in this manner. God speaks to you when God is ready."

I asked, "Ilene, can you help me with what topic I need to do for the next video? I need to know what it is."

Ilene instructed. "Toxic people, removing them from your life. They hinder you from growing."

Relieved, "Thank you, Ilene."

I recalled I posted on Facebook about toxic people, and over three thousand reached organically. I must research the topic to prepare for the live video.

I slept and dreamed about this for seven hours.

Dream Twenty-Seven: Unfortunately, my ex appeared. He showed me a guy I knew. He was kind and generous. People called these qualities "a good man." This man married a woman who nagged, complained often. I sensed they never had sex because of my empathic abilities. A man needed constant reassurance and intimacy in his relationship for him to want to give to his wife. This person was in his late sixties. My ex showed me he died suddenly. I had not seen this person in some time. It shocked me. I wished to go to the funeral. When I arrived, I looked at his wife and she wasn't crying or upset. She did not feel sadness but beamed now. He was dead. I felt horrible. This man did not deserve this.

The next man my ex showed me, I knew. He was in his forties and wasn't happy in his marriage, either. He died unexpectedly.

I struggled to ask Ilene on the other side, "Where are they? Are they okay?"

His wife looked disappointed but moved on with her life like he didn't matter. This behavior unnerved me to see how the women responded to these genuinely kind men, which they had not nurtured.

My ex showed me my current husband died swiftly. My heart sank. "I love my husband and can't live without him." I used my gifts to see if he was in heaven. I heard he wasn't and waited for me.

I thought, "This is untrue. He wouldn't wait for me. He would go to heaven to see his mother and his dog."

The dream shifted. I looked down at my legs and feet walking on the concrete sidewalk in town. I did not know where I was. I looked around. The dark place felt sinister and looked misty, dreary out. I only saw my feet and legs. I strode forward on the gloomy path. I felt dreadful, heartbroken, and filled with worry. I sobbed as I walked into blackness. I heard my ex behind me. I turned and glanced in that direction and observed his feet coming closer toward me. He ran to catch up with me.

He blurted, "I just made sixty dollars. That's not very much money. But I'm gonna spend it."

I retorted, "Well, I wouldn't spend sixty dollars on dinner."

I sensed we would dine together. We arrived at the destination in front of a black brick building.

He taunted, "You can't go inside, you're not a member."

I watched him walk in front of me and enter the dwelling. He glared through a large square window. I spotted a guy sitting there, watching the door. My ex faced me. He wore no shirt. His body looked extremely scrawny. His black, disheveled hair, shoulder length, blown off his face. His eyes looked black, huge with excitement. He held a Ziplock bag containing a half of a cup of cocaine.

He sneered, "I'm not eating dinner with you. I'm going to have a party with my bag and enjoy every bit of this."

He thumped the bag with his middle finger while he smirked and laughed. He turned and sauntered away. I remembered this behavior when he lived. I didn't see where he went then, but now he showed me. My ex strolled into a bar and had spent all his cash on the cocaine. He continued his downward spiral of drugs.

I felt defeated and trudged onward. I recalled the men he showed me who died. I felt the humility he wanted me to feel. I walked barefoot and felt something gooey under my left foot. I stopped and leaned on a white concrete fence post. I viewed my hand resting on the post. I lifted my foot. I stepped in dog crap. It covered the bottom of my heel and the sides of my foot. I scanned around where I could scrape it off. I noticed a small patch of weeds in black dirt. I hopped over on one foot to remove it. The crap did not come off. The residue remained. There stood a man close by.

He scoffed, "Oh, my dog did it."

He appeared not to care. He let the dog crap wherever it wanted to. I knew he never cleaned up after the animal when he lived.

I felt uneasy and hobbled forward on the concrete path. I entered the restaurant. It looked like a dump with no food. I sat at a round dinner table in the corner, completely devastated that my husband died. I struggled to ask for help from my guides and couldn't hear them. Unexpectedly, my ex appeared. He plopped down at the table with me. His face looked hideous, red, swollen, his nose bled. He still wore no shirt. His emaciated body appeared he had not eaten in days.

He muttered, "I finished the whole bag. I did huge bumps."

He struggled to convince me he had a wonderful time. He had a horrible time all by himself. I saw no one in the bar to hang with. My ex was all alone, miserable, and repeating things he did when he lived. He looked incredibly ghastly. I woke shocked.

I thought, "Oh my, I have been dreaming this all night."

What day was it? I felt consumed with grief. I laid in our bed, safe. These men, the ex-revealed, were alive. He sought to hurt me from *darkness.*

Distressed, I asked Ilene, "Why did this happen? Where was he? Where was I?"

Ilene explained, "He is in darkness, trying to hurt God's messenger."

He can't hurt me, but he communicated with me through my gifts. When I slept deeply, it made it easier for him to slip in. *Evil*, I knew, made him do it. I *saw darkness again*. It felt gloomy, desolate, misty, black, and miserable. I sensed evil watching and lurking in the shadows.

I heard something above my head. It sounded like someone deeply exhaled. I thought it was Noodle. She laid on the pillow in the middle of the bed. Rattled, I heard something. When I heard the exhale. The clock beamed 3:33 a.m.

Dad whispered, "It was me, Beck. I wanted to tell you, I loved you."

I wondered, "Why he woke me because it was weird to hear breathing above my head. He did this because the dream lasted for hours. He woke me to let me know my guides, the angels, and God protected me. That is what 333 meant. This is what I must endure, so I can write it for you. God wants **you** to understand **this is real**."

November 26, 2020

Thanksgiving day, I woke, and my tooth did not hurt. I whispered, "Thank you, God, for healing and taking away the pain."

I sipped coffee and wondered how it would feel with no unwanted guests today.

My husband and I enjoyed ourselves on the deck. The turkey baked in the oven. I dressed the turkey with seasoned butter under the skin, stuffed the cavity with dressing and laid bacon over the breast. It smelled scrumptious. I wandered into the kitchen to prepare the yams and mixed the ingredients to pour on top.

Gabriel declared, "God is pleased that you are enjoying your day."

I gasped. "Wow, I'm glad God is pleased. I am enjoying our day with the ones I love most in the world, my spouse and Noodle. Thank you, Lord, for taking away the pain from my tooth. It doesn't hurt. It has hurt for two weeks. I can smile and it doesn't hurt. Thank you for everything."

Later, the meal cooked and ready to eat. Everything, especially the turkey, tasted perfect. It felt amazing to spend this glorious time with just my husband and our dog, our family. With no outsiders, no pity parties for toxic family members. They always made it a drag because you really don't enjoy being around them. Their toxicity took the joy out of the holidays. We hung out and talked throughout the day.

I whispered, "Thank you, Lord, for giving me calmness, tranquility, intimacy with my husband, and no suffering in my tooth. I enjoyed the day smiling, eating, and loving the time with my family. It was a perfect day, Lord, thank you."

Gabriel announced, "Your Lord is pleased that his messenger is happy."

I smiled. "Wow, well, you're always listening. It is breathtaking, thank you."

At 7:30 p.m. I watched a movie on the Brit Channel. "Turn Of The Screw," by Ben Bolt. My husband napped in "the room." Noodle played for a while before the show started. She seemed frolicsome and bright. I grinned and watched her, wanting to play at fourteen. I took a break from the movie and poured a small glass of red wine.

Gabriel announced, "God is glad you're enjoying yourself. He wants his messenger to be happy of the journey you have chosen."

It surprised me and thought, "I am enjoying myself and God is watching me. I am blessed. You want me to be happy. Thank you, Lord."

I finished the flick and started another one at 9:23 p.m.

Gabriel announced, "Your Lord is pleased that you are taking time to rest."

Shocked, it felt great to rest. I had prayed for time with my family. I replied, "It feels good. Thank you, Lord. Thank you, Gabriel, for telling me what God thinks. That is incredible, and he still is watching me. Wow, how marvelous. I sensed many times today I was being observed. Nothing creepy, but I felt my guides, and God watching us."

The movie ended. I prepared for bed and carried Noodle outside to pee. When I opened the front door. Gabriel warned, "There are many spirits out tonight. Do not stay out there long."

My stomach dropped, and I trotted down the stairs carrying her. I decorated the deck with the red Christmas lights my husband bought yesterday. I sensed the lights attracted the in-betweens.

I asked, "Gabriel, keep them away from me." I prayed, "Lord, please remove all spirits from my home and deck. Protect me, Lord. I ask in the name of the Father, the Son, and the Holy Spirit, in Jesus Christ, I pray, Amen."

Gabriel declared, "They have been removed. Do not stay out long. There are many spirits out tonight."

I scooped Noodle out of the grass. I scampered up the steps and locked the front door. I felt relieved and safe. God protected me from the negative spirits who wish to harm me because I am God's messenger.

I turned off the TV. My husband still asleep in "the room." I took Noodle upstairs to bed. I prayed and drifted to sleep.

<u>Dream Twenty-Eight</u>: I examined this place. I sought to understand where I stood. I saw unending thick blackness, misty air. It felt cold, dreadful, and heaviness all around me. I observed women entering a place which looked like a rest stop. It reminded me of a truck stop where truckers would rest and eat. I crept slowly towards the area.

I saw a girl. I noticed her brown skin and her black hair pulled back in a tight ponytail. She looked in her twenties. The young woman wore black clothing, fitting tightly to her body. She strolled into the pit stop. I followed her inside. I glanced around and spotted a large, glass square tank, which held water. It appeared big enough for a person to plunge themselves into the deep water. A light hung above the black, murky water. The woman marched up the ten steps to the platform connected to the tank. She waved her hand under a part of a small box. A card popped out with a stamped code. A person would take the code and plunge into the water. I sensed the young mother believed this would cleanse her sins, but it didn't. The girl stepped closer to the top of the edge of the water. She stood there waiting to jump in.

I noticed a grotesque fetus sliding up the silver metal pole, which held the steel steps together. The fetus stopped as it squirmed, rising to the top of the tank where she would see it. The microscopic eyes looked human in form but weren't. It disturbed me to look at it. The fetus damaged and deformed. It wanted her to see it sliding up the rod, wiggling gradually back and forth. I peered closer. I saw red blood on the flesh, it stopped moving. The fetus wanted me to look at it and it glared at me with its tiny piercing eyes, watching me. I sensed the woman had an abortion. She jumped into the water with her clothes on. She thought this cleansed her and her fears. Shocked, I knew this was untrue. She climbed out of the water. Nothing changed. The fetus temporarily disappeared.

I spotted images of men's faces coming and going through *the darkness*. Their sinister faces watched the mother and relished in her demise. I viewed many wicked faces from different men, and they all felt evil. They had harmed people, especially women. They fed off of her fear.

I panicked and needed to get out of here. *I did not belong here.* The men's faces glared at me and relished in my fear as well. I saw no doors, nothing but solid blackness all around me. I only saw the steps to the tank of water, where the revolting fetus waited.

Noodle shook her collar, and I woke. Rattled and horrified, I glanced at the clock. The time was 3:33 a.m. I drew a deep breath, my eyes wide with panic. God, and the angels protected me. That was why I woke. It took time for me to stop reliving the images flashing in my mind. *I stood in darkness again.* It felt similar to other dreams I had and heard music from Ilene.

I blurted, "What did I dream? What did this mean? It was disturbing and unsettling."

Ilene whispered, "This is how evil torments those who have thought of doing ungodly things. It relishes in tormenting those who do not believe in God."

I sensed these women had abortions from unwanted pregnancies. These sinister men were the ones that violated them. It felt dreadfully wrong, all of it.

I wondered, "What about the children? The fetus didn't look like it was really an unborn child. It looked disgusting."

Ilene explained, "It was an image of a fetus. God protects all of the innocent."

I realized immediately all innocent children were in heaven. Evil played games and tormented those who did not believe in God. Evil wanted the women who thought their abortions were ungodly to relive their pain repeatedly. No matter how they tried to get rid of the pain, this was *darkness*. I did not want to be there at all and couldn't wait to leave. I had never felt such dismal gloom, horror, and dread. Evil harmed you anywhere you went. Evil watched, lurking, and relishing in your torment. Evil continued, making their pain repeat itself. I laid in bed for a while, not able to sleep. I dozed and woke at 7:00 a.m. The dream still disturbed me. I cringed, recalling the wiggling fetus with the piercing eyes, distorting itself up the metal pole. It wasn't even an actual child. *Evil is wicked and vile.* What I experienced was definitely one place you *never* wanted to be.

I thought, "My heart is racing, pounding, recalling how darkness felt. So, I can write this for you. *I saw darkness again.*"

December 8, 2020

I spoke to Jess, Sunday night. During our talk, she suggested I take a break from everything. I cried when she saw through my stress and took her advice.

Monday, I did not realize how exhausted I was. My body felt stiff, my mind weary, and my back ached. I accomplished nothing and laid on the couch for hours. Noodle and I watched a movie together in "the room." My husband came home later from the bakery, and we spent time together. I still required more rest and retired to bed at 9:00 p.m.

I dreamed of many events during the night, but Bob returned for a visit.

Dream Twenty-Nine: I saw Bob's face. He looked in his fifties, like he did when he lived. I noticed his short black hair, dark circles under his eyes, and his skin looked tan. When I spotted him, it felt odd. He stood there. His face changed as he moved towards me. I observed his bald head and his hair long and gray on the sides of his head. I looked at the white, gray hair past his shoulders. His skin looked old, wrinkled, and the dark circles under his eyes looked gray. He appeared worn down.

I thought, "Why are you here? You're not meant to be here."

Bob crept closer. He wore no shirt and had on long white lounge wear pants which tied in the front with a string. No shoes on his feet. He stood only a few inches away from my left arm and walked past me. I glanced at his face, and he glared with anger. I noticed he attempted to tattoo hair on his chest. He wished to have chest hair to attract women. I peered closer. His bare chest had black dots an inch apart along the chest, around his nipples, up to the top of his shoulders. The black dots looked small with red around them. It looked like he drew this on his skin.

I wondered, "Why? When he lived, he always tried to make people think he was a stud and could have any woman he wanted."

I laughed because he wasn't sexy. He was a womanizer, a cheater who thought only of himself.

I sensed he looked for his son while he roamed. He passed my body, and I turned and studied his backside. His long white-gray hair past his shoulder blades pulled back in a loose ponytail. He stopped and shifted towards me.

Bob stated, "I need to use your phone."

I had my phone in my pocket and lied, "It's broken. I don't know where it is."

I did not want him to touch anything I owned. I wasn't about to help him. He must figure out whatever he needed on his own.

He turned and kept walking in the opposite direction, hoping to find something. I felt relief as he moved away. I drifted back into my dream. I was glad Bob left for now. He found me because of my gifts. He looked horrible and haggard. Bob attempted to fake his way on the other side, just like he did when he lived. He always sought for a quick scheme to make a fast buck. This time he drew fake hair-tattoos, hilarious. Bob still wasn't learning on the other side. At 7:00 a.m. I woke.

I needed to prepare for work and heard music from Ilene.

I inquired, "Why does he keep coming into my dreams?"

Ilene explained, "He is a lost soul."

I asked, "Is he ever going to figure it out?"

Ilene answered, "He is trying, but he has much to learn."

I watched Noodle sniffing the yard, "He will never figure it out. He is too arrogant. He has been dead for over twenty years. Wow."

I carried Noodle inside and logged into my notes about the visit from Bob. I recalled how disturbing and worn-down Bob *really* looked. He tirelessly searched for his pathetic son, which he taught him the same things. He would never find him because his son was in *darkness*.

Later in the evening at 9:50 p.m. I laid in "the room" with Noodle. I touched her body and the large tumor on the left shoulder, which was the size of a tangerine. Now, it felt like the size of a kiwi. I pressed down into the lump and felt her shoulder bone. This was impossible before to feel inside the tumor. She walked straighter now since the tumor did not bother her gate.

She had another tumor on top of her right back paw. This tumor appeared the size of a large bean. Noodle licked it because it annoyed her. I searched in her fur and the tumor had disappeared. It was God who healed my baby. God did these things from my prayers. I prayed every day for her. The angels and God instructed me to pray for endurance, longevity, more time with her, strength, and improving overall health. I added, removing her tumors, and improving her sight. I prayed this prayer for over two years daily. My best friend looked and felt better.

I whispered, "Thank you, Lord, for taking care of my baby. It means the world to me. I know you hear me. I feel you watching as I log this into my journal."

I listened to the 528hz frequency tonight on YouTube. It was supposed to cleanse and heal your aura. I wished to learn more about frequencies. I felt extremely tingly all over. My ears rang in a good way.

Dad asked, "Can you hear me better, Beck? Can you hear me better?"

The frequency I listened too differed from the frequency I heard through my clairaudience. I heard Dad better. I felt the negative energy in my aura shattering and dissipated. I felt excited about my new adventure and wanted to share with you.

I whispered, "God you are awesome, I love you."

December 9, 2020

I wanted to listen to the 936hz and laid down in "the room." I grounded, prayed, and meditated to the music. The music sounded wonderful, and I heard a familiar masculine voice.

God spoke, *"You must believe in yourself. Learn to take things in stride."*

I recognized the sound of the voice, masculine, soft, gentle, and loving. I asked, "Is this God?"

God whispered, *"Your Heavenly Father is with you. My messenger has more to do. Balance is key. This is good for you."*

I asked, "Can Noodle hear it?"

God whispered softly, *"Yes, some, it is good for her."*

I tuned into the music more and asked, "Do you want me to put this in the book?"

God answered, *"Yes, write these things."*

Gabriel announced, "God has spoken to you."

I thought, "Wow, I heard from God easily while this played. I meditated for twenty minutes." I felt wonderfully relaxed, tingly in my body and forehead. I would do this again.

December 15, 2020

At 8:30 p.m. Alone on the couch, I wondered, "What does Octavian need to master. I am a man in a woman's body, reincarnated. My soul is two thousand years old. I love watching movies about Italy. The shows remind me of my past life." I recalled the movies I watched previously the day before about Venice.

I asked Ilene as I touched my skin on my arms and hands, "Is there anything you can tell me about myself?"

Ilene responded, "You must remember your God's messenger in this life. The things of the past aren't important."

I gasped. "Wow, that is who I was. This is who I am. I am learning a lot. Can you tell me something to help me with this question?"

Ilene instructed. "These things must come from within."

I stared at my wedding ring on my hand. "This is a symbol of who I am, Rebecca Walters Hopkins. Octavian needs to learn how to grow spiritually from within to help my soul grow."

I needed to be kinder, loving, thoughtful, humble, and patient. I worked at these character flaws. I wished to become softer in my tone and diligent. I tried to think of other's needs before mine and shared how to grow from what I had learned from God. The lessons helped me be a better person and in my relationship with my husband. Our intimacy and how we connected with each other had improved. My soul continued to repair the damage it did in my past life. I struggled with the internal changes daily. I wanted to make God proud of the person I was becoming. I was more aware of my growth and much happier inside. Choices made were difficult, but the outcome rewarded.

God was forgiving, loving, kind, and generous. God wanted me to become these things. I would continue to try each day and understood what God had taught me. It was way deeper than I realized. I had much more to learn from God.

Gabriel announced, "Your Lord is pleased with what you have written."

I choked and laughed. "Wow, God, you really are always listening. Even when I am logging into my journal." I sighed. "That is incredible. God is so powerful and knows everything. It's hard to wrap my mind around it."

Ilene whispered, "Your Lord is smiling, Rebecca. Your Lord knows all things."

I sighed. "Wow, you are absolutely amazing. I am lucky and grateful you are in my corner, God. I have some idea what you want me to do. I am not sure what the future holds. I understand it will be magnificent because of what you have shown and taught me. These lessons have made my life better, richer, happier, more intense, and more fulfilled in the last two years. I have more to do, but my life will be enriched. I am your messenger, and I must work harder for you."

I realized when I spoke it out loud, "Octavian is my essence of who I am. Rebecca has to do the work." I smiled, thinking about the future. My faith felt strong.

Gabriel announced, "Your Lord has spoken to you through thoughts. The words must be written. Your Lord knows all things, with him all things are possible."

I laughed and smiled because it was true, "Thank you, Gabriel. You are exceptional. I am lucky to hear from you." I cried, knowing what I heard was incredibly real.

December 22, 2020

At 7:15 p.m. I watched the series "Death In Paradise," Season 3, Episode 2, on Amazon Prime. My husband worked diligently at the bakery before Christmas. I sat my empty wine glass on the marble coffee table. I strolled into the bathroom to relieve myself and heard, "I'll Fly Away," song.

I smiled. "Hello, Dad, is there anything you can tell me?"

Dad whispered, "I love you, Beck. I miss you."

I cried. "I love you, too, and I miss you. Is there anything you can tell me about my future?"

He whispered, "Beck, I can't tell you these things. You must wait." I flushed the toilet and wiped the tears from my eyes.

I replied, "I realize I must wait. Today was hard. I had some clients that lost their loved ones. Thank you for the messages for my clients."

I remembered the messages from my father. Grateful my husband, our dog, were healthy and alive. I thought about my life and cried. Being a medium was difficult and a blessing. People wanted to know answers, as I did. I received only what God allowed me to know. You really must cherish the time you have with the ones you love.

I hugged Noodle and whispered in her ear, "I love you, and thankful you are alive. I am blessed you are here with me."

Christmas would be here soon. The ones I loved mean the world to me, more than anything.

December 23, 2020

Yesterday I received a Christmas card from Mildred. I didn't realize it was from her because the envelope had no return address. I opened it and wished I never had.

Mildred commented, "You changed after you wrote your books. Maybe one day you will learn the truth."

Reading her manipulating remark enraged me, and I thought, "I know the truth. Authoring my books has helped me grow as a person. God led me away from you and told me the truth. You lied and betrayed me. God knows it. Mildred, deceitful and manipulative, would never change. She enclosed fifty dollars. I immediately removed the cash and threw the card in the trash, where it belonged. Her words pounded in my mind throughout the day.

I took Noodle for a walk to ease my mind. Dad sighed. "She knows she has done you wrong, Beck. She lies."

I wept and remembered the things God spoke. *"These people do not care about thee, only wanting for themselves. Walk away for they do you no good."* Our walk interrupted by the neighbor's Pitbull. I picked up Noodle and quickly raced back home. My instincts did not trust this young dog. I sensed it would harm us. Relieved, the dog stayed some distance between us, but it followed. I needed a bigger stick for our next walk. I felt unsafe and must protect Noodle.

The next day, Christmas eve, I woke and knew what I needed to do. I wanted the tainted money out of our home. I wanted nothing from Mildred ever again. We were out of milk and orange juice. I grabbed the box enclosed with blank Christmas cards and chose the one with joy on the front. I wrote "May God bless you and your family." I placed the fifty dollars inside the card and slid it into an envelope. I drove to the Dollar General, which was close to the house.

I prayed, "Lord, guide me to give this to the person who needs it the most."

I entered the store and grabbed milk and orange juice. I would give the card to whomever was in the checkout line after me. I stood in line and a lady with dark skin in her late forties waited behind me. I paid for my grocery items and turned towards her.

I spoke, "Merry Christmas." I handed her the card.

She responded in a friendly tone as she took the envelope, "Thank you, Merry Christmas to you."

I turned away and wiped the tears from my eyes. Relieved the money would be used for something good and drove home.

Gabriel announced, "God is pleased with what you have done. He is glad his messenger is learning about kindness."

When I heard Gabriel, I cried again. Mildred's card triggered the pain in my heart. I wanted Mildred to stay out of my life. I wished she would live her life without me in it. The trust had been broken forever. I strolled up the steps to the front door and now I could concentrate on Christmas. I smiled and felt free.

Later, I wrapped my husband's gifts and Noodles. I made lunch and had the house to myself. I wanted to meditate and try out my new speaker with the hertz music.

I laid on the couch and meditated. I pleaded. "Will the angels and God guide me."

The angels spoke warmly, "You must remember you are God's messenger and what he has taught you. Walk away. This does you harm. Pray for those you love."

I asked, "What do I pray for?"

The angels replied, "Pray for healing of her soul." I thought, "Why would I do that? Is this a test?"

The angels instructed. "It will help you grow."

I inquired, "Can I speak to my father?"

Dad beamed. "I am here, Beck."

I replied, "Do you have anything to add about what happened?"

He whispered, "She has done many things wrong to you, Beck. God knows."

I begged. "What can you tell me that will help me find joy at Christmas?"

The angels replied, "Spend time with the ones you love. Focus on your future."

I ended the meditation. A fly kept landing on my hand in December. I typed into my journal. I enjoyed the 963hz and 417hz music. I felt calm, peaceful, and looked forward to Christmas Day.

December 25, 2020

Christmas day, I pressed the water button on the refrigerator door. Gabriel announced, "God has been with you today."

I smiled and sensed God's presence most of the day. That morning, I grounded and prayed. I wished God, happy birthday. Christmas morning felt incredible and relaxing. Noodle enjoyed herself to the maximum. My husband gave me fabulous gifts. White cushions for the pool chairs, a nine-foot white umbrella, a huge amethyst and more. Noodle played with her remote-control rats and wind-up bunnies. We shared a tasty breakfast of cheddar cheese grits, scrambled eggs, bacon, and orange juice. We talked about what we loved, and I suggested a toast.

I announced, "Happy birthday, Lord."

My husband added, "And to all that you have given us, your sacrifice of your life." We tapped our champagne glasses together.

We laughed throughout the day, sharing intimate moments to joking around. Noodle played, crashed, and played some more. Christmas was perfect.

Later that evening, Gabriel reminded, "God has been with you today." I smiled, knowing God took time for me.

We watched the last fight on "Spartacus" Season 2, Episode 6, "The Bitter End" directed by Jesse Warn, Michael Hurst and Rick Jacobson. Again, I noticed how one person could make a difference. He won the fight, which granted his freedom. The ending was totally unexpected. I felt freedom in my life because of the choices I had made as well.

December 27, 2020

A bitterly freezing morning, my husband worked. Noodle and I snuggled on the couch and watched TV. Suddenly, at 9:30 a.m. I heard and saw one of her remote-control rats move in the kitchen. I paused the TV for a moment and heard music from Ilene.

I asked, "Did you move the rat?"

Ilene explained, "It was my energy. Do not be afraid."

I sighed. "I am glad it was you. You are with me. It is comforting to know you are always here."

Ilene replied, "I am always with you."

I patted Noodle's shoulder, warm from snuggling. Christmas was over. I felt calm and rested. Fifteen minutes later, the rat moved again in the kitchen. I jumped because it was loud. The house was quiet. I smiled because it was Ilene. I walked into the bathroom and undressed. I grabbed a towel and stepped outside onto the deck and soaked in the hot tub for a while.

I prayed, "Keep all toxic people out of my life, Lord. Help them on their journey without being a part of my life anymore. I don't want them in my life and need to concentrate on my journey. I ask these things in the name of the Father, the Son, and the Holy Spirit, in Jesus Christ, I pray, Amen."

Gabriel announced, "God is pleased with what you have asked for. He has heard your prayer."

I sighed. These toxic people would not be in my life, and I felt relieved. The dread I sensed when I had to see them would no longer enter my being.

I asked, "God, could you help me with these things? It will bring me much joy."

December 28, 2020

My husband and I decided last night the tree looked too dry to leave up for the twelve days of Christmas. I settled on the couch with my coffee. I paid bills and watched TV. I looked at the Christmas tree and knew I must get busy. I removed the ornaments and put them away.

I whispered, "God, I am sorry we are taking it down early. It is a fire hazard."

I received a text from Phil. He wished me a Merry Christmas. I sent one back and hope he stayed strong and did what Gabriel instructed. I recalled God told me to distance myself from Phil. God wanted him to do the work Gabriel instructed. I had obeyed. Months had passed. I believed today it was okay to reply to him.

Phil replied, "Gotcha, I am trying, but lost. Sometimes I feel like I am just passing time away that is lost forever. I don't understand why no one worthwhile has come my way, but I do trust that God will bring me abundance in love and intimacy. Keep praying for me. Don't be a stranger." I prayed for Phil.

I asked Ilene, "Is there anything I can say to Phil that he can pray for?"

Ilene replied, "Reassurance, guidance, intimacy with a new love, strength, and perseverance."

I sent the text and knew God had plans for him. He must do his work first.

Phil replied, "I will."

I added, "Every day."

I gathered the Christmas boxes and carried them into the side attic next to "the room." Noodle's toy played in her toy box. The Mexican puppy that sung "Ba La Bumba," I glanced quickly in the toy's direction. The lid closed, and I listened to it play. I wasn't even in the room. I stood inside the attic storage area. I recalled I burned sage and frankincense throughout the house this morning.

I asked, "Who turned on the toy?"

Ilene replied, "It was me."

I remembered you must press the dog's paw to make it play. I recalled last night before I went to bed. My husband had already turned in. One of the remote-control rats made a noise while I sat on the sofa watching the end of my show. Ilene did it then as well.

I cleaned the house from all the Christmas debris. I hated to see the tree go and usually left it up past New Year's Eve. I had most of the day to rest, write, and enjoy time with my family.

December 31, 2020

Dream Thirty: At 6:00 a.m. I tossed and turned and drifted into a deep sleep. The dream felt horrific and terrifying.

I walked away from family and had no one but my two dogs. I saw my older dog, Speck, and my current dog. Noodle looked different and much larger. I strolled away from my family's house because they did not care about me.

I entered a new property. I glanced down at the dry ground and noticed brown wheat up to my knees. I touched the wheat as I walked up to this house. The dream shifted. I entered a large bedroom and saw the low-piled purple-white carpet. The room went downhill as I stepped inside. I entered a basement, and the area looked clean. I spotted a full-size bed across the room. The bed contained the things I liked, heating pad, fur blankets, soft mattress, and lots of pillows. I sat on the bed and stroked the fur blanket. I glanced toward the adjacent room. The white bathroom looked spacious. I roamed around the bed. I squatted beside the bed and lifted the white blanket to look underneath it. I discovered books and children's toys. I glanced to my right and spotted a white bridal netting draped over the doorway to the deck. I looked through the glass door and noticed the four steps connected to the light-colored wooden deck. I could escape through the netting and be outside. I must not get caught. I sensed the carpet underneath my bare feet and felt my big toe stick to a piece of tape. I panicked and needed to get out of there immediately. I sensed my life was in danger.

A man invaded the bedroom. I peeked over the bed at him. He seemed friendly, even though I sensed he wasn't. His pale white skin looked old and his straight, blonde-grayish hair parted in the middle just above his shoulders. I stared into his black eyes. He appeared to be in his late thirties to early forties. His height looked average and had a slim build. He looked strong, but not muscular. He wore dark pants and a light-colored shirt. The clothes looked blurry. He chuckled and sauntered over to my old blind dog. The man reached down and picked her up. He would harm her.

I shrieked, "Put her down. Do not touch her."

He scoffed and put her on the floor. He boasted, "How do you like the room?"

He walked towards me and tossed makeup and lip gloss on the bed. I grabbed the lip gloss, and it appeared cheap from a dime store. My mouth felt dry, and I applied the gloss. I rubbed my lips together. He handed me a key to the room, and he left. I could stay here and had nowhere to live anymore, no family. The room looked clean, spacious, comfortable for my dogs and me. I should stay, but everything in my being told me to leave. I stared at the metal key in my hand. I raced to the door and slid the key in the lock. The lock fell out of the door. It was fake, and the door opened. The man stood there and snickered. I stepped backward and fell to the floor. The man wanted me to feel I was protected by locking the door. The whole charade took your safety and your dignity away from you.

I noticed a much younger man behind him enter the room. He looked in his late teens and looked exactly like the other man. It was his son who did everything the father demanded. I observed a young blonde girl with a baby doll night gown on enter the bedroom. She looked thirteen, frightened and dirty. I looked around and saw a dark-skinned girl with extremely short black hair. Her face looked sad, angry, and worn down. She said nothing. I had her makeup, and she craved it back. I passed the cosmetics to her. It wasn't a gift for me. He used the makeup to make them feel special.

The younger man stepped towards me and dumped a few clothes in front of me on the floor. I rummaged through the clothes. I saw a white netting see through shirt. Some toys you could hang around your neck. I grabbed the aqua toy soldier with glitter on it. I rummaged through what was there, not much to cover your body. More toys made into panties. The choice you made was how they would treat you. I didn't know which one to choose. The younger man strolled past me over to his father and whispered in his ear.

The father sneered, "I think that is a great idea."

I scanned the naked man walk towards the bed. As he passed me, I observed a busted, round spider vein on the back of his knee running down his calf. His legs looked pale white with no hair. He pushed all the blankets on the floor and stretched out on the bed.

I panicked, "Why did you remove the blankets?"

He shouted, "This is the way I like it."

I glanced over at his son. He sat in a white leather chair across from the bed. They faced one another. The son spread his legs and showed me his privates. He laughed, and they both enjoyed their masturbation. I realized at that moment they did this to last longer during sex.

I freaked, "What are they going to do to me?"

I chose the clothes. The son watched me undress. It excited him to look at my breasts exposed, and I struggled to cover them quickly. I knew they would rape and sodomize me. I glanced at the father and trembled with fear. I looked at him, stroking his enormous pale cock up and down.

I panicked in terror, "*I have to get out of here.* They are going to torment, use and demean me. Strip me of everything that is worth anything inside me. Until I am nothing but their toy to play with." They both did this before many, many, many times.

I spoke, "I don't want to wear this outfit."

The young blonde girl screamed, "You can't say that." I understood my comment made what they did worse.

A door opened. I saw hundreds of girls of different ages, who had been in this house for years. They tormented them all. I saw the pain on their faces, the dirt on their skin. The man branded one girl on her forehead like they do cows. The girls stared at me and strolled up the staircase. I gasped in shock at the horror I saw. *I must get out of here.* I felt trapped. It was my turn next. They finished masturbating. I dressed and was not ready for what they wanted.

I woke. Horrified, my heart pounded in my chest. I gasped and placed my hand over my mouth, realizing the terror did not happen to me. I felt grateful I was home and not in this appalling place.

I pleaded. "Ilene, where was I?"

Ilene answered, "He is in *darkness*. He saw you last night outside. He wanted to show you what he did when he lived."

I gasped. "OMG."

I struggled to retrieve my senses to ground and pray like I do every day. I felt rattled, difficult to concentrate. The man was a serial rapist. He lured girls into his home. Kidnapped them. The son born to one girl he raped, and he turned into his own monster.

I leaned over and kissed Noodle and felt grateful she was okay.

Gabriel added, "Your Lord protects you. Evil tries to frighten you. This man is in darkness for all eternity.

I wandered downstairs to let her go outside to pee. While I waited, my mind remembering the horror I witnessed. Shaken, my heart continued to pound in my chest. I felt the pain and terror these children experienced for years. Thrilled, he would no longer harm anyone ever again and *was in darkness.*

Later that morning, I took Noodle for a walk. The dream still wore on my mind. It was horrifying. I kept seeing the faces of the young women and children this man tortured for years. I realized he showed me what he did. These girls were not in darkness. The evil father took pleasure in raping, capturing young girls, and told his son to do the same.

I asked Ilene, "I thought it was just the in-betweens I had to worry about at night."

Ilene replied, "All spirits can see you. Your light is very bright. That is why you must always protect yourself."

I spun around and looked at a vast twenty-foot holly tree. A bird flew around inside the tree like a bush, eating the red berries. I paused and examined the birds enjoying their buffet. Noodle sniffed and marked. I felt grateful I could take Noodle for a walk. It stopped raining for a while. Relieved, this man who tortured young girls was **in darkness forever**. I sighed and continued our walk. I felt more grounded and understood evil always will try to harm me because of my gift. I am God's messenger. Evil wanted to hurt me the most.

I prayed, "God, please keep toxic people out of my life. There is only one person left I want out of our lives. I hope you will answer my prayer. I need to start 2021 without this person coming around. It is out of my control. I don't enjoy being around this person at all, never have. I dread every time I see them. I wish I did not feel this way, but I do. I am fighting evil and other things. I don't need this person in my home and in our lives and need this worry gone. I ask in the name of the Father, the Son, and the Holy Spirit, in Jesus Christ, I pray, Amen."

Later that evening, my husband and I enjoyed a delightful night together. We ate filets with twice bake stuffed potatoes and asparagus. Dinner tasted divine. We watched more of the series "Spartacus," and flirted, laughed, savoring each moment. We sipped champagne, waiting for the New Year to arrive. The night felt perfect. I gazed into his eyes and sensed how much we intensely loved one another.

January 1, 2021

I woke hung over from the champagne. Later, Noodle and I watched the series, "The Affair," Season 1, directed by Jeffrey Reiner, John Dahl, and Colin Bucksey. I watched immersed in episode after episode all afternoon in "the room." I relished spending time with her, resting by my side. My husband napped upstairs. The first day of the New Year felt cold, damp, and rained. I wondered what 2021 would bring and looked forward to it. God would lead me.

January 4, 2021

I burned frankincense and sage through the house. I extinguished the sage under the running water from the faucet.

Gabriel declared, "Your Lord is pleased you are protecting yourself."

I smiled and asked Noodle if she wanted to go for a walk. She jumped off the couch and ran to the front door. I grabbed my light pink jacket and carried her down the stairs. The air felt damp, cool, and misty. I sensed the dreariness and listened to the wet sand crunch beneath my feet. Noodle ran ahead, full of energy. I felt grateful to have this sacred moment with her.

I whispered, "The LORD *is* my shepherd; I shall not want. He maketh me lie down in the green pastures: He leadeth me beside the still waters. He restoreth my soul: he leadeth me on the paths of righteousness for his name's sake. Yea, though I walk through the valley of the shadow of death, I will fear no evil: for thou art with me; thy rod and thy staff they comfort me. Thou preparest a table before me in the presence of mine enemies: thou anointest my head with oil; my cup runneth over. Surely goodness and mercy shall follow me all the days of my life: and I will dwell in the house of the LORD for ever, Amen."

On our walks, I talked to my guides and God. I whispered prayers for myself, my husband, and the ones I loved. We turned around before the dwelling with the aggressive dog. Midway back, I asked, "Can you tell me anything, the last day before I return to the salon? I dread it. I want to be home with my family. The salon takes all my time."

Gabriel announced, "God wants you to rest today, to be ready for the upcoming week and to do what you love."

I smiled. "Thank you, Gabriel."

I stopped walking while Noodle marked and whispered, "God, I am grateful for you being in my corner, guiding me and giving me strength to do these things."

I knew in my heart I could not have without God's help. I thought about how God taught me to ask for what I needed.

I spoke, "God, I miss seeing you. I wish you could walk with me again. It felt incredible the day you walked with me and touched my shoulder. I miss you." I wiped tears from my cheeks.

Gabriel announced, "Your Lord is always with you. Close your eyes."

I stood in the middle of the road; worried Noodle would wander. I closed my eyes and listened for the rattling of her collar. I saw God's presence form beside my right side through my clairvoyance. God's height looked taller than me, five ten. I noticed his medium wavy brown hair parted in the middle, touching his shoulders. I felt his powerful presence beside me. I peeked at his close-cut brown beard, short to his jawline. I studied further. I observed a thick, long burgundy cloth draped over his left shoulder, which fell to his knees. I noticed a bright light blue tunic underneath, the color of the sky. I observed a thin, delicate gold chain around his waist. It glistened in the sunlight and heard Noodle walking ahead of me.

God spoke warmly, *"Can you see me?"*

I beamed and sobbed. "Yes, I can."

I felt and looked at God's left hand briefly touch my right shoulder. God's touch felt loving, warm, and kind.

God stepped closer, inches from my face, and whispered in my ear, *"You must pray for those who you love. They are weak. Remember, I am always with you. My messenger is strong."*

I cried and begged. "Please continue to walk with me."

God stayed and walked further with me. I looked down and saw the light blue tunic touching his shins. He wore brown leather sandals which wrapped around his ankles. We strolled together down my driveway, Noodle ahead of us.

God spoke firmly, *"Time is of the essence. I must go. Do these things I ask of you. I have blessed you."*

I gasped. knowing God would leave and replied, "I will, God. I will."

I felt God's powerful presence vanish and my body tingled from head to toe. Tears poured from my eyes.

I gasped. "He had done it again. Ask and he is there."

I felt blessed beyond words. My Lord took time to touch, walk, and bless me. I carried Noodle to the front door and wiped the tears from my eyes.

I whispered, "Thank you, Lord. Thank you."

Later in the afternoon, I binged watching "The Affair," Season 2. I finished the entire Season by 6:57 p.m. The acting engrossed me. Octavian loved to research everything. I viewed the bonus footage at the end. The main actor was Dominic West and his girlfriend, Ruth Wilson. In the series, they both were British.

I thought, "British actors and actresses are incredibly awesome."

I searched online for Dominic West. He was married to Catherine Celinda Leopoldine FitzGerald, formerly Catherine Lambton, Viscountess Lambton. She was an Irish landscape designer and gardener.

The name FitzGerald jumped off the page at me because Ilene's last name was FitzGerald. I read further. They lived in the Glin Castle in Ireland. I chuckled as I read the information. This was no coincidence. I hunted on Google Maps, the location of the Glin Castle and the Ross Castle. Ilene lived in the Ross Castle before she died in the late 1500s. I bellowed when the Castles were only one hour and fifteen minutes apart.

I asked, "Ilene, is this woman Catherine FitzGerald kin to you? Is she a part of your family?"

Ilene whispered, "Yes, she is a part of my heritage."

I chuckled. This was no coincidence of me watching this show.

Ilene added, "She is kin to you on your father's side."

I laughed again, shocked to hear it. I removed the cooked pineapple out of the ginger-syrup water. I made a candied snack for my husband. I sat on the couch and logged into my journal of this astounding news. I shook my head, "This is crazy. I haven't had a surprise in a while." My family's lineage lived in two Castles, how stupendous.

In my first book, *Living Life as an Empath and Medium,* my guides showed me crumbs of information about who I was in my past life. This was part of my heritage from my father's side of the family. How wonderful. I prayed earlier in the week and asked for the knowledge to help me understand who I needed to become.

I chuckled. "Thank you, God."

The next day at the salon, Rose arrived for her haircut. She was a long-standing client from England. I spoke of her in my books. I shared with her the story of "The Affair," Dominic West, and his current wife in relation to Ilene living in Ireland. I explained to her during my past research, I learned Ilene was an illegitimate child. I could not prove it, only from using my gifts did I learn this information and from my psychic friend Jon. I filled in the dots from my research in history.

She beamed. "Oh yes, I know who Dominic West is, a fabulous actor. It is common knowledge that the Fitz is before your name, if you are an illegitimate child." She had heard of the Glin Castle and the Ross Castle as well.

Shocked and surprised, I replied, "Are you kidding me? I figured out Ilene was an illegitimate child married to Sir Valentine Browne. He worked for the Queen Elizabeth I. My husband was born on Valentine's Day and his middle name is Gerard. Ilene's dad was Gerald FitzGerald, 15th Earl of Desmond. What about that coincidence? Ilene, encouraged me to watch a different movie months ago about a war with Queen Elizabeth I. She informed me as she gazed out the window and watched the ships pass across the ocean. Catherine was her mother's name, and her father gave his illegitimate daughter to Sir Valentine Browne to appease the Queen because her father lost the battle. They lived in the Ross Castle. It took me months, years ago, to find this information. I had no proof, but today you have confirmed it. I had no knowledge Fitz, before your name, meant you were an illegitimate child. Wow."

Rose listened and grinned. "Yes, you were referring to the Anglo-Spanish War. Ships went across the ocean to England. The ships were set on fire. That would have been the same time period. You are talking about Henry VIII. He declared the Fitz to be in front of the names if your illegitimate, common knowledge in England." She giggled.

I knew how much Rose admired the Queen of England and its history. I whispered, "I asked Ilene after the movie if she met Queen Elizabeth I. She told me she had not met her but knew who she was. She was not a nice person, and the people feared her."

Rose smiled, listening, and absorbing my private information. We gazed into each other's eyes, recalling my conversation. I hoped she believed what I shared. As we walked to the door, I explained to her I prayed for knowledge, and she validated it.

I mentioned as I opened the salon door, "Mildred wanted me to believe my father was poor in his lineage. This information shows me his lineage goes back to two castles in Ireland. He does not know about, but he wasn't poor. This is just incredible."

Rose waved goodbye.

January 9, 2021

Yesterday, I would no longer give readings. The more I learned from God, this was not what my gift was for. I knew other mediums who did these services.

Ilene and Gabriel remarked before, "Use your gift wisely. Don't give of yourself to freely. You are God's messenger."

God reminded me before, *"Your gift is to help others understand God is real and evil is real. You are my messenger. Focus on your future."*

These comments made sense now. The readings helped me learn how to receive knowledge from heaven. Now, I could no longer waste time on readings and had not used my gift wisely. People wanted the answers they searched for. I understood even when I told them what to resolve; they did not always follow through. It was not what they wanted to hear. Then they wanted more. They did not understand the gravity of receiving information from heaven. It was a gift from God. They did not use the information I told them to benefit their lives. I cancelled a booked reading and could not worry about these matters. I must focus on my life and my family's destiny.

I stood in the room where I gave readings and wondered, "What am I to do with this stuff and wasted space?"

I envisioned using it for storage and redecorating the salon with its contents. People did not really notice much. Why buy new things?

Someone asked yesterday, "When did you paint the wall white?"

I replied, "A year ago."

I needed to focus on writing and marketing. My duty to God. Readings distracted me from what I needed to finish.

Later, after sunset, it snowed. The flurries looked chunky and bold. My husband and I enjoyed the snow falling for thirty minutes, then it stopped.

The next morning, I carried Noodle out to pee. Still dark outside, and the steps looked icy. I carefully walked down the steps. Suddenly, I missed my footing, slipped on the slick step, and landed hard on my right hip. I scraped my spine as I slid down the frozen steps. Noodle bounced from my arms into the air. I could not see where she landed. I strained to gather my senses and knew I hurt myself badly. I grabbed Noodle into my arms and checked to see if she was okay. She seemed shaken, but not hurt. I thanked God immediately for protecting her. I asked for her protection in my prayers daily. I removed my slippers and carried her up the steps in my socks. My back screamed with pain. I made coffee and grabbed an ice pack from the freezer because I had to work in an hour.

My mind raced, God telling me, "*balance is key.*" My body exhausted from the busy week at the salon. Relieved it was Saturday. I needed rest and time with my family and wanted *time* to work on the books for God. I must definitely continue to pray for help in these areas.

Later at 4:00 p.m. Noodle and I laid in "the room." I wanted to meditate and focus on answers I needed and recorded everything. I learned it was hard to remember it all. I grounded and prayed, "Please protect me from evil while I meditate. I wish to speak only to my guides, the angels and God. Help me understand what I need to work on. Please give me the knowledge I need. Surround me with the white light of the Holy Spirit. I ask these things in the name of the Father, the Son, and the Holy Spirit, in Jesus Christ, I pray, Amen."

God answered, "*Remember to pray more. These things will help thee, thus saith the Lord.*"

I gasped. "Wow, I did not know I would hear from you, Lord. Thank you, I will pray more. What else can you tell me? I need to focus on my future."

Gabriel instructed. "Pray for the ones close to you to grow with you."

I heard, "Focus on the writings. You have much more to accomplish. He will guide you, rest, spend time with the family. Your Lord has told you; balance is key. Remember to pray for those who you want in your life. Pray for structure, diligence, strength and perseverance, calmness, tranquility."

I asked, "Who is telling me these details?" I sensed more than one speaking.

I heard, "Angels in heaven are speaking to you. We will guide you along with your guides, we comfort thee."

I beamed. "Oh, that is amazing. Have I made the right decision to stop doing readings? I feel I have."

God spoke firmly, *"These things are not for God's messenger to do. They waste time. It takes from thee, use your gift wisely, in the writings. This will help you grow, thus saith the Lord, God Almighty."*

Shocked, I felt a burst of energy enter my heart.

The angels added, "Let the past go, start fresh. Enjoy your new life you have created. Listen to God's love and guidance. Pray for those who are weak around you."

I inquired, "Who is weak around me? What does that mean?"

The angels continued, "Your husband needs guidance, structure, and diligence. He has much work to do. He will provide for thee."

I asked, "How can I help him? Just by prayer?"

The angels continued, "Yes, prayer will help guide him. Pray for strength and diligence in the obstacles he is faced with. You must believe in yourself. You have much more to do. Octavian is strong and determined to do these things. Your Lord has been watching. He understands your desires."

I whispered, "Wow, I'm glad, and try my best. I could do more if I had time. I don't have enough time."

The angels instructed. "Pray for these things."

I whispered, "I understand but have to work to pay bills. The books aren't making any money. Will it ever happen? I have to sell many books to make a few dollars. What am I to do?"

REBECCA WALTERS HOPKINS

The angels explained, "Focus on your path, the path of righteousness. The Lord will provide for you, you are his messenger. Your Lord is pleased that you have made changes."

I whispered, "I'm glad. It felt wrong, just started feeling sinful."

The angels added, "People must do their work for their lives to change. You know these things."

I added, "Change is difficult."

The angels instructed. "Remember to pray often. He will guide you."

I spoke, "Thank you to the angels, God, Gabriel and Ilene. Thank you for guiding me, talking to me during this meditation."

The angels sounded warm and loving and spoke in a group. They sounded more than one voice speaking. Gabriel sounded not as firm as God's voice. God sounded firm, warm, and kind when he spoke today. "Thank you, God, for speaking to me. I will do my best in the writings. Please continue to protect me, surround me with the white light of the Holy Spirit. I ask in the name of the Father, the Son, and the Holy Spirit, in Jesus Christ, I pray, Amen."

I glanced at the clock, 4:20 p.m. I smiled, haven't seen 420 in a while. I learned it represented the angels. Wow, I did not realize God would take the stage to speak today. I had worked hard in raising my vibration, cleansing myself daily, wearing crystals and living cleaner. This made it easier for God to speak to me. I did my work and continued to do my work. I felt grateful, it has completely changed my lifestyle. I never felt happier. I didn't know I could be this happy. You must do the work. God did not rescue you and sweep you off your feet. He showed me how to do these tasks in his teachings. Your soul lives in the body, which can walk and do things. God did not knock on your door and rescue you. You must do the work towards something, and you must remove toxic people from your life. They hindered you from growing. I wasted over twenty years of my existence. I had no clue the people I was around were toxic. Now I did. My time felt precious. I needed to make more changes in my life. I would do what God, Gabriel, and the angels instructed today.

234

January 19, 2021

I drove home. The silence from my guides was deafening. I heard music from Dan "Still The One," by Orleans.

I begged. "Hey, can you talk to me?"

Dan whispered, "We love you."

I pleaded. "I love you, too. Is there anything you can talk to me about, Dan?"

Dan beamed. "I've learned so much from Ilene. I am glad I am your guide."

Shocked, I wondered, "What did you learn?"

He replied, "She protects you fiercely."

I shifted the car in park and stepped out to unlock our metal gate. I focused on driving into the garage. My husband and Noodle greeted me at the door. I wasn't able to finish my conversation with Dan. I desired to write it down. I grabbed my iPad and logged the message. I heard Bon Jovi song, "Livin' on a Prayer."

I inquired, "What else has Ilene taught you?"

Dan added, "She lived a long time ago. She's beautiful, Rebecca, gentle, kind, loving, charismatic, caring, diligent and fiercely protects you daily. God instructs her what she is to do to help you. She's brilliant at how she shows you things. I am by her side watching and observing."

I gasped. "Wow, I did not know. That is amazing to learn. Thank you for sharing with me. That is how I feel about Ilene, extremely kind and loving. Anything else you can tell me you are learning?"

He continued, "She is patient and kind, extremely diligent. She's filled with love. I'm learning to be a better person in heaven."

Dan chuckled. I saw him smiling. I looked at his hands, face, and his sandy blonde hair to his shoulders. He wore a yellow-beige long-sleeved T-shirt. The sleeves pushed up to his elbows. Dan looked twenty. I recalled he wore his shirts in this manner when he lived. It felt wonderful to see and hear him again.

I added, "I didn't know she was teaching you. You mentioned one time you were under her. You meant spiritually. So, she is teaching you to help me. Wow, how incredible."

I sensed a strong chill run down my right arm into my right leg.

I beamed. "I'm lucky to have Ilene as a guide. I can't wait to see her in person. It will be a glorious day."

I continued, "To see Gabriel would be freaking outstanding."

Gabriel announced, "Your Lord is pleased with what you have written."

I choked. "Wow, I forget God is always listening. Of course, to see God in all his glory would be magnificent. I cannot wait to see God in person."

I felt another big chill all the way down my right breast, side, arm, and thigh towards my calf.

I grinned. "Wow, this was great to hear. I needed to hear from you guys. It has been quiet. I wasn't expecting all this and smiled. I had forgotten the details of what you look like, Dan. It felt grand to see you again and to hear wonderful descriptions of Ilene. Knowing God is pleased with what I wrote too."

I pulled up my sleeve and looked at the chill bumps on my right arm. I enjoyed the chill flowing down my right side. The chill felt powerful, and my side cramped. It was them and could feel their energy.

I whispered, "Thank you, Lord, for all you've done for me today. This is the best day I had in a while."

At 8:15 p.m. I had no wine in the house and my husband worked at the bakery. The wine stored in the garage outside. Noodle slept on the top of the couch in the window. I grabbed my grey jacket and stated, "Ilene, please protect me and keep the in-betweens away from me."

I heard music from Gabriel and Ilene as I opened the front door. I mumbled, "Thank you for being with me."

I trotted down the steps towards the garage. The garage door rose loudly. I reached in and snatched a bottle of red wine from the shelf. I tapped in the code to close the door. I feared the in-betweens could hear the noisy door. I waited for it to close and hurried towards the front door.

Gabriel announced, "You are safe. We are with you. The in-betweens are starting to see your light."

I took a deep breath and opened the front door. I locked it and sighed. I was inside safe. It felt frightening to realize there were spirits outside at night who saw me, which wanted to harm God's messenger.

I logged into my journal and asked, "Can the in-betweens hear noise?"

Gabriel instructed. "Yes, Rebecca, they can. It attracts them."

I sighed and realized everything I did attracted them. I must prepare ahead in the future to have wine in the house before dark.

Gabriel announced, "Your Lord is pleased with what you have written. He has protected you."

I gasped and exhaled, "I'm glad I have all of you to protect me. The gift you've given me is strong. I don't want to have nightmares and be harmed. Thank you, God, for always protecting me every day. Thank you, Gabriel, and Ilene, for watching out for me."

I turned the TV to "Million Dollar Listing Los Angeles, Knock Knock Who's There?" Season 8, Episode 6. I wondered why I have been drawn to California. It had nothing to do with Octavian's past. Why?

I asked Ilene, "Why am I drawn to California? I need to know. The group on Zoom were from California. I did not join in anymore because someone had three demonic attachments."

Ilene answered, "These things are not for you to know. Not at this time."

I gasped. "Wow, there is something about California supposed to happen in my future? I sense it. I wanted to go to California sense I was a teenager and never understood why. I lived in North Carolina. Why can I not know?"

Gabriel instructed. "These things are not for you to know at this time. You have much work to do. Your Lord is guiding you."

I chuckled. "Wow, I am speechless. I didn't see this coming. I have work to do before I know the answer. I have been drawn to California all my life." I speculated if it had to do with John.

I added, "You know how curious I am about details. This is unbelievable. You threw me a curveball. Now I must wait, and the anticipation is wonderful. The last several days I felt weary from the COVID-19 restrictions at work."

I sensed my heart fluttering with joy. I had prayed for guidance for days and it was happening. I needed to cook dinner. It was already 8:45 p.m. I loved the conversations with my guides. I heard more when I felt relaxed and needed no more wine.

I stated, "Thank you, Lord, you are awesome. Ilene is brilliant. Gabriel confirmed it, and Dan added to it. Wow, I feel blessed and full of anticipation of good things coming. I need this. Thank you, God. I know you're the center of it all."

I strolled into the kitchen and started dinner. I flipped on the exhaust fan above the stove. Ilene played "Santa Claus Is Coming To Town," I chuckled and grinned, knowing this meant a gift. I enjoyed her presence and love. I pushed Pica Italian pasta into the boiling water. In another skillet, I browned ground beef with red sauce and beef broth. I included the spices and waited for the pasta to finish cooking. I sensed another wave of chills through my midsection and parts of my arms. I wasn't cold. It was their energy.

I whispered, "Thank you. I love you, God, Gabriel, and Ilene."

January 20, 2021

My husband and I sat on the couch and watched *Forrest Gump* by Winston Groom and Eric Roth. The rerun made us laugh hysterically. We discussed, like in the movie, how there were followers that ran with Forrest. They desired a leader. We snickered, joked, and recognized we both were definitely not followers. We both led in every aspect of our lives.

Gabriel declared, "Your husband lived when you did. He led his own legion in Rome under your command. That's how you knew one another."

Shocked to hear from Gabriel. I urged my spouse to be quiet so I could hear. I asked Gabriel to repeat it and relayed the message to my husband.

He stated, "That's why I want to kill people who piss me off."

We laughed because this was a joke between us. I thought we knew each other from past lives. Then tonight Gabriel confirmed we did. Jon, my psychic friend, informed me over a year ago during a reading. He felt my husband was a Roman soldier, and we knew each other in a past life. Gabriel confirmed my spouse was a leader of a Roman Legion under my command. Wow.

Gabriel announced, "Yes, Rebecca, you were great friends."

I asked, "Can I know his name?"

Gabriel declared, "Marcus Vipsanius Agrippa."

I pleaded. "Can you say it again?"

Gabriel spoke, "Marcus Agrippa is your best friend."

I immediately knew who this was. I asked years ago was Marcus Agrippa, my husband. I was told no through using my pendulum.

I inquired, "Why, Gabriel?"

Gabriel answered, "Your Lord did not want you to know at that time. This is his gift to you."

Flabbergasted. I smiled. "Oh, God, this is outstanding. I felt this before and sensed it. I married my best friend."

I shared the exciting information with my husband. He retorted, "That sounds so gay."

I blurted, "This is the most incredible news I have heard in months. I must show you a picture of what you looked like. I have it on Pinterest. You did many things and were brilliant."

I grabbed my iPad and searched for his name. I showed my partner the picture. I continued, "See, he looks like you. It is you, your soul."

He squinted at the sculpture and mumbled, "He looks like me."

I added, "It is you. You have been reincarnated. You don't look exactly the same, but very similar. I asked to be a girl when I was reincarnated. This is not wrong in God's eyes because we are not gay. That is why God sent you to me. You were my best friend and died before I did. It broke Octavian's heart. He loved you deeply. I read all this information in my research when I wrote *Living Life as an Empath and Medium*. You were a brilliant Roman general and architect. You renovated aqueducts so everyone could have water and many baths. You designed gardens, and the Pantheon which stands today in Rome. You won many victories in several battles. You loved to fight wars, and you were magnificent in winning them. I gave you the money and power. You were a mastermind at killing people." I giggled. "You fought against Cleopatra and Mark Antony, and we took Egypt from them." I continued, "Wow, what a gift. God allowed me to marry my best friend and be with you again, wow."

I knelt on the hardwood floor, astonished, "You were way ahead of your time, brilliant. Octavian could not have accomplished what he did without Marcus Agrippa's help. I can't accomplish what I am doing in this life without your help. How freaking outstanding is this. It is mind-blowing. I am speechless. I have been praying for knowledge of things to help me grow."

I struggled to recall my research of the history I relished reading years ago. I strolled into the bathroom to pee.

Gabriel announced, "God is pleased you're happy."

I exclaimed, "You are incredible. I am still in shock. How wonderful, how you surprised me, God. We are together again. Thank you."

I smiled and sensed this information years ago and felt it was true. But when I inquired about it. My answers were no. I thought about how Agrippa and Octavian were inseparable and great friends. They accomplished so much during their past life. My husband and I mirrored different accomplishments together in this life. I must work on patience and trust. My husband needed to work on anger issues and giving too much to unappreciated people. These attributes did not aid us in growth in this life. We needed to amend our wrong doings. I remembered Gabriel asked me to pray for the ones I love to grow with me. I did. This was the best news ever. My husband really did not understand the vastness of this information.

I asked, "Gabriel, is there anything I can ask to help my husband understand?"

Gabriel announced, "Your husband will in time. God has shown him the way."

I beamed. "Thank you, Gabriel."

January 23, 2021

I woke. Gabriel announced, "Prepare the house. God will speak to you this morning."

I bounced out of bed at 8:29 a.m. I chugged my warm coffee. I did not want to make God wait. I burned frankincense and sage throughout the house, especially in "the room" for my protection. I felt anticipation, wondering what God would say. I missed God's voice and powerful presence.

I laid on the bed in "the room" with Noodle. My excitement churned in my belly. I grounded and prayed for protection for the meditation. 8:55 a.m. I heard music from Gabriel and Ilene.

Gabriel exclaimed, "Your Lord is preparing. Thee must be ready for your Lord is coming."

Dad beamed. "He's almost here, Beck."

God spoke softly, *"Hello, Rebecca, it is your Lord and Savior that comes to you. I have been watching my messenger working diligently of the things I've asked of you. You must remember to pray for the ones that you love. They are weary, weak. They need steadfastness, endurance, and strength, thus saith the Lord.*

My messenger is dutiful, kind, and obedient. I hear your prayers daily, for there are many. Do unto others as you would have them do unto you. Remember, these things I have taught thee, thus saith the Lord.

Be kind and merciful to those who are weak. They do not understand the things I have taught thee. Pray for the things that you need, and I will grant them. My messenger is strong and vigilant. You have not tarried in your work. This is why I come to thee, for there is much more to come. The things I ask of thee to do for your Lord and Savior. You must remember to pray for what you need, and I will help thee. Your Lord has given you many gifts, blessings because of your dutifulness and unwavering faith. Remember to pray for those that you love. They need guidance, strength, perseverance. These things I say to you, your Lord, God the Almighty speaks.

There will be many changes in your future that will bring you joy and happiness, for I have granted these things through your prayers. You must be dutiful and kind to others. Show mercy when needed. These things I teach thee today. These things will help Octavian grow of who he needs to become. God's messenger is all of these things. You must listen when I speak, for I am God the Almighty here with you, guiding you, and showing you the way as you have asked. These things are important. Ask and I am there, says the Lord, God Almighty.

My messenger has not been weak. You have been dutiful, kind, diligent and persevered, through your prayers have been answered by me, your Lord and Savior, Jesus Christ, himself.

Do unto others as you would have them do unto you. Remember these things I have taught thee. I am showing you the way. These things are important. These tasks will help my messenger grow. Pray for what you need, and I will grant these things to thee, thus saith the Lord.

Remember, I'm always with thee. Ask and I am there. Does my messenger have any questions? You may ask them now. I am waiting."

I felt God's extremely powerful energy and tears swelled in my eyes. I cried. "Lord, you want me to be merciful to whom? I thought I was merciful?"

God continued, *"These things I say to you to help others see how to show mercy. You will be teaching them how to be kind and merciful in their lives."*

I inquired, "Lord, when am I to publish the third book? I don't know when to publish it."

God answered, *"These things will come to pass when you are ready. I will show you the way. Now is not the time. You have more work to do before when the time is right. Be patient, Rebecca, these things I say to you, your Lord and Savior, Christ the Almighty."*

I asked, "Are me and my husband on the right path of the choices that we are making in our lives?"

God whispered, *"Yes, the changes are coming are your prayers answered by your Lord and Savior. These things will affect your future and make your bond as husband and wife stronger. These things I say to my messenger, says Christ the Lord."*

I pleaded. "Is there anything I need to pray extra for Noodle? I know she is getting older. Thank you for all that you do for her."

God spoke firmly, *"Pray for strength, endurance, overall better health, more time with her, improve her sight, these things I say to you, thus saith the Lord, and I will grant them."*

I sobbed. "Thank you for all that you do for me. Is there anything I need to pray for myself?"

God continued, *"Strength, perseverance, diligence, unwavering faith, dutifulness, calmness, tranquility, guidance for your future, these things will help thee, thus saith the Lord."*

I asked, "Lord, what am I to do to shift my job from the salon to just being an author? I want to make these changes, but I don't know how."

God answered, *"You're not ready for these changes to come to pass. You have much work to do before these things can happen. The studies and your diligence, these changes, do not worry. I will provide for thee, thus saith the Lord. Ask for what you need, and I will grant these things to my messenger, the Lord, God Almighty speaks."*

I begged. "Is there anything I need to do to help my husband?"

God spoke firmly, *"Your husband is strong and vigilant. He will take care of thee. I will provide. You must believe in these things, for they are true. I have answered your prayers for thee. I am showing thee the way.*

These things I say to my messenger, Jesus Christ, speaks these things to you."

I sobbed. "I'm honored to hear from you. Thank you for coming to me. I've missed you talking to me."

God whispered, *"You are welcome. Your Lord loves you. I have chosen Octavian for these tasks because of his strength and diligence. It requires great strength to be God's messenger. Pray for these things and I will help thee. Be dutiful and kind and merciful in your teachings."*

I asked, "Am I marketing the right way? To show people how to be better and lead healthier lives? Is that what you mean?"

God continued, *"I will guide thee. Listen to your heart. You have helped many. There's more to come. Time is of the essence."*

I knew God would leave soon. That was what time of the essence meant. I blurted, "Lord, is there anything else you can tell me about my future that will help me, my family, my new life that you've helped me find?"

God instructed. *"Be diligent in your studies. This is God's will. These things must be done. You will help thousands of people understand that I am real. Thee will save their souls from eternal damnation through the teachings I have taught you. Continue this work, there will be difficult times ahead. Ask and I am there. I will help guide thee. I must go. Time is of the essence. It takes from thee when I speak to you."*

I bawled. "I know, Lord. I can't stop crying. Just feeling your powerful, magnificent, presence and it is surreal all at the same time. I will do these things for you. Please help me. Be there for me, help me."

God whispered, *"I must go now, Rebecca. Your Lord is pleased with the things you have done. Continue on this path, the path of righteousness, God's path. I will provide for thee. Do not worry. I love thee, goodbye."*

I begged. "Oh, God, I don't want you to leave."

Gabriel announced, "Your Lord is leaving."

I sobbed uncontrollably. God's energy felt so incredibly powerful. It overwhelmed me and laid there howling for several minutes. I cried tears of joy, recalling how wonderful and powerful God is. I glanced at the clock. It was 9:27 a.m. God talked to me for thirty minutes. My pathetic body could only handle that amount of time with God. I was too weak. I noticed shortness of my breath and felt the swirling of God's love in my heart. My face numbed from his power. God's energy felt further away in the beginning. Then God's energy came closer and closer to me as God spoke to me. My puny existence of a human could not take God's energy all at once. I took several deep breaths. My chest filled with God's love.

I thanked my guides and God for protecting me during the meditation. I prayed, "Please continue, guide me, and help me learn mercy. So, I can teach others. I ask in the name of the Father, the Son, and the Holy Spirit, in Jesus Christ, I pray, Amen."

January 25, 2021

I slept deeply, and *darkness* crept into my slumber.

Dream Thirty-One: My ex and his father, Bob, visited again. His dad stood in a black room, only enough light above to see him. The space felt damp, dreary, a basement. I studied him across the room from me. I hid on the ground in a half open dirt tunnel. He wore a long black satin cape. The interior of the cape appeared bright red. The cape draped around his wide shoulders and clasped underneath the center of his neck. It reminded me of a magician's cape. He tried to escape this place. He wanted to become a magician, to disappear from this dreadful place. I peeked closer and did not know I was there. He turned and faced me. I looked at his face inches away. He looked like the character, Herman Munster, on the TV show "The Munsters," by Allan Burns and Chris Hayward. I looked at the drawn on black eyelashes underneath his eyes. His top eyelid looked heavy and filled with black lashes. His skin looked pale and sullen. He slowly blinked his sad eyes and said nothing. I noticed his lips were thin, painted red and his head wasn't square like the character on TV. He prepared for a magician's show to try an escape from this horrendous place.

The dream shifted to where his son stood in *darkness*. My ex had a tremendous performance coming up and his father would perform in his band with him. The father would perform the vocals since his son did not sing. I chuckled and knew this would not happen. His dad remained in limbo, preparing his magician's act. Bob was not in *darkness,* but his selfish son was.

I looked at the area where the band staged their equipment. I noticed a three-inch bright yellow sponge for the stage floor. I viewed the men who played the other instruments. They wore wedged shoes. The heel made of thick yellow sponge. It looked like a cartoon cheddar cheese wedge. I spotted the texture of the sponge. The men seemed excited about the softness under their feet. My ex stormed into the room. He played the drums and didn't have on the same outfit or shoes as the others. He scoffed at how the shoes looked and the stage. He thought it looked ridiculous. I studied him. He wore a type of lounge wear clothes. I only saw from the waist down. The red and black wide plaid pants had a sheen to the fabric. I glanced at his feet and laughed. His feminine shoes made of the same fabric to match the plaid pants. The shoes looked like an open-toed slide with a two-inch Sabrina heel. I used to wear shoes with Sabrina heels a lot when we dated.

I chuckled. "How can he press the petals of the drums with these shoes on? Wow, *evil* made him wear feminine shoes like I did to humiliate him. I believed this to be true."

I viewed. He appeared stressed and out of sorts, wondering why his father had not arrived. He needed him there and could not perform without him.

The Ex screamed, "Where is he?"

I understood, "This will never happen. You're in *darkness* and he's in limbo."

The dream shifted. I observed the toxic people I removed from my life inside a restaurant. Some were family, clients, and friends. I discovered the owner, a woman, was sick and could not open her establishment. These people took over her restaurant to help her.

One of the older ladies asked me, "Did you bring the spaghetti and salad?"

I questioned, "What are you talking about?"

She explained, "Everyone was expected to bring part of the menu. Did you bring the spaghetti and salad? That is what you were supposed to bring."

I retorted, "No one told me."

I spotted sneers on the faces of the others behind her.

I laughed. "You're kidding me. You're going to run a restaurant for this lady, and you have to provide the food too. I wanted no part of this because the owner should have provided the food."

Since I brought nothing, they shunned me. I felt an outcast because I did not bring what they expected. I strolled out of the restaurant and felt lost. I turned and bumped into my current husband outside on the street in front of the business. My husband looked young, like he did when we first met years ago. He appeared unhappy, hurt, and heartbroken.

I whispered, "I'm sorry I chose my ex and not you. I miss our home, where we used to make love."

I saw a flash of our current dog lying on her back in our yard. Noodle's back broken and laid there in pain. I rushed over to see if she was okay.

I woke. My ex attempted to make me feel humiliated, hurt, and an outcast again. He even strove to make me think someone injured my dog. I looked around our bedroom, grateful I chose the right man to marry, and Noodle laid beside me unharmed. When I slept deeply, spirits communicated with me through my gifts God gave me. They could not hurt me but tried. My Ex will never be happy. He remained in darkness because he did not believe in God. His father will stay in limbo until he learned what he did wrong. Then his next step to transition where you repent for your sins and misdoings. I did not believe he would figure it out because he was arrogant. He still attempted to fake his way out of limbo by dressing up like a magician. Really? He wasn't getting anywhere doing that and must learn what he did wrong when he lived.

I recalled, "He tried to fake his way through life then and he still repeating the same thing in limbo. Wow. I am happy. I have a wonderful life with my husband and now I know he is Marcus Agrippa, my best friend."

I took Noodle outside and looked around at the buildings in our yard. All the buildings have A-framed roofs. Most all the structures in Rome had A-framed roofs. It cost less to build. We had many steps to our front door as well. I smiled and realized the similarities. When reincarnated, you did not realize these things because you had no memory of them. You created things in your life but were drawn to parts of the life you lived before. You must learn what you did not learn in your past life.

God chose if you were reincarnated. That was what God told me.

January 30, 2021

I finished my video, "Books about Heaven and Spirits." Few people responded on Facebook, which discouraged me. I turned on the TV and watched a show about Egypt on Amazon Prime.

I asked, "Is there anything you can tell me? I am discouraged."

Gabriel announced, "You are drawn to these places. You have been there, conquered them with others."

Shocked. I asked, "Does God want me to write this in the book?"

Ilene instructed. "Yes, your Lord, wants you to write these things."

I did not know what the documentary would show and wondered, "Was there something new about Octavian I would learn?"

Gabriel added, "Your Lord is pleased that you are listening."

I watched the program for a couple of minutes and Gabriel instructed. "This will help you grow."

Anxious about what I would learn. There were several things about how the Egyptians worshipped many gods. I read about these months ago in my research, but this information was in greater detail. The Egyptians showed extreme diligence, wealth, and power.

Later the next day, my husband moved his bakery to a new location. While he worked, I finished the last of the series. I spoke to Gabriel, "I thought this might be something about Octavian. But these events happened before Octavian."

Gabriel announced, "These are the places you conquered and its people."

I understood, "They worshipped other gods and built magnificent structures because of their Pharaoh's guidance. Their gods aren't real. I thought how pathetic it is how the people were manipulated. The Pharaoh had complete power and control of the region and its people. Today we find their treasures they thought would go with the Pharaoh to his afterlife. Well, that did not happen."

February 2, 2021

I prepared a delicious dinner, baked chicken, cream spinach, and cheese. I pondered of the things I learned today. I heard music and felt the *nag*.

I inquired, "Did Tracy see my work online? Why will she not comment or support me?" I needed clarification of my instincts.

Ilene answered, "She is unsure of some things. She is unsure how it will affect her future. She sees your texts and watches your videos. She wants to stay neutral."

I smiled because that was what I sensed. She had her own agenda, which had nothing to do with me. I sighed, and the house felt silent. Noodle slept, waiting for her daddy to come home.

I sobbed. "It is difficult to love family, and not all back you. I feel as if I don't exist and never thought my family would do these things to me. God wants me to show mercy. I understand, God, what you have taught me. These pitiful individuals do not realize. I have done nothing to them and that hurts the most. But you have taught me mercy, walking away, distancing myself, forgiving, no judgment of how others live. I am grateful you have shown me mercy. I love you for all you do for me, my husband, and Noodle, which *is* my family. Thank you, Lord. I know you are listening right now."

Ilene instructs, "God wants you to write these things." I logged into my journal.

Gabriel announced, "Your Lord is pleased with the things you have written and spoken to him. These things are true."

I smiled and sobbed because *I knew it was true.*

February 6, 2021

I woke and realized immediately God sent my thoughts. I needed to understand what the next video God wanted me to do. I heard through the impression of a thought, "Kindness and Mercy." God would show me the way, and God did. I knew what I needed to share about kindness, but mercy felt difficult for me to discuss.

I closed my eyes, "Ilene, please tell me the definition of mercy. I want it to be perfect."

Ilene instructed. "Mercy is a form of forgiveness of others' wrong doings."

I smiled. "Wow, perfect." I remembered God explained about people's shortcomings and not understanding things. God had showed me mercy. I pondered what God spoke before to me, *"Be kind and merciful to those who are weak. They do not understand the things I have taught thee."*

I used God's name in vain by accident when I lost control of my temper months ago. God showed me mercy and wanted me to teach others. I felt excited about my video. I gathered my notes about mercy. Noodle and I went for a stroll.

Home from our walk. Gabriel announced, "God is pleased with the choices of your work today. He is showing you the way."

I grinned. "Thank you, Gabriel. It is wonderful to know I pleased God. I never want to disappoint him."

I remembered I heard from angels last night. They told me to believe in myself and something else. I could not recollect.

I asked, "Ilene, can you tell me again what the angels said? I was tired and can't remember."

Ilene whispered, "Believe in yourself, pray for those that you love. God is showing you the way."

I asked, "Please tell me if I described in the video what the angels sounded like. I stated they sounded childlike. Was that a correct adjective because a part of me believed it could be taken the wrong way? Can you tell me again what you said last night?"

Ilene replied, "Your Lord is pleased with your work; the angels are children of God."

I smiled. "Thank you, Ilene. It shocked me last night when you told me how God felt about what I said in the video."

February 8, 2021

I showered and heard a new song. "Holy, Holy, Holy," by Audrey Assad. I shampooed my hair and listened to the words. I asked Ilene, "Are you playing the song?" Ilene whispered, "Yes." I smiled and enjoyed the tune.

February 12, 2021

Dream Thirty-Two: I woke in the middle of the night and realized my friend Macky visited. He died on July 8, 2020. I never knew what he died from.

I viewed the outside of a red brick apartment. I noticed a large swimming pool to the left of the entranceway. People hung out around the pool. I observed them stroll through the shallow end of the water. The pool a luxury in this heat. I felt the warmth of the air on my skin while I sat on the edge of the concrete wall at the pool. I looked at Macky walking towards the pool with a male friend. Macky held a beer in his hand. He wore no shirt, slim build, medium length light brown hair, thirty. He wore beach shorts to the knee. I peeked closer at the shorts and noticed a light blue and white swirl pattern. The blue cloth bright as the sky. He walked casually through the water. I watched the water engulf his body. His head stayed out of the water. He turned and faced me with black shades on. He smiled but his face looked blurry. I recognized him. He said nothing. He swam in the pool, got out, and wandered away.

I jumped off the ledge and strolled into his apartment to get a cold drink in the kitchen. Macky returned. I sensed his presence and stood close beside me in the unlit kitchen. He opened the refrigerator door, and the bright light filled the room. I saw his soft hands reach in. He pointed at his stash, his secret hiding place for beer. He grabbed the box and opened the lid of a square container. I peered inside and two slim cans of beer, not beer I usually would drink. I did not recognize the label. He gestured to share one with me. I declined because I already had a glass of water. He closed the box and took one can of beer out. He placed the container inside the back of the refrigerator. No one knew it was in there, hidden. It was his stash.

I wondered, "Why is he hiding beer?"

His demeanor seemed calm, passive, quiet, loving, gentle and kind, just like he did when he lived. My dream shifted, and Macky vanished. I searched for him, but to no avail. I woke and thought about the dream. His body looked and seemed relaxed. I struggled for an hour to sleep. I tossed and turned and finally slept a little more. I woke.

I asked, "Ilene, I had a visit from Macky, right?"

Ilene replied, "He misses his family."

I questioned, "Is he in heaven?"

Ilene added, "Yes, he is in heaven. He wanted to visit you. He wants you to write about him."

I whispered, "Thank you, Ilene."

I finished in the bathroom and walked downstairs. He died young; we are the same age. Last time I saw him was in high school. I talked to him on the phone when he contacted me on Facebook. He showed me his nasty habit, drinking. Why? He lived at the beach. He showed me he enjoyed the warm water in the pool and had many friends. I would love to share this dream on Facebook. But I would write it in my book instead. It thrilled me he came for a visit. Macky was a good man and died too young.

Later, I drove home for lunch and asked Ilene, "Is there anything you can tell me about Macky?" I felt the nag. "I sent his son a message to friend me on Facebook and hope he does. Does Macky want me to tell his son about my dream? Can you tell me anything?"

She answered, "Yes, he wants his son to know he misses him and wants to see him again. He is unsure about God."

I gasped. "Now I get it. If he doesn't believe in God, Macky will never see his son again. I hope he contacts me. I will give him the message. You are my friend. I can at do that for you. I hope he reaches out."

Ilene added, "This was God's gift to him to visit you."

I replied, "Wow, I hope his son calls me soon."

He never did.

February 14, 2021

I glanced at the clock at 5:55 p.m. I smiled, wondering what changes were coming.

Later that night in bed, I woke. I felt my purple velvet blanket slide slowly off my left shoulder towards where Noodle laid. I watched the cover move off my skin. I looked at Noodle and she had not moved. She slept deeply. It unnerved me because nothing had moved in the bedroom in a while. I glanced at the time, 5:55 a.m.

Startled. I asked, "Who moved the covers?"

Ilene whispered, "It was me. I didn't mean to frighten you."

I saw the covers slide away, and it frightened me. I believed it was her, and she confirmed it. Ilene wanted me to see the clock.

I wondered, "What changes are coming? I wish I knew what they were."

My husband slept downstairs when it got too hot in the loft. He fought to stay asleep nightly. I realized when it happened, he was not even in the room. Noodle never moved.

February 21, 2021

Dream Thirty-Three: I met my friend Jess in a tavern for a drink. She was moving and selling her house. We enjoyed talking and sipping our cocktails. I noticed the tavern had dark wooden walls and floors. I spotted many round wooden tables and chairs. It appeared small and nothing fancy.

I needed to wash my hands. I strolled toward a dark wooden hallway where the restrooms were. I entered the hallway, and heard a man's voice, "Your Dad is behind the door."

I stepped towards the left back corner of the tavern and pushed the door open. I saw Dad. Thrilled to see him. He sat at a small table with two men. Dad wore his outfit from Burney Hardware, where he worked when he lived. He removed his blue-jean cap and looked at me and grinned. I observed a bright light shone around him and not the other men. Dad appeared in his thirties. I peered closer at his short, dark brown, wavy hair combed off his face. He sat quietly, grinning. I observed his creamy, youthful skin.

I beamed. "I didn't know you were here."

I glanced to my right and noticed a young man in his late twenties. He wore the same cap and his red curly hair pushed out from the sides of the cap. I looked at his bright, long, curly beard, several inches long. His eyes looked bright, clear blue. The other fellow had not much hair, almost bald and small in stature. He sat between Dad and the other guy. I sensed they were friends and worked together at Burney Hardware. No one spoke to me. It felt odd. I sat down in a wooden chair with a round table to my left. I checked my phone for messages to ease the awkwardness. I woke.

I heard music and asked, "Was it you? Dad, please tell me."

Dad exclaimed, "It was me. I miss my friends, Beck."

I snuggled into my soft pillow and smiled. I felt Dad's presence, but he did not speak. He showed me he missed his friends who were like family when he lived. It felt incredible to see my father again. He looked happy, glowing, and young.

February 22, 2021

I chilled on the couch, watching a series on TV. Gabriel announced, "God is pleased his messenger is happy."

I smiled, rubbed my feet together, and enjoyed God's love in my heart. I whispered, "God, thank you for all you do for me. I am happy because of your lessons. The things you have taught me, guiding me. I pray daily for what I need. My life is better all because of you and your guidance, love, and blessings. Thank you, Lord."

I sipped red wine.

Gabriel added, "God is pleased that his messenger understands these things."

I felt blessed for the past several days and enjoyed time with my wonderful husband. I sensed myself growing into the person Octavian needed to be. It required diligence, and I have more to accomplish. Octavian had no patience when he lived. I must strive for more. God's messenger must be kind, calm, generous, and show mercy. Staying calm and patient was difficult for me, and I fought it often. I managed not to get angry, upset, impatient and rude like I had in the past. The kindness God spoke of did not mean you had to give a gift to someone. It was as simple as the sound of your voice, meant being kind.

I cancelled our cable for TV and did not become angry. It took over twenty minutes to cancel the service. I felt calm and peaceful. If it were five years ago, I would had been angry for waiting and spoken in a sharp tone. Today, none of these feelings happened because I did what God taught me to do. I prayed for calmness and tranquility every day. I learned self-control and awareness of my behaviors. I felt fantastic when I ended the call. One must handle matters with integrity and kindness.

I whispered, "Thank you, God, for helping what Octavian needs to learn to heal my soul. I am sure there is more. I will do my best for you because you are showing me the way. I have never been happier in my entire life. It is all because of you. Thank you, Lord."

Gabriel announced, "God is very pleased with what his messenger has stated."

It felt awesome to hear God's validation.

February 28, 2021

Dream Thirty-Four: Joy visited me, and I stood in the salon. A client sat in the hydraulic chair. She did not want the heating pad on her back anymore, which laid on the back of the chair. I noticed to my right another hydraulic chair formed. Joy sat in it.

I asked, "Do you want the heating pad on your back?"

Joy cheered. "Yes, but can you take the cover off of it?"

I peered down at the dark blue velvet cover and replied, "No, I cannot take it off the heating pad. The pad will be too hot for you and burn the chair."

She whispered, "Okay."

I placed the heating pad behind her, and she snuggled into the warmth and smiled with pleasure. I recalled she enjoyed the heating pad when I did her hair when she lived. She always commented on how wonderful the heat felt.

Joy inquired, "Beck, can you look at my skin? I think there is a spot on it."

She called me Beck instead of Rebecca when she lived. I saw my magnifying mirror on a stand from the facial room appear beside the chair. I pulled the mirror closer over her face as she leaned back. Her skin appeared radiant, smooth, and creamy in texture. I searched for the spot and saw nothing. Her skin looked perfect.

I spoke, "I see nothing. Your skin looks beautiful." She smiled.

I remembered she used to comment about her skin, how it had changed as she aged. Joy looked in her fifties while she sat in the chair. Her aura glowed. She smiled and appeared happy, patient, and calm, as she did when she lived. I woke and drifted to sleep.

Joy appeared again. She stood and looked in her thirties. Her platinum blonde hair cut close and framed her face. She wore an extremely long huge cloak for a queen. I looked closer at the cloak. The material made of bright orange-red velvet. I spotted gold embellishments adorned throughout the cloth. The length of the garment puddled to the floor. I noticed the weight of the garment on Joy's shoulders. A braided gold strand of cloth draped the front of the cloak and fastened at each side of her collarbones. I laughed and watched her being treated as a queen.

I recalled when she lived. She wanted to be treated like a queen. Her husband did everything for her. He shopped, made dinner, washed the laundry, and drove her anywhere she wanted to go. She took advantage of her husband and appeared lazy. I looked at her standing there, glowing in a queen's outfit. She looked beautiful. I woke and realized I dreamed of Joy for hours.

I asked, "Ilene or Gabriel, why did Joy come to me again? Why did she visit me? This is the third dream I have had from her. Her husband wasn't with her this time. Why?"

Gabriel explained, "She came to visit you because she missed you and she is repenting for not being kind to God's messenger."

I gasped. "Wow, she was kind, but always talked down to me like a servant. I did not like it. She wanted you to feel beneath her in status. I knew I was not and did not know I was God's messenger then. My gifts blossomed in the early stages when she lived."

March 9, 2021

On my drive to the salon, I thought about clients. My friend Jess was coming in today. She talked about moving to Brazil. I felt concerned about her moving far away from everyone she knew and wondered if it was a good decision.

I inquired, "Ilene, may I ask a question?"

She replied, "I am here."

I questioned, "Is there anything you can tell me today about Jess moving to Brazil?"

Ilene instructed. "This is not for you to know. It is not your decision."

I sighed and parked the car. I thought, "I hope she is making the right choice. She is determined to move away."

I had several last-minute changes in my schedule and asked Jess if she could come in earlier. Jess arrived at noon, and we started her nail service.

Dad interrupted. "Her husband Bob wants to say hello. He misses her and loves her."

I stopped, "I am hearing from your husband. Do you want to know?"

She beamed. "Yes, please tell me."

I relayed the message I heard. Bob continued through my father, "She's making the right choice. There will be many things that will be difficult for you."

Jess whispered, "I felt my choice was right. Well, everything in this life is difficult. I should prepare."

I added, "Me too. Everything I do in this life is a struggle. But we do it, don't we?"

We both chuckled. Jess beamed. "Yes, we do. That's what life is."

I explained, "I was worried about you moving. I asked this morning and was told I could not know. Then later, Bob comes through and tells us both the answer through dad. It surprised me."

She laughed.

I thought, "This will be much more difficult than she realizes. I want her to be happy. We are old souls and knew each other two thousand years ago when we lived before."

March 11, 2021

I woke and Gabriel announced, "Prepare the house. God will speak to you, soon."

Groggy, I asked, "Ilene, did I hear Gabriel correctly?"

Ilene instructed. "Yes, you need to prepare the house. God will speak to you in a few days."

I laid in bed, marveling at what God will talk to me about. I worked hard and sometimes believed I had gotten off track. God's guidance always kept me focused and diligent. I hoped I had not made God angry not working fast enough. I showered and prepared the house. My husband's schedule had changed since he relocated the bakery and was home more. I hoped God would speak to me when he was not home. If so, I would ask him to stay outside and keep busy for an hour. I must have the house quiet and with no disturbances. I knew he would not mind if I requested him to do this.

March 12, 2021

I prepared the house after I woke. Later in the evening, I watched TV alone and Ilene played a new tune. I paused the TV and heard, "Let me call you sweetheart."

I searched online for the lyrics. The voice of the song sounded female. My husband and I had a slight disagreement since he was home more. It was a change for us both, and Noodle. He did not realize how much me, and Noodle adjusted to him being gone. We had a different routine. Now he wanted more time. I never had enough time. My tone sounded sharp and gave him an attitude. I looked at TV alone since I hurt his feelings. He laid in "the room" and watched TV there.

I found the song, "Let Me Call You Sweetheart," by Patti Page. I played the video of the song. Ilene reminded me he was my sweetheart.

I asked, "Is this why you are playing this music for me? Please talk to me."

Ilene whispered, "Yes, Rebecca, these things are true. Be kind to one another. I am reminding you how much you love each other."

I whispered, "Thank you for reminding me. We love each other deeply."

Gabriel announced, "You must remember to pray for each other."

I gasped. "Wow, this is new." I meant him popping in to help me like Ilene did.

I whispered, "I will, Gabriel, now."

I prayed, "God, I pray for my marriage to be stronger, kinder to each other, listen to one another, more intimacy and guidance for these things. I ask in the name of the Father, the Son, and the Holy Spirit, in Jesus Christ, I pray, Amen."

I added, "Thank you Ilene and Gabriel for guiding me in strengthening my relationship with my husband."

I sent him a text while he slept, "I hope you slept well, my sweetheart. I love you deeply, forever. Enjoy your morning." He would see it the next day and we went to bed.

The next morning, I prepared the house before for work.

While I dressed, Gabriel announced, "God is pleased you have prepared the house. He will speak to you in a few days."

March 13, 2021

My husband and I watched a movie together. I walked into the kitchen to prepare my dinner; he wasn't eating.

Gabriel announced, "Your Lord is pleased you are spending time with your husband." I gasped.

My husband inquired, "What? Who is talking to you, Ilene?"

I responded, "No, Gabriel, do you want to know?"

He answered, "Yes."

I sauntered over and whispered in his ear what Gabriel said and kissed him on the cheek. He smiled. He expected something else. But I had prayed for help in these matters, and God had listened to my prayers.

Later, my husband fell asleep in "the room." I went in and laid beside him and heard music from Dan, "Shot Through The Heart," by Bon Jovi.

While I laid there, I asked, "Can you tell me what he is thinking or anything about my husband?"

Dan whispered, "He loves you more than I ever could." I smiled and held him tight. "Thank you, Dan."

The next day, Sunday, Gabriel announced, "Prepare the house. The Lord will speak to you tomorrow."

My husband had left to run a quick errand. I burned sage and frankincense throughout the house. When I finished, Gabriel added, "The Lord will speak to you in the morning."

I replied, "Thank you, Gabriel. I will be ready and can't wait to hear what God has to say."

Later that evening, my husband worked at the bakery. Gabriel seemed chatty, which felt odd. Ilene interjected. "It's totally normal, not to worry."

Gabriel added, "God is excited about talking to you about many different subjects tomorrow."

I checked my food cooking and wondered what God would say. I felt anxious and excited. "What would God tell me tomorrow?"

Gabriel announced, "Your Lord is pleased with what you said this evening and written."

I gasped. "Wow, I thought about how much I love my husband and cried. I prayed to help keep him in my life longer, to keep him healthy and strong. I need him in my life."

I knew Gabriel referred to this. I wept, knowing God listened. I had ten minutes before my dinner was done. I watched "Downton Abbey," Season 4, Episode 3. I missed my husband, and he would be home soon. I missed God and sensed I was running out of time in many areas of my life.

March 15, 2021

I woke. Gabriel announced, "Your Lord will speak to you when you are ready this morning. Prepare the house."

I whispered, "Let me get some coffee in me to wake. I need to burn sage and frankincense. I'll be ready."

At 7:59 a.m. My husband delivered the baked goods and would not arrive home for a while. I would have the house to myself and gulped my coffee.

Ilene added, "Your Lord is preparing to speak to you. Do not make him wait."

I looked into my coffee cup; half gone. I finished and prepared the house. I set up everything in "the room" with Noodle. 8:10 a.m. I prayed and meditated.

Ilene announced, "Your Lord is preparing."

Gabriel exclaimed, "Your Lord is coming. He is almost here."

My heart pounded with excitement and nervousness.

God spoke gently, loving, and softly, *"Hello, Rebecca, it is God. I am here with you, beside you. You did not make me wait. This pleases your Lord. Time is of the essence. There is much to do. You have been diligent in your studies like I have asked of thee. Time is on your side. You must pray more for what you need. I will grant these things. I hear your prayers daily, for there are many. You mustn't worry. I have plans for thee. My messenger is strong, not weak, diligent, forthcoming, and teaching the lessons I have taught thee. Do unto others as you would have them do unto you. You mustn't worry about the future. I will take care of thee. Many things must unfold before you are ready for these changes to happen. Be patient for the unfolding. Be diligent in your studies, for time is of the essence. I am showing you the way. You must remember to pray for what you need, and I will help thee, my messenger. You must listen when I speak. Write only what I say, for I am God the Almighty."*

God spoke firmly, *"Those who do not believe in me shall perish in eternal damnation. Those who do believe in me shall have everlasting life in heaven where I reside. These things must be written. I say these things to you, my messenger, for I am your Lord and Savior, Jesus Christ, God the Almighty."*

God spoke softly, *"There will be many changes in the next few months. Be prepared. These things will bring joy to your life. I have answered many of your prayers. I want my messenger to be happy. This is God's will, the writings. I ask of thee many things that are difficult for you. This is God's will. You must do these things for your Lord and Savior, Christ the Almighty.*

Do these things and thee will be rewarded in my kingdom of heaven. There will be many changes coming the ones you've prayed for. Prepare thyself and enjoy them. Your husband is strong, and he will help thee on this journey, as you have requested. Remember to pray for those that you love, for they are weak and need guidance. It will help them grow with you on this journey. They do not understand the things I have taught thee. Teach them. My messenger has been dutiful, kind, loving to others like my messenger should be. You have shown mercy for other's shortcomings. My messenger is learning these things I have taught thee. Do unto others as you would have them do unto you, says Christ the Lord the Almighty, himself.

I must go now, for time is of the essence. Do you have any questions for me? You may ask them now."

I gasped. "Oh, wow, you've said so much already, Lord. I know you've been listening to my prayers. I have lots of worries. Please tell me what I can pray for to help Noodle. I see her aging. What should I pray for?"

God answered softly, *"Longevity, endurance, more time with her, overall better health, strength, these things I say to you."*

I asked, "Lord, what do I need to pray for myself that will help me with these changes coming for me to be a better person?"

God replied, *"Strength, guidance, mercy for other's shortcomings, steadfastness, perseverance, calmness, tranquility, dutifulness, these things I say to my messenger."*

I sighed. "Oh, Lord, I am blank. I did not know what you would say to me today. I have missed you talking to me. I'm glad you're with me. Is there anything else you can tell me about my marriage, my husband, the changes coming?"

God answered, *"Your husband loves you deeply. Marriage is sacred. Be kind and loving to one another. He will be with you for many years to come, by your side, helping my messenger. I have granted these things because I love thee."*

I replied, "Thank you, Lord. I have prayed this many times. I cannot do this by myself. He is my best friend and need him by my side."

God spoke, *"I must go now, for time is of the essence. Do you have any more questions for me?"*

I struggled to think, "How does this COVID-19 virus still hinder everyone's lives, many months, years? What am I to do with my work?"

God replied, *"Thee must be patient. There will be many changes in the next few years. Things are unfolding. It will affect many people in their lives."*

I pleaded. "Do I need to save more money? What do I need to do? I know you will provide for me. I just don't know what to do."

God answered, *"You must pray for what you need, and I will grant these things. Remember to ask and I am there."*

I whispered, "Can you tell me anything about the people that have harmed me? Will you keep them away from me? I don't want to see them again, especially Mildred."

God spoke firmly, *"These people are callous and unkind to thee. They will be punished by Lord, God, Almighty, himself. These people have angered your Lord. They do not deserve thee. Walk away, let them go. These things I say to my messenger. They will harm thee."*

I sighed. "Thank you, Lord. I know that's what I should do. Sometimes I wonder about death and obligations I don't want to have. I am excited about the things you've told me about; the things happening in my future. Thank you for blessing me and granting these things. Will you please take care of my baby Noodle? I need her, Lord. I know she's aging; it breaks my heart. Can you tell me anything about her?"

God answered, *"You have more time with her because of the many blessings I have granted. Remember to pray for her often and I will help her. She loves you very much. I must go now. Remember to work on your studies like I have asked of thee. These things must be done for your Lord* and Savior. *You're dutiful and kind, my messenger. Your Lord is pleased with your work. I must go now. I love thee, goodbye.*"

I blurted and sobbed. "Oh, God, I don't want you to leave. You're so loving and kind. It's overwhelming to hear anything from you."

Tears rolled down my cheeks while God spoke. I felt the swirling of God's glorious presence and love in my heart. I couldn't think when God spoke, "I feel humbled, meager. I love you, Lord. Thank you for granting all of these things to me. Thank you."

Gabriel announced, "Your Lord is gone."

I bawled. "I don't want you to go, please come back." I could not stop crying and ended the meditation. God knew all my worries.

It was 8:41 a.m. I needed to proofread. Thirty minutes again, and it felt like five minutes. It seemed crazy how for me to hear what God spoke took so long. Then when I looked at the time and I saw how much time passed. *It felt like five minutes.* This boggled my mind.

I reread after proofreading, "Wow, God talked about all the things I thought about which I shared with no one other than my guides. My worries, uncertainties, God addressed them all. God is always listening, watching, knowing everything I feel. I felt relieved I did not upset God. I worked hard and needed to work on patience for things to happen."

I whispered, "I am blessed. Thank you, God, for all you do. Most of all, thank you for speaking to me. I am honored to feel your presence, and I know you're real. There is no doubt in my mind and being. I've seen the things that you can do. I've seen you answer my prayers. I'm glad you've taught me to pray."

March 22, 2021

At 11:00 p.m. I finished watching TV and my husband slept in "the room." Noodle needed to pee. I dreaded going out at night and carried her outside. The air felt balmy, still. She appeared groggy because she had slept on the couch for hours. It took Noodle a moment to get her bearings to pee. While I waited, I glanced over my right shoulder at the sky behind me. It looked clear with a few clouds, stars, and the moon appeared half full, glowing. I distinctly sensed someone behind me watching. She finished. I lifted her and marched up the stairs, wishing I were inside. I remembered I left the tender tomato plants on the deck my husband gave me for my birthday. The plants sat in a white plastic tub by the front door. The night would be cool and did not want to stress the young plants. I placed Noodle on the deck and opened the door. I reached down and picked up the bin. The *black metal wrought-iron chair slid on the deck*. It made a distinct sound when you shoved the chair on the deck. I recognized the sound instantly because I moved the chair frequently. The chair was only a foot behind me. I freaked out. It took force to push the heavy metal chair. I sensed a large male spirit stood behind me. Noodle waited by the door. I shoved her inside with my foot. I placed the tub of plants inside the house and slammed the door. The noise woke my husband.

He asked, "Is it cold outside?"

I replied, "No, it is rather warm."

Rattled, I forgot to even tell him goodnight. My heart pounded in my chest. I sensed the male spirit came inside the house behind me. I carried Noodle up the stairs to the loft and placed her on the bed. I moved the puppy gate across the top of the stairs. I switched the light off at the stairs and wandered in the dark to my side of the bed. I turned on the lamp and climbed into bed, terrified.

I prayed, "God, please remove all earthbound spirits, in-between spirits that came inside the house. Please remove them and protect me while I rest. Protect my family and Noodle. I ask these things in the name of the Father, the Son, and the Holy Spirit, in Jesus Christ, I pray, Amen."

Gabriel announced, "Your Lord has heard your prayer. The spirit has been removed. Do not worry."

My heart pounded in my chest. I took several deep breaths. I knew God removed the spirit, however I felt unnerved. I recalled how the chair moved behind me, just a foot away. There was no wind, and it felt warm and calm outside. The wind couldn't move the chair. It took strength to push it. I laid there for over thirty minutes, struggling to fall asleep.

I slept horribly throughout the night. I dreamed people chased and tried to harm me all night long. It was not important enough to write it down. I sensed the spirits in my dream were in darkness, aiming to scare me. They did.

I woke and asked Ilene, "Was the spirit last night an old man? Why was he on the deck?"

Ilene explained, "He lived in the 1900s. He was interested in the plants. That is why he was on the deck."

I remembered his presence felt dark, heavy, and large. He stood right behind me and followed me inside. I was thankful I had God in my corner to protect me. The gift he gave me was powerful, and it attracted things. Spirits saw me. I felt him staring when I waited for Noodle to pee.

This morning I carried her outside and examined the chairs. My husband and I sat out on the deck yesterday and enjoyed the sunshine. The chair I sat in had moved a little. I shuddered, remembering how it felt to hear the chair scrub the wood. It rattled me again.

I asked, "Ilene, what does God want me to do today?"

She instructed. "Work on the writings, rest, and enjoy yourself. Finish them, it will be time to publish soon."

I gasped. "Thank you, Ilene. I have been wondering when to publish because God told me to wait. I am almost done with the final edit of *Experiences Never Stop Part 2*. I am determined to find balance in life, work, salon, time with my family. I am seeing a pleasant rhythm. It is a lot. I will do it for God."

March 24, 2021

I woke and heard, "All You Need Is Love," by The Beatles. I had a visit from my dead sister-in-law. She inserted herself into my dream. She looked thirty-five. I looked at her long brown hair and dark brown eyes. I stared at her long eyelashes while she sat beside me.

Dream Thirty-Five: I arranged a big gathering for the family. I planned a wonderful meal, and we would exchange gifts to show gratitude to each other. It didn't go as planned. Everyone sat scattered and did not wish to sit with one another. They weren't interested in the food or being there.

I reclined in a soft, white lounge chair. I wore a long black spaghetti strap dress, calf length with a deep V-neckline. The dress wasn't very revealing, but it looked sexy and tasteful. My client appeared. He looked six-foot tall, short gray hair, slim stature and in his seventies. He knew about the party and wished to help. I mentioned him before in my last book *Experiences Never Stop Part 2*. I had a dream visit from his uncle. He had not listened to anything I told him because he did not believe me. He handed me a massive magazine which contained photos of proper party dresses.

He commented, "I can see your breast." He struggled to peer down my dress. "I think I see your nipple. Yes, there it is."

I glanced down at my dress and saw my nipple, but you had to *look* down my gown to see my nipple. I adjusted my dress and sat upright. Since he was tall, it was very easy for him to peek down my clothes. This is when I spotted my sister-in-law sitting right beside me. She watched the man.

I sassed, "It's just a breast. Get over it."

She defended, "You must not look at her in this way. It's not polite."

I recognized her voice and watched her. She looked incredibly happy, calm, and extremely serene, which was not her behavior when she lived.

I woke and inquired, "Ilene, it was her?"

Ilene explained, "Yes, it was her. She wants you to know she watches over you. The things they do are wrong."

I sensed my sister-in-law protected me in the dream because he stepped away from me. I noticed Ilene said "they" which meant the family, too.

Unfortunately, I dealt with this man in the salon. He did not scare me. He was a womanizer and didn't like his comments. I corrected him when he stated things inappropriately. I did his wife's hair, and that was the only reason I put up with his foul behavior. What qualities his wife saw in him, I did not know. He was extremely shallow and self-centered.

It felt wonderful to know she watched over me. When she lived, she usually made snide comments to me and wasn't kind. The man did the same thing. Was she learning in heaven? Yes.

I asked, "Ilene, does God want me to write these things?"

Ilene answered, "Yes, God wants you to write these things."

I recalled how happy, young she looked. Her energy felt warm, loving, kind, and gentle. I laid in bed and remembered the details. This was the fourth visit from her. She was learning and growing in heaven. I still heard the song, "All You Need Is Love." I needed unconditional love. That is what my soul really needed. I grounded and prayed.

I whispered, "Thank you God for all that you do for me."

March 28, 2021

Dream Thirty-Six: I saw a man I did not know. I stood in a nightclub, and I am a young girl. I observed lots of people at the bar, drinking, laughing, and they enjoyed the live entertainment. I noticed bright pink and red flashing lights surrounding the bar's ceiling. I stayed for the duration of the event. The girl realized she was too drunk to drive home. She knew there was a room upstairs above the bar. She had a crush on the bartender, and he lived upstairs. I watched her feet walking up the stairs to the door. Unlocked, I entered. The room looked dark inside. The bartender had not arrived yet. I spotted an older, balding man with long, gray hair on the sides. I sensed his demeanor was calm and nothing to worry about being alone with him. He knew the bartender and waited for him as well.

I asked, "Is he here?" I knew the answer.

The old man replied, "Come sit with me and wait."

The old man seemed lost, sad, lonely and didn't have anyone that loved him. He had been married before, but she left him. I observed the young girl. Her hair dyed black and had a petite figure. She wore a short black skirt, heels, and short top, all black. I noticed her fingernails and toenails painted black as well. She thought it looked hip and modern. This happened many years ago. It was not the present time.

She sat on the couch beside him. They talked and laughed. She still had a buzz from partying. He knew all about the partying. As they chatted, this man knew someone I knew in present time. I watched them sitting on the gray couch. He slid a soft blanket over their legs because she was cold. Under the cream blanket, she relaxed. I watched his feet with socks on, sliding around underneath the blanket, bumping into her legs and her feet. She felt warm and comfortable with the man, but her buzz dissipated. He reached over and grabbed her right wrist. I noticed her small fingers spread wide. She did not want her hand placed anywhere on his body. I sensed he was going to put her hand on his erect penis, but he placed her hand on his upper chest. I could feel her fingers touching the old, wrinkled skin. I watched the thin gray chest hair moving around between her fingers.

The drunk girl stood up and yanked at her small black top, and her breasts fell out beneath her top. She wore no bra. Her breasts looked large and perfect. I observed her rock-hard nipples erect. She leaned over and shook her breast from side to side, so they bumped into each other and bounced around. The old man loved large breasts.

Suddenly, the man's demeanor shifted. He jumped to the edge of the couch. He was naked and grabbed his erect penis and aggressively masturbated. His eyes turned red; his hair disheveled. His face red from excitement. I heard him grunting. I watched foamy slobber building around the edges of his mouth and dripped from the sides. He looked like a wild animal unleashed from his cage. I felt fearful for the young girl. She did not know what she unleashed. He crawled over to her and placed his mouth on her right nipple. He relished how it felt in his mouth.

She instantly felt this was wrong and pulled her shirt down. The girl stepped backward and grabbed her things. She wasn't drunk anymore; this behavior jolted her awake. She knew she must escape before he raped her. She struggled to put on her black heels. I looked at the man and saw his backside. I noticed his long stringy gray hair and reminded me of a hippie. He sat on the edge of the couch, disappointed this would not go any further. He had his own ideas of what he desired.

He grunted, "Damn, girl, you made me pee on myself. I am a sixty-five-year-old man."

She realized he had done this before. He enjoyed playing games and making you feel comfortable. So, he could take advantage of you. She desired to flee. Disheveled, I watched her walk down the steps. It looked dark outside. I saw the green grass and the streetlights lit in front of her car. I woke.

I looked at the clock and realized I dreamed this for hours.

Disturbed, I asked, "Ilene, what am I dreaming?"

Ilene explained, "He is in *darkness* and showed you how he molested girls when he lived."

I struggled to not recall the dream. His face crazed and foaming at the mouth. I laid there, remembering how the man's energy felt. I sensed it was my client's deceased father.

I asked, "Ilene, was it him, her father?"

Ilene replied, "Yes, it was him."

I knew he died in his eighties. His daughter called me a few days ago to make an appointment. She told me years ago that her father molested her. I laid in bed and felt her pain at what this horrible man had done to her. I cried, sensing no telling how many times he violated her. Relieved, he was in darkness. He hadn't gotten away with anything, and he will hurt no one again. I recalled what she expressed when I shared with her my publication of my first book, *Living Life as an Empath and Medium.*

She said, "I am not sure if there is a God."

I understood why she said this now. Her father was evil and did horrible things to her. God had nothing to do with his actions. People made their own choices of what they did, even if it was extremely wrong. His faced flashed in my memory and I shivered. I could still hear his disgusting grunt. He felt vile and evil.

I asked, "Ilene, why did he visit me from darkness?"

Ilene replied, "He misses his daughter and wanted to show you what he did when he lived."

I answered, "I am not telling her anything for this wretched creature."

Later at 9:55 p.m. Noodle and I laid in "the room." I watched "Downton Abbey," by Julian Fellowes, Season 6, Episode 3 and heard, "I'll Fly Away," song.

I responded, "Dad, I haven't heard from you in days." I paused the show and walked into the kitchen for more red wine.

I asked, "How am I doing with these changes of my husband being home more?"

Dad replied, "There will be many more changes coming, Beck." I stopped in my tracks.

I questioned, "What do you mean, more changes? Are they good? I have been trying. Don't leave me hanging, tell me what they are?" I heard nothing for five minutes.

He added, "You'll be very happy with the changes that are coming."

I took a deep breath and sighed. "Good, I am glad and relieved. I want things to be happier between us. If I can get one last toxic person out of our lives. The person's energy feels like a heavy, dark umbrella hanging over my head. I feel trapped every holiday. COVID-19 has been a blessing for this person not able to pop in unannounced. I don't want our lives to return to the old ways. I wish it were different, but every fiber of my being tells me to run in the opposite direction from this person. If these are the changes, it would be fantastic."

April 1, 2021

Easter was in a few days, and tomorrow was Good Friday.

In bed I cried. "Lord, I am sorry you felt so much pain when you died. I feel it; no one believed you. I feel pain which no one believes me as well. I hear from you. It is true." I bawled.

God spoke firmly, *"This is God's will, Rebecca. Your Lord is with you."*

I sobbed. "Thank you, God for speaking to me."

I asked, "Am I to write this?"

Gabriel instructed. "Yes, your Lord wants it written."

I asked, "Gabriel, please remind me of exactly what God spoke to me in the morning. I am tired and want it to be correct."

Gabriel answered, "I will."

In the morning, Gabriel spoke the words of my Lord to me as I wrote in my journal.

April 3, 2021

I edited the final draft of *Experiences Never Stop Part 2.* It took five hours but finished. I wanted it completed by Easter weekend. I turned off the computer and walked downstairs to get something to drink. My husband watched TV.

I explained, "I am almost done editing and need to be in the sunshine for a while."

I strolled onto the deck and drank my water. I absorbed the warm sun on my skin.

Gabriel announced, "God is pleased with your work today. Do not overdo. He wants you to enjoy Easter."

I smiled and knew I was on the brink of overdoing. Noodle and I strolled toward the garden. I prayed, "Lord, please give me strength and calmness. I ask these things in the name of the Father, the Son, and the Holy Spirit, in Jesus Christ, I pray, Amen."

I opened the new cream umbrella my husband gave me for Christmas. I watered the flowers in the garden. As I watered the rose bush, God spoke Psalm 23. I listened to every word God said. When God finished, he whispered, *"I have blessed thee."*

I smiled and knew God heard my prayer, I just said. I felt better already and replied, "Thank you, Lord for all that you do for me."

I relaxed in the sun on our sandy beach around our pool and enjoyed the break. I listened to my guides playing music and watched Noodle enjoying herself.

I whispered, "Thank you God, for all that you have done for her."

April 11, 2021

Noodle and I laid in "the room." At 9:00 p.m. I heard "I'll Fly Away," song.

I asked, "Hi Dad, can you talk to me?"

Dad replied, "Don't worry, your husband loves you very much. He's thinking of you now."

I smiled. Today was a wonderful day, but later this evening he snapped at me about not taking care of things in the garden. He hurt my feelings and wanted me to do more. I did so much already. How much more could I give? This was what Dad referred to.

He added, "Yes, Beck, he wants you to do more, but he's frustrated with his own lacking not being able to provide."

I asked, "What do you mean? We split our finances. Has Octavian done something wrong again?"

Dad answered, "No, Beck, he needs to be loved, admired. He needs to feel like a man."

I replied, "I admire him. I tell him I love him all the time. This is not enough?" I heard nothing.

Ilene added, "Your father is sharing his fatherly advice."

I whispered, "I need to adore my husband, more than I already do? I am focused on work. I feel he focuses more on his work than me. Marriage is hard."

He answered, "Just love him, Beck, with all your might. He does adore you. He needs to feel worthy."

I added, "Really?"

Dad replied, "Your husband needs to be reminded how much he is adored by you."

I whispered, "Thank you. I am going to send him a text right now and tell him how much I adore him."

It was wonderful to hear these things. I love him deeply with all my heart.

I added, "Thank you, Dad, for reminding me."

April 13, 2021

Early this morning, I waited for Noodle to do her business. She pranced around the yard. I noticed the last several days her eyes looked clearer and the tumor on her left shoulder appeared even smaller. My husband noticed she heard things he said to her. A couple of weeks ago, she heard nothing.

I stood barefoot in the cool green grass, smiling. I whispered, "Thank you, God, for answering my prayers. Thank you for blessing and doing all the things you do for her. I need her healthy and happy, thank you, God."

Noodle's health improved.

Gabriel announced, "God has heard what you have said and is pleased." It was incredible to know God listens to everything.

On my drive to work, I enjoyed the cool breeze on my face and heard music.

I inquired, "What have you been doing in heaven, Dad?"

Dad whispered, "You're not allowed to know, Beck."

I grinned and knew I should not ask but was curious. I asked, "Are you happy? How does it feel? Do you miss living?"

He replied, "Sometimes, Beck, but I'm very happy." I sensed sadness in his voice.

He added, "I wasted time with people. I should've done more."

Dad wished he had done more when he lived. He regretted his choices.

Dad replied, "The choices we make are very important."

The wind felt fantastic. I felt pleased with the positive choices I made with their help. I knew more choices would come.

Later that evening, I bought red Sun-Inpatients and bright pink Vinca flowers at lunch for the garden. I found exactly what I needed. These flats were the only ones left. I sensed the flowers not bought, for me to find. I carried the three flats into the garden and noticed the sunset. I needed to hurry and heard "I'll Fly Away," song.

I smiled. "It is wonderful to hear from you. I am blessed."

Dad beamed. "They are beautiful."

I added, "I can't wait to plant them."

I watered the flowers and placed them in the shade. I glanced at the sunset and turned off the water. I marched inside before the in-betweens came out. They would want to harm me.

April 14, 2021

At 8:53 p.m. My husband and I enjoyed time on the deck having a glass of red wine. We shared what happened during our day. I noticed Gabriel seemed very chatty, which he rarely does. Gabriel spoke to me about my husband.

I asked, "Do you worry about me?"

He frowned, "I do worry about you a lot."

I replied, "You haven't shared your concerns with me. Why? What do you worry about?"

He answered, "I think you overdo sometimes with writing. It worries me. I just think you do too much. I worry about your safety and our health." I noticed concern in his eyes and sensed worry in his tone.

I whispered, "God asked me to do these things and I must. He wouldn't ask me if I could not handle it. It is a lot. I don't mean to worry you."

We talked about other topics, and we went inside before sunset. I prepared salmon and thick cut fries to bake. I sliced thin tomatoes and sprinkled salt and pepper on them while the fish baked. My husband worked on his taxes and seemed aggravated. I felt exhausted from work and needed "the room" after dinner. I am an Empath, and it is difficult to juggle everything God asked of me.

Gabriel reminded, "Write these things. You are God's messenger."

I work hard and did not realize my husband worried. It was difficult when people were not interested in my books.

Gabriel announced, "Prepare for the changes coming. Your prayers have been answered."

Shocked, "I can't remember what I prayed for, there were many."

Gabriel reminded, "The changes will make you happy."

I replied, "I need some happiness. All I do is work. I am exhausted. People want what they want when they want it. They really don't care about my time. I feel I am passing time to make money. I dread being there often. Am I amending Octavian's misdeeds? I am sure he had a heck of a lot to amend. God told me things were unfolding. It is difficult to wait but I am trying. I need more time with my husband, Noodle, to stay grounded and safe. What is to come?"

Ilene answered, "Things will become better, richer, you must endure these things."

I asked, "What do you mean?"

Ilene instructed. "Things will get better. Your future is bright. You must prepare."

I questioned, "How do I prepare, Ilene?"

Ilene added, "Believe in our Lord and Savior. He has showed you the way."

I sighed and knew she was right. Gabriel added, "Your Lord has been listening. He is pleased his messenger has worked hard for these things. God asks, not to worry. God is by your side showing you the way as you have asked."

I smiled and prayed this morning to show me the way.

April 18, 2021

I woke and heard music from Ilene, "What does God want me to do today?" I felt spent.

Ilene answered, "God wants you to rest. You are overworked and finish the book."

I sighed and smiled. Thankfully, God understood. I desperately needed rest.

Later, after lunch, we enjoyed the day together gardening and sunning at the pool. I heard little from my guides throughout the day. I struggled to rest but felt unsettled. I was not used to resting. At 3:30 p.m. We came inside because my husband needed to work at the bakery. I gave Noodle a bath and took a quick shower to rinse off the suntan oil. I had an hour before our time on the deck. Our new ritual I loved.

I carried Noodle upstairs and filled out the forms of the changes to *Experiences Never Stop Part 2* by Rebecca Walters Hopkins. I needed to remove the italics from Psalm 23 when God spoke to me. I laughed as I filled out the documents. God spoke this in the bible and to me but should not print it as he did. I sent the needed forms, and I had finished the book.

Later on, the deck, we enjoyed our time sipping wine and talked about the day. My husband looked exhausted and needed a nap.

He said, "I am going to go lay down."

I added, "Sure, get some rest. You need it."

I pounded out a chicken breast and seasoned with herbs and salt. I baked the chicken and some potatoes with cheese in the oven. The house was quiet and heard music.

I asked, "Dad, will you please talk to me? It is quiet. I know you guys want me to rest, but I am not used to this."

Dad joked, "I've been busy, Beck, doing things for God. You've been busy resting." My Dad loved to joke around when he lived.

I replied, "Yes, I have been resting. I forgot what it was like to rest. I wish you would talk to me more. I miss you."

He answered, "Beck, God is pleased with your work. You have been diligent, forthcoming. God is smiling beside me. It will be printed. God's words spoken to his messenger to help others believe in him."

I gasped. "Well, I was wondering how God felt about everything. I have heard little. He's smiling, happy. I have done my best and will try harder for the next book. I know it will help others. My only concern, how will they find it? If they can't find the book. How can I help them? These are the things I need help with, Lord. I am trying to wait for things to unfold and be patient. I need encouragement. It is hard for me to be excited about the book to be published. Most people I know aren't interested. Family doesn't care, friends are drifting away. It is like old news. New people are hard to find. I feel they really don't believe me. God warned me this would happen, and it is. I will continue no matter what. I believe in you and know what I hear is true. Please help me Lord."

Gabriel announced, "Your Lord is with you. He has shown you the way. These are God's will. There is more to come. His messenger must be ready."

Tears formed in my eyes. This was true. I was not even halfway done and asked, "Please give me strength, Lord, guidance and mercy for my weaknesses. I ask in the name of the Father, the Son, and the Holy Spirit, in Jesus Christ, I pray, Amen."

Gabriel answered, "Your Lord understands all things. His messenger is strong and vigilant, understanding God's will."

God spoke firmly, *"These things must be done, thus saith the Lord."*

I replied, "I am confused, Gabriel. When I hear thus saith the Lord, means God Almighty is speaking to me. Who spoke this sentence?"

Gabriel added, "Your Lord has answered you."

God spoke firmly, *"Time is of the essence. Work on your studies, thus saith the Lord, God Almighty. These things will help you grow, which you have asked for. I come to you. You will begin book 3 Experiences Never Stop Part 3."*

Gabriel announced, "Your Lord has spoken to you. You must remember your Lord is with you and forgives those who are weak."

I gasped. "Wow."

I sat for a moment and did not know Dad, Gabriel, and God would speak to me. I did not even know if my chicken was done. I had rested and must work tomorrow. I was getting behind and would start in the morning. I felt pressure and fear of wasting time.

Gabriel announced, "Do not be afraid of the Lord. This is God's will."

I sighed and plated my dinner. My ego hoped for more acknowledgment from God. I needed to keep my ego in check because I was God's servant.

April 19, 2021

I walked outside with Noodle and heard music from Ilene.

I whispered, "Good morning, what does God want me to do today?"

Ilene answered, "God wants you to prepare for the many changes that are coming. The ones you asked for. They will happen quickly and work on the writings."

Surprised, I thought God would want me to work on the writings and nothing else.

I asked, "What changes are coming? I don't remember what I prayed for. I need time with my family and to sell more books. I am weary working at the salon."

Noodle and I walked back inside and heard nothing from Ilene.

Later, after lunch, I strolled into the garden with Noodle to lie by the pool. I transplanted three lavender phlox from one bed to another. I laid by the pool and meditated. I asked God, my guides, and the angels to speak to me, to help with the worries I had.

I meditated and heard from the angels, "You must pray for those that you love."

I prayed for them. God spoke warmly, gently, *"Prepare, for there are many changes coming that I have granted to my messenger, thus saith the Lord. Your Lord has answered many of your prayers. These changes will make my messenger very happy. You must end book 4 soon. Your Lord is pleased with your work and must begin book 5, 'Experiences from the Lord God Almighty'".*

Shocked, I asked, "God, please repeat the name of book 5?"

God answered, *"Experiences from the Lord God Almighty."*

I ended the meditation and thanked God, the angels, and my guides for their guidance and protection. I smiled absorbing the knowledge and how the sun felt on my skin. God answered all the questions I had. When to end book 4, what was the name of the next book and changes to help me for my future to grow. I would have to wait for what I prayed for to unfold. I marveled at how God knows everything and guides me. I wondered what would happen to me to write the experiences in book 5. The title, people would definitely read it or not at all.

April 25, 2021

Noodle and I hung out on the deck while my husband worked. I had a few moments before sunset to enjoy. I recalled when a client came in this week. She was the one who had been molested by her father. While I colored her hair, I could not help but remember the dream visit I had from her father. He did horrific things. I must say nothing to her.

Gabriel warned, "You must not speak of her father."

I replied, "I will not because I know he wanted to give her a message."

It bothered me during the appointment. I wanted to hug her and reassure her he paid for his evil crimes. I refrained and did not speak a word. I felt her pain.

I forgot to log this into my journal. God did not allow evil into his kingdom. I knew you did not get away with your horrific transgressions. I saw it in the dreams I had from *darkness*. God had told me no rapists or murderers were allowed in his kingdom.

I felt peaceful staring at the sunset. We had a wonderful day together. I pondered what changes would come. I felt strongly what I am writing will be a movie.

Dad whispered last night, "Will be many years before it happens. Don't tell your husband. Men need to feel important in money making."

I thought about how a movie was directed. I suspected they would want to change it. I would never allow a director to change what God spoke. I would sign no documents that gave them the freedom to change my work.

I felt grateful and enjoyed the day with my family. My body needed a break. We worked on the pool, adding the salt generator equipment. My family was the most important thing. COVID-19 had been a blessing regarding no unwanted pop-ins. I loved my serenity, for I had little of it. I am an empath and desperately need time to recharge.

April 28, 2021

I installed an SEO on my website and needed a break. My brain ached. I gathered Noodle, and we strolled to the pool. I reclined in the lounge chair and saturated the SPF on my skin. I enjoyed this gorgeous day. It was the most beautiful day so far in the season. I poured water from the pool on Noodle's back to keep her cool. I turned on the big drum fans and gazed at the intense blue sky. I absorbed feeling the beauty within my soul and heard music from Ilene.

I inquired, "How am I going to end this book? What is going to happen?"

I examined the top of the Poplar tree's blooms of orange and yellow blowing in the wind. She spoke nothing and heard "I'll Fly Away," song.

I spoke, "Hello, Dad, can you talk to me?"

Dad sighed. "You're getting very brown, Beck. Don't overdo."

I smiled and knew he looked at me. I answered, "I know it isn't good for me. It feels wonderful to my soul. The sun warming my skin."

Gabriel announced, "God is pleased with the work you've done today. It will help people find you."

I heard Dad's music again, "Can you tell me anything?"

He whispered, "I love you and miss you, Beck. I miss all of my children. They all could do much better, including you. God loves you, Beck. God loves his messenger."

I gasped. "Wow, that is incredible to hear what God thinks. It is marvelous."

I gazed up at the poplar tree. It's ginormous foliage, bright green against the clear blue sky. I confided, "I understand now why you guys tell me to pray all the time. I understand it helps me. The more I pray I know it keeps evil away and strengthens me. I realize I am a work in progress but am trying my best to be a better person."

I prayed, "Lord, please give me encouragement, signs to help and guide me. Lord, help me have more time with my family, more intimacy with my husband to strengthen our marriage. Help me, Lord, with these things. I ask in the name of the Father, the Son, and the Holy Spirit, in Jesus Christ, I pray, Amen."

I grinned. "How far away are you from me, Dad? How far away is it, really?"

Dad whispered, "You're not allowed to know these things, Beck. I am closer to you than you think."

Surprised, I pleaded "What do you mean?"

He beamed. "I'm standing right beside you."

Shocked, I replied, "I've heard other mediums state that your loved ones are right beside you and are there with you always. I wondered if that was true. So, you are right here beside me?"

I struggled to feel his energy. I sensed a presence on my left side and not my right. It felt faint, but it was there. I asked, "Which side of the lounge chair are you on?" A wasp hit me on the left knee and flew off.

He added, "I am on your left. I made the bug touch you."

I gasped. "Wow, I know you can move things." I looked to my left in hopes of my Dad standing there. I saw nothing, just the garden flowers and fence.

I requested, "Can I see you, Dad?" I recalled he revealed himself once on my sofa while I was not dreaming. "Am I allowed to see you? Will God allow it?"

He answered, "Close your eyes, Beck, and think of me, Beck. Think of me."

I closed my eyes and thought of my father. I saw nothing.

Dad joked, "Can you see me, Beck?"

My eyes closed, I replied, "No, Dad I cannot."

He instructed. "Look to your right, Beck. Open your eyes. Can you see me?"

I opened my eyes and glanced to my right, hoping he sat on the other lounge chair. I saw nothing. I replied, "I can't see you, Dad."

He laughed. "Look to your left, Beck."

I turned my head and looked to the left of my chair towards our old six-foot gray fence. I saw nothing. He asked, "Can you see me, Beck?"

I whispered, "I can't, Dad. I can't see you."

He instructed. "Try harder, focus. Can you see me?"

My eyes open, I allowed my clairvoyance to open. I saw my father leaning on the fence. He had on cream colored pleated dress pants with a light blue, almost white, top. The short sleeves rolled up over his biceps. His dark brown hair looked thick and wavy, combed off his face. I glanced at his brown leather shoes and leather belt. I studied his face. His light blue eyes glistened as he stared at me. Dad smiled showing his white, perfect teeth. He appeared twenty years old, younger than me. He rubbed his hand over his forearm. I recognized his arms and hands. He looked absolutely beautiful and happy.

I beamed. "I see you, Dad. You look fantastic." I combed over the image in my mind he place before me. He leaned on the fence with his shoulder. He looked happy, and his eyes twinkled.

He sighed. "I can't stay long. God doesn't allow it."

I viewed his soul shoot upward towards the blue sky. The bright beam of light appeared round, 3-feet wide, which flashed upward. The light and Dad vanished.

I cried. "God, thank you for letting me see my father and giving me encouragement. Thank you for letting me see him. He looks beautiful and happy."

Tears rolled down my cheeks. I still felt the warmth of Dad's love and the happiness in his voice. I sensed how he watched me while showing himself to me. I knew God allowed it.

I sobbed. "God, thank you for my gifts you have given me. It comes with a great deal of sacrifice, but I am blessed. I can hear my guides, Dad and especially you, God."

My husband entered the garden, and I shared what just happened. It felt incredibly marvelous. He looked young and charming. I had never seen my father look this young and happy. I savored the moment, gazing into the sky. God allowed me to see my father in my garden. How incredibly fabulous.

At 9:07 p.m. Noodle and I laid in "the room" watching "Lark Rise to Candleford," directed by Susan Tully, Patrick Lau, and Alan Grint, Season 2, Episode 12. I heard music and hit pause. I listened to my father's voice. It sounded childlike.

The voice stated, "I adore you, Beck. I love and miss you."

I immediately felt apprehension because my father never would say he adored me. This was not my father.

I prayed, "God, remove this evil spirit from my presence and my surroundings. I ask in the name of the Father, the Son, and the Holy Spirit, in Jesus Christ, I pray, Amen."

Gabriel declared, "The Lord has removed this evil presence, the imposter of your father. Evil will always try to hurt his messenger."

Shocked, we had a wonderful day at the pool. It did not sound or feel like him. I felt no love in the words I heard. I heard Psalm 23 and recited it out loud. I sensed God blessed me when I heard Psalm 23.

Gabriel announced, "Your Lord is by your side. He has protected thee from evil which tried to fool thee."

I whispered, "Thank you, Gabriel. My Dad would not speak that way. Keep this evil presence away from me."

I heard songs from Dad, he added, "Beck, it wasn't me. Evil was trying to trick you. It wasn't me, Beck. I love you. I want you to be safe, Beck. God removed it."

I whispered, "Thank you, Dad. I can hear your voice and feel your love that is always there. What I heard earlier was different."

I asked, "Gabriel, why did this happen? How did evil sneak in?"

Gabriel instructed. "Your Lord has protected his messenger. Evil never gives up."

At the end of the series, a couple married in the church. She looked stunning in her wedding dress, and the groom grinned. The friends and family were there in the church, watching. I realized at the moment God always observed when one marries along with everyone else. While they exchanged their vows, tears ran down my cheeks.

Gabriel announced, "Your Lord is pleased you understand how powerful God's presence is."

April 30, 2021

I prayed for encouragement, protection of my energy, and guidance for my clients I had today. I asked God to help me because I had a long day ahead. The morning seemed uneventful, but the afternoon was spectacular. I felt God's glorious presence. I sensed God's love and guidance through the words I spoke to my clients.

At lunch, Dad reminded me to focus on my future and not about upcoming holidays. I thanked him while I ate vegetable soup, olives, and fresh strawberries. The three clients I had in the afternoon; Dad shared knowledge from heaven for each one.

The first client I instructed through Dad's words to pray for guidance and help for her father. She explained he stayed in a nursing home temporarily because of his health. I explained what Gabriel spoke, "He would come home soon if she prayed. It would be faster."

She shared, "He wants to come home. He hates the food and isn't listening to the caregivers."

I reminded, "Pray for him, he will come home faster."

She understood, and I saw the relief in her eyes.

The second client, He instructed. "She should walk away from her husband. She will be happier."

I replied, "I can't say that to her."

Dad joked, "Yes, you can. You can."

I sighed and turned off the blow dryer. I gazed into her eyes, "Have you ever thought about leaving your husband?"

Surprised, she looked at me, "Yes, I am on the struggle boat every day."

I shocked her. I explained what I heard was from heaven and these things would make her happy.

Dad added, "She will meet someone in the future."

I laughed. "You're going to meet someone in the future. If he is still hanging around. How are you going to meet someone? You are miserable, unhappy, and you're going to retire in the next few months. How are you going to live the next phase of your life, happy or unhappy? You know he will not change. He will get worse."

She agreed and shared an outing she had with a girlfriend. What fun they had at lunch and shopping. She bought a new outfit and wore it home. Her husband did not notice.

She sighed. "I had such a wonderful, fun, exciting day and came inside the house. I felt the doom and gloom."

I asked, "Do you think your life will change? Do you think he will change? Wouldn't be wonderful to come home and feel happiness?"

I saw the answer in her eyes. I reminded as she walked out of the salon, "Remember, do you want to be happy or unhappy. That is the decision. It will be difficult, but a decision you must make. They have guided you from heaven today. Don't take it lightly." She smiled.

The last client chatted about her aunt she spoke to a day ago. Dad shared, "He's with us, Beck. He loves his wife. He wants to tell her hello."

I interrupted and explained. I added how important it is for the person to receive a message. God allowed these things.

I asked, "Do you feel comfortable in giving the message to your aunt?"

She hesitated. "She is very conservative."

I replied, "If you don't that is okay."

Dad interjected. "These things will help her."

I explained, "Sometimes you must give the message and put your feelings aside. This will help her. It is important."

She whispered, "Okay. She was not able to say goodbye to her husband when he died."

I knew how it would help her when I heard this. While I made her next appointment, I explained how I felt a spirit's essence through what I heard from Dad giving me the message.

I asked, "Was your uncle a large broad man?"

She replied, "Yes, he was tall and Scandinavian."

I smiled. "Was he a gentle man? He felt gentle, soft spoken in his words."

She beamed. "Yes, he was very soft spoken."

I reminded her how important this was. I hoped this gave the encouragement she needed to make the call. This helped him in heaven as well.

I locked the salon and drove home. God had answered my prayers today. I felt incredible, not tired. I recalled how God told me not to help others for my own needs, but to honor my gift. It was for them.

May 1, 2021

Noodle and I laid in "the room" and watched "Lark Rise to Candleford," Season 3, Episode 5. I heard, "I'll Fly Away," song.

Dad explained, "Beck, many things will be happening soon. You're gonna love them, Beck. God has answered your prayers."

I asked, "What am I gonna love, Dad? Can you tell me more?"

He answered, "Beck, these things take time for you to understand, but God has allowed me to tell you these things. God has listened and answered your prayers for your future."

I questioned, "Why can I not know about it now, Dad?"

He instructed. "Now is not the time, Beck, but you will know what in a few days. He wanted me to tell you this. He wants his messenger happy."

I replied, "I can't imagine what it would be? Prayers, God answered. I said many. Is it about me or someone else close to me?"

He answered, "Beck, it is about you."

Surprised, I added, "About me? The only things I can recall I prayed for are my books. I need people to find and want to read them. I don't see that happening soon."

Dad beamed. "Beck, it's gonna happen in the next few days."

I thought, "I should receive my books from the publisher in the next few days. People will want to read them, only five. It's better than none. I asked for thousands of people to read my work. I have to start from somewhere. Is that what you are talking about, Dad? Is that the prayer?"

He replied, "Yes, but this is one of them, but there is more. You'll have to wait to find out."

I answered, "I am learning when prayers are answered. It makes you happy and surprised. I'm just not sure if my work will ever be read. I hope so. I am gonna need God's help to make that one happen. I'll have to wait and see. I am not getting my hopes up. I don't want to expect too much."

Gabriel interrupted. "Your Lord and Savior is with you. Do not doubt your Lord."

I sighed. "I don't doubt my Lord. I just don't have any idea what he has prepared for me. I don't want to get my hopes up."

Dad beamed. "You're gonna love it, Beck. You'll know in a few days. God is pleased with your work and is showing you the way."

May 2, 2021

Dream Thirty-Seven: The nightmare lasted all night and woke at 7:30 a.m. The place felt like a rundown hotel. I saw only a couple of 20x20 rooms. I saw no carpet or furniture. The walls painted grey. The space looked gloomy, shadowy, and dreary. I spotted two small groups of people trapped. I counted four individuals in each group. I sensed the groups were gang related and not to be trusted. I stood in this place with Noodle. She looked two years old and only weighed a couple of pounds. She stuck close and protected me. I wore nothing but a long, soft pink coat and clothes underneath, which kept me warm. I sensed the cold in this dreary place. I felt trapped inside the two rooms with these horrible, violent criminals. The two groups consisted of all men. One group terrified of the other group. They all had done appalling things. I didn't know what they were, but it wasn't good. I felt unsafe here and was the only woman with a tiny puppy. I watched the one group cram into the elevator to leave. The elevator did not work. I found a corner and crouched down. I kept my coat tucked in around me and Noodle. I placed my arms on my knees and tucked my chin in. They watched me, and I peeked at them. The groups took turns walking to the elevators to see if they worked. As they passed one another, the men taunted each other with sneers and comments. The bully group wanted to fight, and the docile group walked away. This went on for days, weeks. We were stuck in these two adjacent rooms. I noticed the men were African American and Caucasian. They looked young, in their twenties. I glanced inside a leather bag which held three black whips. This was their weapon of choice, ready to use at a moment's notice. I saw bandannas on their heads. It looked dark. I could not make out the color. Some guys had on black sunglasses. They did not want you to see their eyes, but they scrutinized everything. They wanted to pounce. I sensed their hostility toward one another and desperately needed to get out of this dangerous place. I saw there was no food, heat, or money, and no way to escape. I felt intense oppression and doom. The heaviness in the air so oppressive I could not breathe and could barely see. It was dark and shadowy. I glimpsed at their clothes. They wore black. Everything dark and dismal. I had an idea of how to escape. I tried the stairs instead of the elevator. I frantically sprinted up the stairs to a dead end. I had to turn around and go back. I noticed you could walk out onto a deck near the room. I touched a wooden railing. The thick, misty gray air outside felt as oppressive as the air inside. I couldn't see through it. I saw no end, *just darkness.* Trapped with eight criminals. They wanted to harm me, but they didn't touch me. I felt protected. They stared through me with their piercing eyes, stalking my every move. I stayed to myself and observed their movements.

The hotel provided once a couple of tiny boxes of cheese, popcorn, and very little to drink. Not enough for nine people. I ate a couple pieces of the popcorn and gave a piece to Noodle so she would not starve. I marched back to my corner. I didn't want to push my luck with these unsavory hoodlums. They wanted all the food and I let them have it.

I woke and felt depressed, sad, overwhelmed by what I witnessed. I heard music from Ilene.

I pleaded. "Where was I? I felt it was *darkness.*"

She answered, "You were in darkness. You saw these people repeating things over and over for eternity."

I had felt darkness in other dreams. You could not escape and knew you could not leave. I still felt their horrible misery. I looked at Noodle and felt the covers beneath me. Relieved, I was happy, in my bed, alive and well. I stood inside this horrible place for eight hours. I could not imagine what eternity felt like. My heart sank knowing these people paid for their sins and would for eternity. I could not get the oppression which still hovered in my heart out of my mind.

I walked downstairs and saw my husband on the couch. I made coffee and said nothing of the dream. I struggled to shake how *darkness* made me feel. I felt trapped in prison, starving and scared.

I needed to enjoy Sunday with my family. I wondered what God had in store for me. I cried myself to sleep last night, whining about my books. I apologized to God this morning about my whining as I rose from bed.

Dad whispered, "I didn't mean to upset you, Beck."

I explained, "You didn't. You were telling me things that God wants me to do and know."

I struggled to smile. The oppression lingered in my mind, hovering. I soaked in the hot tub for a while and needed to cleanse the dirt off my aura. I scrubbed my body with a salt scrub in the shower to remove the filth which lingered. My husband noticed I wasn't myself and hid what happened.

Later in the evening at 6:52 p.m. My husband worked. Noodle and I relaxed on the deck. I asked Dad, "What can you tell me about now?"

He joked, "I can see my daughter. I love you."

I asked, "Just how far away are you, Dad? Are you right above me?"

He answered, "You're not allowed to know these things, but I can see you from where I am. How you are absorbing and learning what's going on around you. How you listen to God. You had a rough night last night, Beck. You must remember to pray for protection. God will help you."

I sighed. "I had a rough night, and it was scary. It was horrible and ruined most of my day."

Dad replied, "There will be many changes coming. The ones that I spoke of last night. God is right beside me, reminding me to tell you again. Embrace them, Beck. It will make you very happy. I am very proud of you, Beck, my daughter. You've accomplished so many things for our Lord and Savior. He's very pleased with you, his messenger. Don't doubt our Lord, Beck. He's right here beside me, telling me what to say to you."

I listened, and the words made me cry. The conversation was from God. The sky close to sunset, and I must go inside. I had nightmares last night. It felt horrific just to know that souls who do not believe in God would live that way for eternity. It took half the day to get it out of my brain. Evil watching the whole time. Now Dad told me God by his side, telling me things. It felt beautiful, loving, warm, the complete opposite of what I experienced last night. Dad sounded loving and kind, just like he did when he lived.

I whispered, "Thank you, God, for telling my father what to say. It helps me. I need to go inside and prepare dinner. I don't want to be out in the dark. I love you."

May 6, 2021

I drove into our driveway and noticed my husband holding Noodle. She appeared thrilled to see me. I stopped the car and rolled down the window. I touched her face and gave her a kiss. My husband smiled at me while she squirmed in his arms.

I stated, "Let me get the car in the garage."

I pulled in and Noodle greeted me at the car door and dashed towards the yard. I hugged my husband and glanced to see where she was. I noticed her on her back, thrashing around as if rolling in something. Something was wrong and my husband ran over to help her. She had a seizure. He picked her up, and her body went limp in his arms. I rushed over to see how she was. She looked at me, not fully aware. I watched him carry her inside and followed.

He demanded. "Take my pants off and turn on the water in the shower."

I did. He held her close and stepped into the shower, letting the cool water run over her back. I grabbed a towel from the linen closet. She got too hot after a walk and fainted a couple of weeks ago. He put her in the shower then. It helped her. I turned off the water and draped the towel over her back. My mind raced. It was only seventy-two degrees outside today. Noodle gathered her senses. He gently dried her off. She looked shaken and unsteady. I could think of nothing, but God told me he had given me more time with her. This could not be happening. This was not what God said. I had more time with her. He granted me these things. She meant the world to us both. She would be okay. This is not how my Lord is. He would not let her be harmed and take her from me.

My husband, terrified, took her out on the deck and placed her in her bed. While he made her dinner. I changed quickly out of my work clothes while I watched her from the bathroom. I washed my face and poured a glass of red wine. I marched on to the deck and sat with her. My husband worried to death, but in my heart, I knew she was fine. This is not what God told me.

I searched online for information about seizures. We needed knowledge and awareness of this problem. I glanced at my husband; his face haggard with worry. She seemed better. As time passed, she ate her dinner, and we relaxed. It was getting late, and he needed to work at the bakery. He carried her inside, and I started my dinner. My husband kissed us and left for work.

Later after dinner, Noodle and I laid in "the room." I heard music from Dad and Ilene.

I begged. "What happened tonight? What happened?"

Dad and Ilene answered, "God is preparing you."

Shocked, I replied, "What?" I knew this meant Noodle's death coming. I knew in my heart this was untrue. God had blessed her. I had more time with her."

Gabriel explained, "You have been tested."

It felt difficult to hear because of what happened earlier.

I inquired, "Why would God test me with her?"

I passed. Gabriel instructed. "Pray more for her."

I asked, "What do I pray for?"

Ilene and Dad answered, "For her to be healed."

I prayed and struggled to relax and watch TV. I turned off everything in "the room" and my husband sat in the living room watching TV there. I carried Noodle outside to pee. She seemed like herself. My husband wanted to stay up for a while before I went to bed with Noodle. I placed her in her favorite spot and prayed for her and us. I turned off the lights and thought about the evening. God listened to my prayers.

I begged. "God, please heal, protect, and keep her safe. God, please explain what happened. You said ask and I am there. I am asking. I need to hear from you, Lord. What happened tonight? Please explain things to me. Please Lord, help me." I sobbed. I heard nothing.

God spoke softly and sounded far away, *"Time is of the essence. Your Lord is with you, beside you, thus saith the Lord. You have been tested greatly by your Lord."*

I wept. "Why have you tested me? Why?"

Gabriel announced, "For your uncertainties of your Lord. You must pray for her more."

I knew this meant how I felt about the changes coming a few days ago.

I gasped and placed my hand over my mouth. I cried and pleaded. "I am sorry, Lord. Please forgive me for my weakness. Please forgive me." I bawled.

God spoke softly, *"Your Lord has forgiven you. I have granted you many blessings. She has been blessed by your Lord. Remember, you are my messenger. You have asked for the ending of the book. This is it. You are my messenger. I will ask many things of you. Will you do these things?"*

I felt horrible. I had let God, my Savior, down. I bawled. "I will, Lord. I will."

REFERENCES

World Collins. "Holy Bible Concordance," Red Letter Edition, King James Version, accessed March 31, 2020, June 1, 2020, January 4, 2021.

Walters Hopkins, Rebecca. *Living Life as an Empath and Medium.* accessed April 11, 2020, page 213, Balboa Press 2019.

Walters Hopkins, Rebecca. *Experiences Never Stop.* accessed June 15, 2020, July18, 2020, July 28, 2020, August 21, 2020, September 15, 2020, Balboa Press 2019.

Walters Hopkins, Rebecca. *Experiences Never Stop Part 2.* accessed May 25, 2020, June 15, 2020, July18, 2020, March 24, 2021, Balboa Press 2021.

DISCLAIMER

This book is a memoir. It reflects the author's present recollections of experiences over time. Some names and characteristics have been changed, some events have been compressed, and some dialogue has been recreated. To protect persons privacy

CPSIA information can be obtained
at www.ICGtesting.com
Printed in the USA
BVHW031030161221
R12959200001B/R129592PG623915BVX00003B/3